To

Guj

CW00659938

Hamish Engelberg

First published in 2015

Copyright © Hannah Engelkamp 2015

ISBN 978-0-9932136-0-1

No part of this book shall be reproduced, stored or transmitted in any form without written permission of the publisher

Published by Hannah Engelkamp
www.seasidedonkey.co.uk
hannah@hannahme.com

Edited by Lucy Ridout
Designed by Isobel Gillan
Cover photo by Rhys Thwaites-Jones
Cover magic by Jasia Warren
Maps by Hannah Engelkamp
Photos by Hannah, Rhys, Alan Hale and Rob Browne

Although everything that happened in this little tale was true in my eyes, it is entirely possible and rather likely that I have misremembered all sorts of things. Any inaccuracies in people's stories are entirely down to me and my stack of fallible notebooks

This book was made possible by the generous and enthusiastic crowd funding pledges of 831 people

The poem 'Tirlun' on page 66 is reproduced with the permission of Gwasg Gomer on behalf of the estate of TH Parry-Williams

WELSH PRONUNCIATION

This book is full of Welsh place names, and if you don't speak Welsh but would like to know how to pronounce them, there is a full and fairly entertaining glossary, plus some general tips, at www.seasidedonkey.co.uk/welsh

I decided to mix Welsh and English spellings of place names to reflect the most common usage.

PLACES WE STAYED

If you'd like to know more about the places we stayed, or go and stay there yourself, there are details at www.seasidedonkey.co.uk/stayinwales

SEASIDE DONKEY, THE MOVIE!

There is a full-length film of this adventure. To find out how you can see it, in glorious technicolour, look here www.seasidedonkey.co.uk/film

SEASIDE DONKEY

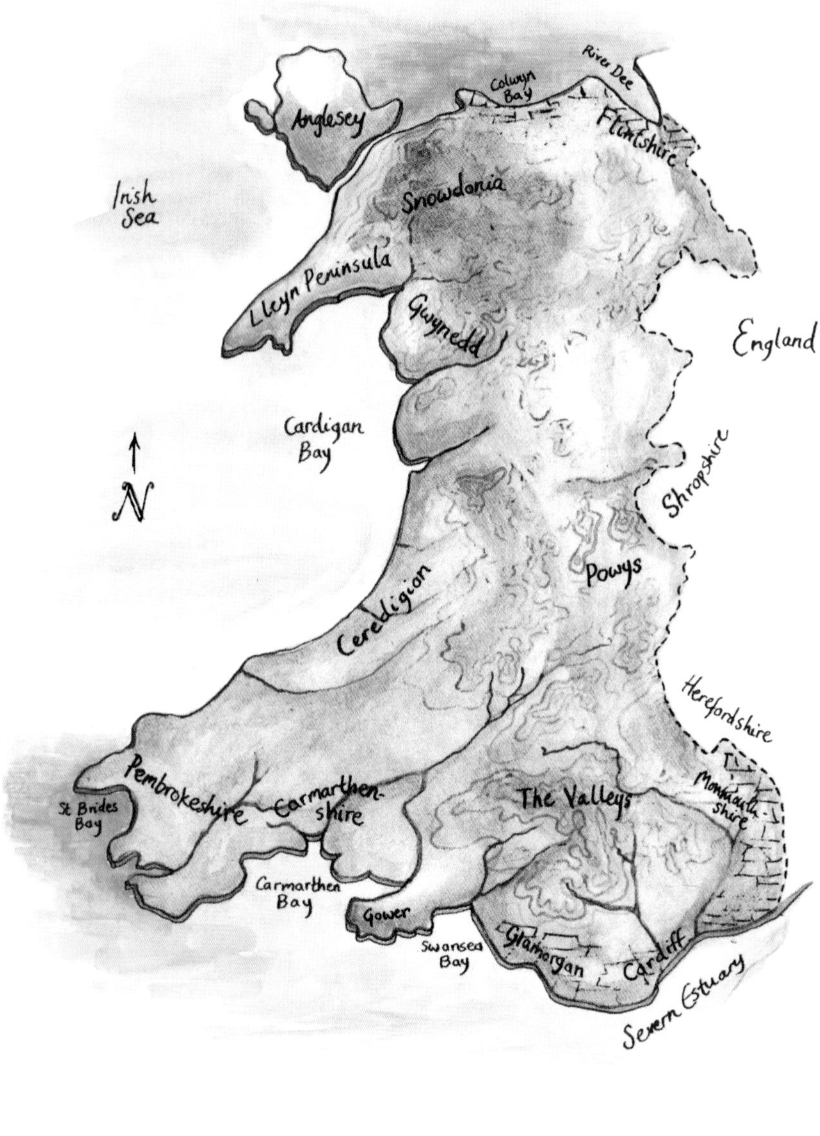
River Dee
Colwyn Bay
Anglesey
Flintshire
Snowdonia
Irish Sea
Lleyn Peninsula
Gwynedd
England
Cardigan Bay
N
Shropshire
Powys
Ceredigion
Herefordshire
Pembrokeshire
St Brides Bay
Carmarthen-shire
The Valleys
Monmouth-shire
Carmarthen Bay
Gower
Swansea Bay
Glamorgan
Cardiff
Severn Estuary

SEASIDE DONKEY

A WAYWARD WALK AROUND WALES

Hannah Engelkamp

PART ONE

FROM ABERYSTWYTH TO THE END OF THE LLEYN

ONE

Until we hit Aberystwyth town centre, the list of things that frightened Chico had consisted of birds and butterflies, cows and horses, a black lamb, and a dry leaf skittering menacingly along the tarmac. Suddenly that list was multiplying; cars crashed through puddles, plastic sheeting flapped against scaffolding bones, rain roared and murmured in the guttering. A man opened an umbrella just a few feet away. What was wrong with him? Couldn't he see I was barely in control of a rattled donkey?

Despite the heavy rain, Aberystwyth was stuffed full for the late May bank holiday. I heard the occasional breathy 'Donkey!' to left and right, but I kept my eyes forward, stiffly blinkered to the new dangers that darted and shied around us. Chico's ears swivelled wildly. Children and dogs surprised us as we surprised them – they were delighted, Chico and I were not. We stalked along together but were each alone in our own panic. I didn't once glance at Chico, and he took no obvious notice of me. I waved my arms around at the traffic and hoped that my face would convey that people should keep their distance but not be alarmed. *Everything was under control!*

We rounded the last corner and I spotted familiar faces: the stalwart farewell committee, standing in the rain, collars up and backs to the sea, sheltering amongst the Welsh flags and foil windmills outside a souvenir shop.

Dai strode towards us, a wiry, rustic archangel in his full-length tan-coloured oilskin riding coat, the shoulder cape sitting like neatly folded wings. His encouraging smile faded as he saw what I hadn't yet noticed. Chico's packsaddle – Dai's own creation – was sliding sideways, the disaster largely hidden by his rain sheet. As we surged forward the last few feet into Dai's reassuring arms, the saddle upended against Chico's side, depositing one of its panniers on the ground. Chico freaked out.

Fifteen or so people flinched as my donkey leaped forward in terror, the whites of his wide eyes showing. Dai grabbed his headcollar and crooned to him in his high-pitched Welsh accent, 'Hey, gw-boi... Hey, gw-boi...' With one hand he unfastened the rain sheet and remaining pannier and piled them on the ground, then pushed the packsaddle back into position and tightened the very loose girth straps. I watched in impotent horror, the relief at having Dai take control just emphasising the sick knowledge that I was scarily out of my depth. The last remaining sorry clods of my confidence dissolved in the rain and washed between the sand-coloured paving slabs. I'd barely managed half a mile, and there were still nine hundred and ninety-nine and a half to go.

Then Chico's bowels opened, releasing a great, green, spattery poo right onto his rain sheet and those paving slabs. The farewell committee groaned, a tender note between sympathy and revulsion. Dad sprang into action, scraping up the poo with two cardboard boxes and running down to rinse the rain sheet in the sea.

Scared though I was to be alone with Chico, a quick departure might be the only way to retain any dignity. I hugged each person in turn, whispering, 'I think it's best if we, um...'

'Yes,' they agreed, and wished us a good time, and *good luck*.

I took Chico's rope and we plunged around the corner, onto Aberystwyth's wide and deserted promenade, heading north into the salty wind. It had already occurred to me that Chico, acquired only a month before, might never have seen the sea – just one of the catalogue of worries that had plagued me throughout a sleepless, appetite-diminished May. And now that we'd got to this point, the waves weren't helping. They crashed and spat, flinty grey and foaming. Chico quaked.

There's an Aberystwyth tradition of walking along the full length of the promenade and kicking the railing at the north end of the seafront, before turning on your heel and strolling home. It's a physical punctuation mark repeated so many times over the centuries that the paint is always scuffed away to the metal. Rather than turn back, however, I was apparently going to go the long way around. I would continue north, making a 1000-mile clockwise lap of the entire country, before returning to kick the bar a second time, from the south.

I had never embarked on anything with such deep-seated self-doubt. But somehow, despite the several calamities over the previous weeks, and the fact that the weather, my own instinct, many people and Chico were all telling me clearly that this was a very bad idea, there I was.

I kicked the bar and burst into tears.

TWO

I was ready for an adventure. I'd drunk in the New Year full of optimism for an exciting year ahead, but for the next six months direction hadn't been forthcoming. Then one day in June came an unexpected gust of inspiration. The Wales Coast Path had opened a month before and I was writing a news story about it, looking at an aerial photo of Criccieth Castle. Suddenly I knew: I was going to walk around Wales. For more than a decade I'd been meaning to walk the Pembrokeshire Coast Path, but finding three weeks together had proved pretty much impossible. But three months? One thousand miles? Raising the stakes made it seem more attainable, not less. Rather than clawing a long holiday out of a busy life, I'd just have to stop the busy life, say no to everything. No, sorry, I'm walking. It sounded delicious.

My usual walking buddy, Sarah, was concerned. We had a walking ethos that we'd built over many years which balanced the challenge with the pay-off, the hardship with touches of luxury. We'd used bag-carrying services and often felt totally vindicated as we passed haggard hikers who seemed determined to suffer. Eating, drinking, chatting (Animal, Vegetable or Metaphysical Concept? made its debut somewhere in the Yorkshire Dales), having baths – these simple pastimes were so enhanced by a day of fresh air and exercise as to legitimise walking just for the pleasure of stopping.

Sarah pointed out that I'd go crazy alone, and that I'd hate carrying a big backpack. It sounded like deliberate and unnecessary hardship to her, a contravention of all we stood – and walked – for.

Three weeks later I was sitting under the stars in Dorset, watching 1920s footage on a big outdoor screen of a man travelling the world on a motorbike, cumbersome film equipment buckled on, all sepia and intrepid. Some people walked into the desert with horses. I wasn't paying much attention, but suddenly I was blindsided. I sat up, colliding with Rhys, spilling a little beer. 'Rhys! I've got to take a donkey! I'm taking a donkey!'

I incubated the idea gently but firmly. It would have to be the following summer, I'd have to find a donkey. I'd need to speak to the coast path people, and wrap up work commitments. There'd be some beautiful panniers, hand-tooled leather, waxed canvas and brass buckles. I'd be a romantic figure, wandering through landscapes of magical realism with my burro, gathering tales and ancient wisdom. I'd be able to take my ukulele!

A donkey would be a porter, a companion, a crowd-pleaser and a good story. There'd be jeopardy, of course, but that would be expected, and necessary for the yarn. Very excited and very badly informed, I hit the internet and began to learn about *Equus africanus asinus*. On the whole it wasn't good news, but I refused to be discouraged.

Firstly I learned that donkeys don't like the rain. They are desert animals, and their fuzzy hair has evolved to trap a layer of air for insulation, keeping them cool in the daytime and warm at night. Horses have oily hair that allows the rain to run off; donkeys don't. They can handle heat and cold, but they just really hate the rain. Wales… well, it's famous for its rain at the best of times, but as I googled further ('donkey evolved hair oil?', 'donkey lightweight gazebo?', 'donkey Gore-Tex wax?', 'donkey umbrella hat?'), the wettest summer in 100 years flung itself against the windows. Then I learned that donkeys could actually die of wet. The jeopardy had already begun.

Next up: donkeys are buddy animals, it turned out. Although in the wild they hang out in herds, they still have a particular companion too. They operate on trust and friendship rather than hierarchy and force. That trait made me really like the idea of donkeys – a human characteristic that I could identify with. But I didn't think I could handle taking two donkeys; they'd have an unfair advantage over me. And what do you know – donkeys can die of being alone. Of course they can.

Also, donkeys are slow. They average 1.5 miles an hour, while people stride along at 2.5mph or more. Walking unnaturally slowly is much harder than walking too fast, as I knew from accompanying my friend Beth, who has pretty short legs and is generally relaxed. It's tough on the body, and it takes a change of mindset too. Could I really *amble* for 1000 miles?

Still, these things were surmountable. But then, a whole three weeks later, whilst monopolising yet another social event with my fledgling idea ('So why the donkey?' 'Well, as a porter and companion and a good story, really...'), I was suddenly floored. Harriet, mother of my goddaughter, said in a casually delivered blow of disaster, 'What about stiles?' Three weeks since the introduction of the donkey idea to the walk idea. Three weeks in which I had thought about all angles, talked the hind legs off all sorts of people, and not one person had come up with this thought. Not me, not the internet, not the dozens of friends and relations. Not even the woman at the Donkey Sanctuary. (For ages I'd put off ringing them in case they told me it was not just a bad idea but also irresponsible and illegal and that they would pursue me with a donkey abuse cessation order if I tried dragging a lonely, absorbent donkey around a surprisingly corrugated coastline. I'd finally called when a two-day power cut in my studio left me robbed of all other avoidance channels. They thought the idea sounded cool.)

What *about* stiles? I grew up in Wales – I knew all about stiles. Some of them were really high, taller than a person. Lots of them were rickety, or just lumps of rock sticking out of drystone walls. There was no way a donkey could get over a stile. For the first time the whole dream retreated, and I was alarmed. Worst of all, it had captured the collective imagination at the table, and I was forced to joke along with alternative solutions. Get the donkey to carry a lightweight aluminium ramp? Or two ramps, since I doubt it would be keen to jump off the top... Take wirecutters and a portable welder to break and mend the fence as I went? Or a chainsaw? 'Pack goat,' said Rhys, who was quite excited since he'd discovered that such a thing existed. In America, mostly. Did they have stiles in America? Could I carry a goat? 'A hydraulic lifting platform?' said Harriet. I could hardly summon a smile.

Maybe there were no stiles? Maybe stiles had gone out of style and been replaced with... well, what? I'd be no better off with a kissing gate or cattlegrid. On the train home I googled 'donkey stile' on my phone. Note: never google donkey stile. Especially not in public. The results were mostly videos.

I tried 'can a donkey climb a stile?' No answers, of course, but a sponsored link called 'Donkeys for sale' led me to a website called Horsemart and a little retail therapy to help me ignore the big problems. The first result was for Susanna, a 'trad-style donkey, with a cross'. 'Good bones,' it said. Alarm! Was it a glue-makers' website? 'Should make 12,' it said. Twelve? Sausages sprang to mind. No, it was 12h, which must be hands, like horses. Aha. So if two hands were about a foot, 12 would be... six foot? Not possible! Well, I guess she could leap stiles, a giant six-foot donkey.

What an amateur I was! I knew nothing about donkeys! Or in fact the Wales Coast Path, or the Offa's Dyke Path. Rhys declared a little obstacle to be a good thing, and nodded off, leaning against the train window. He couldn't have done much walking in Wales, I thought; stiles were a big obstacle, regularly. It was sheep country, for crying out loud!

I looked out into the darkness, and the bleak wind of a dead dream blew through the open window.

THREE

I went along to a weekend for aspiring adventurers, staffing a stand for a friend. One of the talks was on risk assessment. In the theatre of the Royal Geographical Society I listened to warnings about tropical diseases and altitude sickness and then made my own risk assessment, using the scheduled 15 minutes to plumb the depths of whole new calamities that hadn't yet occurred even to my overactive mind. I'm very obedient, and this was the task at hand. Some passing adventurer asked if I'd heard of a woman who'd ridden her horse across Ireland. 'I think the horse might have been struck by lightning, actually... Maybe that's something you need to think about?' I didn't really need to think about it, I was too busy chewing over a different horror scenario of my own devising: imagine being stuck on a beach with the tide coming in. Say we'd been walking along the sand for hours, and then discovered that the only route out was a ladder. Or sheer cliffs with just enough foliage for a frightened creature with opposable thumbs to scale but not for one with hooves. The tide coming in, no time to go back, oh cruel world! Oh cruel, incompetent muleteer! ('Donkey swim?' I asked the internet, but the search was inconclusive.)

Maybe the donkey would accidentally knock me off a cliff to my death. At least that would balance the scores. My risk list also included donkey illness, worms, bucking, biting, running away, being benighted, rapists, cattle, scary dogs, getting lost and blisters. There was a prize for the best risk assessment; I didn't get it.

I went on to a route-planning workshop, almost entirely men, almost exclusively discussing getting into Tibet in overland vehicles. There was a stack of maps and an air of testosterone, dust and privilege. It was impossible to tell who was the tutor – everybody seemed to be throwing pieces of hot information and conjecture at each other, waving their willies about. I flicked through an ancient road atlas showing some vast brightly coloured region with few roads, murmured something about Wales and donkeys, and was laughed out of the room.

Outside, a pinboard map of the world invited people to reveal their adventure; my pin was in scant company, on our own green isle. But I had pinned the tale of the donkey, pinned the donkey on the map of Wales, and I felt quietly bolstered – this was something else.

I emailed the Wales Coast Path people, a laboriously crafted enquiry that I hoped would charm them into responding with good news. But no, it was all bad. And not only that, but the reply came, grimly, from a man called Grimley:

'This idea has been received with much interest here but I'm sorry to say that I do not think it is really feasible for two main reasons:

1. *Much of the Wales Coast Path and Offa's Dyke Path (around 75 per cent) is on public footpaths and other routes upon which there is only a public right for people to walk – leading or riding a donkey would be trespass against the landowner. It would be necessary to get permission from every landowner in advance to avoid this.*

2. *As you suspect, there are numerous stiles and kissing gates to negotiate. We expect to have data on exactly how many in the next few weeks but it is probably in the thousands.*

May I suggest the Pennine Bridleway?'

I was beginning to feel like a very unreasonable dog with a bone. I emailed back to say that was fine – I wanted to walk the path more than I wanted to take a donkey, donkeys were slow anyway, he'd done me a favour. I tried to smuggle in the final line: 'What about a pack goat? Pack monkey? Pack guinea pig?'

Nothing got past Grimley. He responded: 'Good luck and have fun! By the way, dogs – however big – are the only furry things allowed on public footpaths as they are deemed to be a "usual accompaniment" of a walker!'

That exclamation mark rang out like the hammering in of the last nail in the coffin. I got on with ordinary life.

Two months passed and although far from resolved, the donkey idea continued to live side by side with the Wales Coast Path idea in my mind, proven impossible, but neither agreeing to die. An unsuitable animal and an impassable route.

And then, at last, a bit of good news. Hallelujah! After several days of looking at a phone number for a Wales-based donkey dealer, I summoned the courage to call it. I so desperately needed someone to think it could be done. This person would clearly know about donkeys; if they were sceptical or wary I might just… well, I didn't know what. But they weren't. Oh happy day! Zoie thought about it for a moment or two and said, 'Yes, I've got the donkey for you. Mali. She's strong and fast and needs something to occupy her mind.' Er, great! In my mind, me and Mali – which rhymes with Sally and is Welsh for Molly – were instantly firm friends. Faced with this unexpected result, I paused, and then dared to unpack a few other concerns from the giant sack of worries I'd begun to haul about the place.

I was thinking of fifteen miles a day…? 'She could do fifteen miles *standing on her head*!' Carrying bags would be fine too, once she'd had a bit of training, and her online profile also reassured me that she would be good with children, traffic and other animals, that she came to call, was willing to please and was easy to box, bath, catch and so on. A 'chunky, strong-boned jenny', it said. Bingo! The perfect donkey, and with my very first donkey-shopping enquiry! We didn't talk money; I got the impression I'd be doing Zoie a favour by giving Mali something to do.

'What about food? Should I feed her something in addition to grass?' Zoie suggested she might need a handful of nuts each day. Yes, yes, of course – I nodded down the phone and made a note, as my mind boggled quietly. Donkeys ate nuts? Who knew? Presumably something cheap like birds eat: peanuts rather than cashews or pistachios. Sounded heavy, one to look into later.

'And does she have a companion donkey already? Will it be okay to take her away from the others?' Zoie reassured me that she wasn't already buddied up and that loneliness wasn't a worry as I'd become her companion.

We agreed that I'd visit before long, and take Mali for a walk. 'And a ride,' said Zoie. I'd never thought about that! Would it be a good idea, having that option? If I could ride my steed, why would I ever choose to walk?

The dream was renewed. My imaginary donkey – a feeble creature that could die almost immediately from a variety of common occurrences, that would dawdle slowly, with worms and bad hooves, thinking up ways to knock me off cliffs – was straight away replaced by Mali the trouper. Strong, sturdy, hungry for activity. Yes! At last! And she was handsome: her online profile showed a shiny chocolate-brown donkey with a grey nose and belly. I would be delighted to be her companion.

I saved her picture onto my mobile phone and set to learning some more donkey facts. They are curious and not easily startled. They have incredible memories, remembering faces and places for up to 25 years. They can get sunburn. Their ears help keep them cool and they can hear other donkeys up to 60 miles away in the desert. Sixty! No way! They have an average life expectancy of 27, although Lively Laddie of Blackpool, the world's oldest donkey, may have been 62 when he died in 2005.

They groom each other, their presence can calm nervous horses, they have a natural aversion to canines and can be used to guard sheep and goats. They eat a lot of fibre and are efficient at extracting all the nutrients. They came to Britain with the Romans in 43 AD. They have been used for cockling, and there have been beach donkeys since the 1830s.

There were currently 850 beach donkeys in the UK, I discovered. The Donkey Sanctuary recommended that they had to have a lunch hour, and a day off per week. They shouldn't be sold until they were at least six months old or ridden before they were four. And they shouldn't be made to carry people who were over 16 years old or weighed more than eight stone.

Ah. I was over twice the former and nearly three-halves the latter. Good. Maybe I could still lean on her, though.

With the donkey situation now comfortably under control, the year came to an end. 2012 may not quite have been the year of adventure, but it was the year of adventure planning. For Christmas I got 29 Ordnance Survey maps from Mum, and an engraved farrier's knife, a pony headcollar, and a blue plastic My First Grooming Kit from Rhys. The knife said 'Hannah &' on the wooden casing, and 'A Seaside Donkey' on one of the blades. Unlike ordinary penknives that have lots of useful things and one puzzling implement that might be something to do with horses, this one had one ordinary knife and dozens of strange tools. I loved it.

I started jogging with a view to being able to run away from dogs, if Mali wasn't as good a guard donkey as I hoped. Somewhere at the back of my mind it nagged me that I'd not actually seen a donkey in all the five months of this dream, so I jogged past Hackney City Farm, craning my neck for a glimpse of Larry the donkey. No sign, so I followed him on Twitter instead.

The beginning of a new year ushered in a new level of reality. The damp pressure of financial unease began to weigh on my solar plexus – I'd saved almost nothing. But it brought with it a hardy cheapness that I was happy to welcome back. I stopped buying the expensive edible treats of busy urban life and began to long for an enamel mug and a camping stove. I pictured myself slicing up an apple onto my morning muesli with an awesome sea view from my chosen bluff, Mali grazing calmly nearby, and everything tasting better in the fresh air than anything from a patisserie ever could. Begging hot water for my flask, eating fish and chips on quaysides, a pint of ale in the evening, buttery, floury welshcakes as I walked. I couldn't wait.

I emailed Grimley again to see if he knew where the stiles were. Maybe I *could* contact all the landowners of the stile-free sections? There might be hundreds of them, but if it was the only way to salvage the dream… Grimley replied; the bad news was in at last: 410 stiles, and they didn't know where they were. 'However, given that kissing gates are also a problem to a donkey – and there are 783 of these – I still don't think you'd get very far on the actual WCP route!' Another killer exclamation mark, backed up this time with an attached map of the sections of path that were designated bridleways. They were shown in red, and looked like a mere few dozen flecks – of very little comfort. The WCP part of the journey was around 800 miles, which meant more than one and a half obstacles per mile, on average. 'Ah well, roads it is then,' I emailed back. 'Good to see you and your donkey are determined!' Grimley replied.

Yes, me and my donkey. At least one part of this plan was coming on well. A visit to Mali was long overdue.

FOUR

There are good reasons why donkeys are companion animals. Horses and dogs need to know who is boss – you show them it's you, and then they'll do what you say, even if it's sometimes counterintuitive to them. Donkeys have a different logic, which appealed to me much more. They have a strong sense of self-preservation. ('You're really taking a donkey?' said Sarah one evening. 'Aren't they famously stubborn?' 'Ah!' I replied. 'That's a myth. Donkey people say it's actually just a well-honed sense of self-preservation – donkeys won't do anything that they perceive to be not in their best interests.' 'Yes…' said Sarah, who is a barrister and as such finds holes in arguments for a living. 'Isn't that kind of the definition of stubborn?')

To train a donkey, you become friends with it. You show it that you can be trusted, and that you also have its best interests at heart. You have to be confident. Donkeys – and probably all creatures – can tell if you are nervous.

I was deeply, deeply nervous. It was early January and I planned to leave on the 1st of May. There were less than four months in which to make Mali like me. Not to mention her owner! Despite her enthusiasm on the phone, I knew I was going to have to make an effort to win Zoie over too; it seemed highly likely to me that she'd change her mind.

What if Mali was grumpy? I was going to try to take her for a walk, but what if she just wouldn't? My 1000-mile journey had to start with a single step, but it was going to be Mali's journey too, and what if she just didn't fancy it, wouldn't take a single step?

Equipped with Marks & Spencer pre-cut carrot batons and a packet of Polos, Rhys and I hit the M4 and eventually crossed the Severn Bridge, taut harp strings slicing the grey sky. Greetings, oh land of my... well, my father is from Germany, and my mother is from England, but I was born amongst the velvet, sheep-bitten hills of Mid Wales, 10 miles inland from Aberystwyth, where my parents had settled in the 1970s.

I decamped to London at 20, and although I felt comfortable now in the city amongst the 24-hour noise and hectic anonymity, the air muddied with distant beats and sirens, and the pavements with puddles of neon, Wales would always be home. Crossing the bridge made this bold homecoming plan all a little real; I sat upright in my seat.

This was like a blind date. But a blind date with someone mute who would see right through me and not feel the need to be polite; whose assent I really, really needed. To make matters worse, Rhys was about to film proceedings.

I'd asked Rhys if he'd come and cheer me up on the walk, if it turned out to be an awful mistake. With a filmmaker's glint in his eye, he'd turned towards me and said, 'If you're miserable, I'll be happy.'

And then, there they were. Donkeys, at least a dozen, milling around completely oblivious to me having a 'big moment' at their gate. These were the first donkeys I had seen since having the idea – it had crossed my mind that I might even find I was allergic to them. They were all shaggy and sweetly dishevelled, and most trotted up to the gate to nudge at us with their noses. One big, dark brown donkey stood at the far edge of the yard, unmoved by the excitement. Of course, that was Mali.

Zoie and her uncle let themselves in and went to fetch her, and Rhys and I watched as she jerked away from them, giving them the runaround, back and forth along the breezeblock wall. When they got hold of her she pulled against them and skidded in the mud on her clattering hooves, her strength and sudden movements inspired by fear. They got her tied and beckoned us over, and I came to stand a few feet away, looking her kindly in the eye. 'Hello Mali!' Her eyes were wide, and she backed away from me, pulling so hard on her rope that one of its two thick strands snapped with a twang and unravelled suddenly, making us both recoil. I turned my attention hastily to Zoie, warm and friendly in full make-up and waterproofs, and reassuringly relaxed about the performance.

'There's nothing nasty in her. You only start working them at three, and she needs more training because she's so strong, you see, but I haven't had much time. And it's been so wet. She needs something to keep her busy, keep her occupied. She is normally better than that.'

Of course, of course, I'm sure it's all fine. My default setting was to pretend I wasn't alarmed and to issue relentless positivity. We discussed donkeys in general, and Mali calmed down a little, once we weren't looking at her. Donkeys can commit suicide, said Zoie. 'Their body can just sort of shut down, it suffocates the organs in its own blood.' Interesting! I said. 'From stress, or if they've bonded with another animal and that bond has been split,' says Zoie. I sneaked glances at Mali. She looked pretty stressed.

Meanwhile Teddy, one of the sweet little white donkeys, sidled up and rested the full weight of his huge head on Rhys's arm. 'You'd like to go on an adventure, wouldn't you, Teddy?' said Zoie. 'But you can't, because you are my favourite.'

'They won't show you if they are in pain,' she added. 'That's another reason you need to get to know her, so you can tell.' Well, fascinating, I said. 'Then there's pneumonia from getting wet, and you'll have to be careful with the hooves.'

The hay man arrived and Zoie went to move hay about, giving me a few moments alone with Mali. She was beautiful – a brown so dark it was almost slate grey, with a soft, ashy grey nose and belly. She looked like a perfect storybook donkey, handsome and noble, with a bold red headcollar. I would be proud to be seen with her, if she'd ever let me near her. I leaned in very slowly and stroked her wiry cheek gingerly with the backs of two fingers, and she let me, in stiff defeat.

Hay man bustled in, scaring a wild, bug-eyed pony, which galloped towards me across the muddy concrete. I flinched, and he laughed and said what we were probably all thinking: 'Well accustomed to equines, then?'

But to my relief, Zoie didn't seem to be put off by my total ineptitude, and we began to make plans. She suggested I notify vets all along the route so they would be expecting us. 'Yes! I'll do that!' And I'd need to spend time with the donkey before departure, to walk together and get to know each other. Daily handling. 'Yes, yes. No problem!' I was willing to be absolutely dutiful, just as long as she would keep faith in me as a future donkey owner. Everything would be alright, wouldn't it? 'You've seen her from scratch now,' said Zoie, twice.

We drove home, without having taken Mali for a walk, let alone a ride. I ate the carrot sticks pensively – it hadn't seemed the time to offer them to her, somehow, and they'd stayed in the car. She hadn't liked the Polos, she hadn't liked me.

I would persevere.

I'd known that this wouldn't be easy, and that first nuzzle would be all the more wonderful for this hiccup. We'd be sitting by a hedgerow, looking at the view, and Mali would give me some sort of unexpected snuggle with her nose, accepting me as her buddy. It would be a soaring moment. We'd get there.

FIVE

I turned my efforts to other things, like working out that walking uses something like 100 calories per mile, so I'd burn 100,000 additional calories over the walk. That's 167 portions of fish and chips, or 556 welshcakes. The average person's stride is two and a half feet, that's two thousand steps in a mile, or two million steps altogether. Taking into account fast bits and slow bits and breaks, I could expect to cover two miles an hour, so that would be 500 hours of walking. Sitting at my laptop day after day, through a bitterly and relentlessly cold February, with a layer of snow across the whole of the British Isles, I felt unequivocally good about the impending outdoors.

I made a website and a Facebook group. I showed people a picture of Mali on my phone. She looked beautiful, and terrified. 'Welsh for Molly,' I'd say. 'Isn't that sweet? Yes, she can walk 15 miles a day standing on her head, apparently.' I ignored the little demon of foreboding that tried to haunt me.

Packsaddles – that was the next challenge. More internet time told me that donkey packing was alive and well as an activity, just not in the UK. Of course the vast majority of the world's 40 million donkeys are in poor countries, where they are used for work, providing the cheapest, strongest and most stoic assistance it's possible to buy, or breed. The packsaddles used on those donkeys looked cheap, homemade and functional.

On the lifestyle-choice end of the donkey-packing scale there were two players: America and France. On a French website I found beautifully made packs that were fully customisable to allow the carrying of various combinations of children, picnics and parasols through landscapes that no doubt smelled of herbs and hot sap. Their menu of accessories was informative

– my shopping list included the kindest hobble ever invented, a plastic-covered tethering cable that wouldn't get caught on clumps of vegetation, a peg, a 'couveton' (padded cushion!), a rain sheet, and two handsome canvas packs, for a grand total of 1000 euros. Ouch. In their defence, they did explain that the quality was exceptional. Their canvas bags, for example, were '*not among the least expensive*', they wrote, Frenchly. This was because they would be '*your safeguard against the vagaries of the road. They resist to rain and bear the most difficult terrain, the more rocky and more thorn.*'

I opened a new browser window.

From America I found advice on taking your burros or mules long distances. These were clearly a different breed of packers, who wouldn't leave their bedrolls for anything less than guaranteed 'more rocky and more thorn'. There were no wickerwork padded baby carriers on offer, but bags came with optional bow or rifle scabbards and bear-proof panniers (that thankfully did meet the 'Interagency Grizzly Bear Committee requirements for bear-resistance'. Phew).

Both suppliers would need Mali's measurements, but I put off asking Zoie to measure her. Was I stalling? I couldn't help thinking that Zoie wouldn't survive an encounter with Mali and a tape measure.

Weeks passed and I came across a man called Peter who made inflatable saddles for Afghan donkeys to carry women in labour. After we had exchanged a few emails, Peter said very gently that he didn't think Mali was the one. He was just words on a screen to me, and yet I knew immediately that he was right, and sank with utter gratitude into his advice. 'I would specify a mature (eight-years-plus), calm and sensible donkey with plenty of road experience,' he wrote. 'The other thing is the size and strength of Mali – she will pull you as if you weren't there… You could easily get killed from something stupid like a leaf falling onto the footpath and the donkey pulling you into traffic.'

The relief at having untethered my future from wild Mali's kept me cushioned, for a few days, from the great worry of having an impending donkey adventure but no donkey. Peter gave me some leads though, recommending a Shropshire-based donkey dealer called Dave, and a forum of donkey lovers, for help and advice. And suddenly everything got much, much worse.

Forums, I realised quickly, are for people to show off their knowledge unhindered by the constraints of tact or manners. It's a fool who wanders in, as I did, waving my inexperience like a cheerful flag of surrender. There came an alarming barrage of firmly held, fiercely expressed but highly contradictory opinions, and in shock and self-defence I erected a firewall of false promises. I reassured them that I had the whole of April set aside for donkey familiarisation and training, a backup donkey in the wings, a schedule of appointments with vets and farriers, a support vehicle, and the ability to identify a yew tree. None of these things were true; inwardly, my resolve faltered.

I also began to call up donkey dealers. Shropshire Dave was very encouraging, said he'd have a think about whether he had a suitable donkey, but warned, 'One of you needs to know what you're doing.' He chose to spell it out: 'And it's not you.'

Deep down I knew it could be done, but some days it felt very, very deep down. The donkey worries at least obscured all of the other things to think about, like the route and the overnights. I'd not even settled on the basics, but made notes that I never followed up, like: 'Clockwise or anticlockwise? Ask meteorologist about prevailing winds…'

One person remained unflappable. Rhys, any time I declared the latest list of possible freak occurrences, or just my shaken confidence, would reply, 'People have been walking about with donkeys for thousands of years. You'll be alright. It's a great idea.' Often he didn't even look up from his work. 'But do find a picture of a yew tree.'

SIX

As I cowered, bare and defenceless in the battleground of the forum, it delivered me an angel. Carol lifted me up and dusted me off, dispensing practical advice with great heart and in a Yorkshire accent that was like being affectionately scrubbed with a hot flannel. She had several donkeys and often took one out for a weekend's walk, staying overnight at guesthouses with stables. She was just as worried about me as everyone else, but much, much wiser.

'You are young, Hannah, full of enthusiasm for this trip, and that is exactly as it should be,' she wrote. 'I don't know if you are an animal person, but donkeys are a bit special. They can read you for sure, and when you spend time with them you will find they have the ability to see into your very soul.' She followed this with brisk advice on webbing straps, including the catalogue reference number.

Somehow I could take it all from Carol – I suppose because she was knowledgeable rather than just opinionated. Rather than just tell me, several times, that donkeys don't like the wet, Carol told me that donkeys are good at finding hedgerows for shelter. She told me I'd need a pocket spring balance to make sure the packs were even, and that the most she'd ever had her donkeys carry was 14kg each side. She said that the dead weight of a pack is much heavier than the weight of a human, as a rider will stand in the stirrups and help the animal along. She said the speed of a donkey isn't really to do with the length of leg, and that we'd need lots of rest stops – every two hours or so. She recommended going for a beach donkey aged between seven and eighteen. If we were going to stay overnight somewhere with no grazing, I'd have to take hay – a donkey couldn't be without food for that long. I could take pony nuts. (Oh! *Pony* nuts! Yes, of course.) When frightened, horses run and keep on going, but donkeys freeze and assess, and often look a bit embarrassed.

As Carol poured out her experience, every now and then the sheer thousand-miley-ness of it would occur to her anew: 'I don't know if you'll do it, I really don't,' she said. And I didn't mind hearing that from her. 'I don't know either, Carol. But if we don't manage it, if we have to give up, it'll be for the right reasons. We'll have tried.'

Donkey owners invited me to visit, and friendly meetings with tense undercurrents took place around the country with people who loved to talk about donkeys. While they worked out my intentions for their beloved beast, I soaked up their knowledge and advice and tried to fathom their motives in return. Were they more interested in money than getting me the right creature?

Until the recession, donkeys had commanded a good return. £1000 wasn't unusual, and for something you could make yourself with two other donkeys, that was pretty good. But prices had dropped, bringing a new urgency to the sales process. Donkey breeding is a lifestyle choice, and the dealers I met were sentimental about their animals, but there was also something of the used-car-salesman about them. It was a weird, weird mixture. Many of them loved their donkeys dearly, but could never quite remember their names. They were simultaneously hungry to make a sale and loath to lose a friend.

I called donkey dealer Dave now and again. 'I know just what you need… You need a donkey that will stride on… One that's sharp. And dark hooves – they're stronger than white hooves. Hm, I'm trying to think…' He told me to call him back in a few weeks.

But weeks were getting scarce.

'You'll just *know* when you find the right one,' said the online donkey advisors, but how on earth would I? It was like highly inefficient dating, with silent and standoffish candidates, deeply concerned chaperones, and hundreds of miles between encounters. I was the bumbling suitor, nervously proffering a bouquet of carrots.

Donkey owners talked quite a lot about how a donkey could change their mood and their priorities. How spending ten minutes with their donkeys could get them their poise back. I learned that donkeys are used for therapy, that autistic kids can find them comforting, and that they're often taken to care homes. I looked forward to a time when donkeys would be a source of calm and perspective for me too – right now they were causing me nothing but worry, and a nagging toothache from clenching my jaw at night, through dreams of disapproval and heavy responsibility. The persistent cold spring wasn't helping – frozen, brittle puddle shells hoarded hard grains of snow; cold lambs and ragged daffodils and hunched people all wondered when a reprieve might come.

One recce took me to my home patch, to meet the hard-as-nails Borth donkeys who live by the train line. Borth is a seaside village just north of Aberystwyth, and it is almost always cold. A single wind-bitten street runs between the sea and a hinterland of blonde bog and in the distance stand the mountains on the far side of the Dyfi estuary, in all the shades of green and purple, with a stark beauty like Mongolian steppes. Costa del Borth, my sister Naomi calls it.

When we got there it was the bitterest I'd ever experienced. The wind ravaged my exposed fingers until they felt like bare bones, stiff and awkward and unable to direct themselves into my pockets. The ear flaps on my hat beat me around the cheeks as I shook hands with Bill Doyle, the stout and elderly Irishman who had been running the Borth donkey racket for 47 years, ever since it cost tuppence a ride. Bill's bread bag broke free and whipped off into the distance, only to whip back later from another direction. The donkeys' bathtub drinking trough had frozen over, been broken up, and then frozen over again.

The dozen woolly donkeys ran over and surrounded Bill, Mum and me, and went for the bread. They were all big animals, but not frightening – calm and friendly and shaggy. Some sweet soft brown donkeys came right up to say hi, but Bill pointed out his pick for me: Lily; as usual, the introvert donkey skulking behind the gang. 'You can't have that one – that big, friendly one – he's my favourite,' said Bill, whose initial suspicion of me was cast aside when he took a cuddly shine to Mum.

I dearly wanted to take a Borth donkey – they were donkeys from my patch. Mum and Dad had lived in Borth when they were first married. While they were away on honeymoon, the sea flooded their rented house and drowned the pile of wedding presents and belongings they'd not yet unpacked; the neighbours broke in to let the sea out of the back door. I was brought up with a very wrinkled dictionary that survived – an antediluvian remnant of a time before my parents were parents. As a child, I swam in the chilly sea at Borth with visiting aunts and uncles and drew mazes on the beach. I learned to drive on the hard sand of the next beach along.

I was cautiously optimistic about Lily. She was rough and lousy-looking and sturdy, but maybe that was exactly the sort of beast I needed. There weren't any thunderbolts of true love, but perhaps that would grow.

Even so, I called Dave again. After a few moments he remembered who I was, and said, 'Yes! I think I might have a good donkey for you…' Really? What is it like? 'A female… Sharp. Walks on. Brown.' And, er, what's her name? 'It's… it's… um… Jenny!' he said, sounding rather like he was clutching at straws.

Um-Jenny? Wasn't Jenny just the name for a female donkey? Was this for real? Still, I wasn't about to complain. Um-jenny might be just the donkey I was looking for. The just-know, thunderbolt donkey. 'Can I come and see her?' I began to bother him with desperate travel arrangements.

No, said Dave. He was chocker-block with ecclesiastical bookings. It was Easter – the peak season for donkey hire, for heaven's sake.

Back to Lily. By now Bill Doyle also had a second option for me, called Dolly. He agreed to let me take them each for a walk, provided that Tamlin, the Donkey Sanctuary's welfare officer for Mid and North Wales, was there too. Many people had advised me to get in touch with Tamlin – so many that securing her approval began to look very important and I was getting nervous about seeking it. When I finally worked up the courage, she was expansive and excited by the idea, and what's more she already knew who I was. It turned out she was from the village of Bontgoch, the remote T-junction and scattering of farmhouses where I'd spent my childhood. For a decade, she'd been our closest neighbour and she still lived in the next house along the track from our old Welsh longhouse.

Without any fuss she met me in Borth and got down to the business of teaching me how to check Lily's and Dolly's hooves. A tall, practical, strong woman, she had pockets full of minty horse treats, training in animal behaviour and a great deal of love for the donkeys. Under her tutorage I picked out two of Dolly's hooves, coaxing each one up and cradling it while clumsily scraping the underside clean of mud and stones. Then Dolly lost interest and refused me the next hoof. It was rooted to the ground. Dolly didn't seem to be fighting to keep it there, it was just a simple, steadfast fact – hoof and ground were as one. Tamlin advised that I had to really believe the hoof would lift, and then it would. But crouching by a donkey's knee, soft skull close to hard hoof, I didn't believe it, Dolly didn't believe it, and Tamlin took over.

Still, it was real donkey experience at long last, and as Tamlin and Bill chewed over the issues of the donkey world, I walked Lily and then Dolly up and down the lane to the optimistic sound of a distant ice-cream van in the encouraging fresh sunshine.

I took Lily first, but it was not to be. The whine of a lawnmower eroded her confidence, and 20 steps further on, when we rounded a corner that gave her a brand-new view of the world, it was all too much. She stopped and I got my first taste of powerlessness, tethered to an immovable beast with no faith in me.

Dolly next, and I chatted to her breezily in the hope of concealing my fragile state. Past the lawnmower, past Lily's point of no advance, she flinched only slightly at a distant pickup truck but ambled on, paying no heed at all to the leopard, draped on a branch 10 feet above us.

Hang on, *what*? I snuck a second look, trying to hide it from Dolly. Yes – it was a leopard. We were passing along the back of the Borth Animalarium and there really was a leopard. Did Dolly not notice or not care? Either way, as soon as we were a sensible distance from the zoo, I felt confident enough in the new relationship to get my phone out with one hand and take a Hannah-and-Dolly self-portrait. She might just be the one: rotund and a bit ploddy, walking behind me rather than alongside, obedient and unquestioning, a little bit mangy but kind of attractively gingery. And not afraid of leopards.

I went back later with Mum's tape measure and climbed the gate in the evening light. I needed to measure Dolly to get the packsaddle ordered. The donkeys had retreated to the far side of the field and eyed me as I approached. Which was Dolly? There were several brown ones… The friendly half a dozen came over – the huge one that was Bill's favourite, the tiny pushy black ones that looked like they had legwarmers on. They jostled me a bit scarily, egging each other on. Finally I found the one, loitering around the back, that was most likely to be Dolly. With patience, carrot slices and more than an hour, I managed to get close enough to measure around her belly and note down some fuzz-covered approximation of her hip and shoulder.

At the end of our little walk I'd seen Dolly surge forward when she caught sight of her field and her donkey buddies and I had sensed the reserves of power running through her sturdy frame. Once I had torn her from the place she knew, forced her to be my friend and impressed upon her the mission at hand, maybe she would bring that power to bear in the eating up of coastal miles. I seized hope where I found it, and chewed on it through the nights.

And then everything changed.

Donkey dealer Dave had a free morning, and after all that time it seemed worth going to meet his donkey, Um-Jenny. But as I drove through the bright Mid Wales countryside, heaving with the green energy of long-delayed spring and spattered with riotous daffodils, I hoped it would be an easy decision. Mum came too and we had a powwow in the car. 'I just pray that I'll either fall unquestionably in love or can rule this donkey out completely and go back to placid old Dolly and be content.'

Dave tried to prepare us by apologising that Jenny, a strong Bulgarian, um, jenny who 'walked on', hadn't been as 'sharp' that morning as she usually was. Then he led her out of the stable. She was somehow covered in her own poo, and proceeded to drag me all over the place as I gripped the knot I'd tied at the end of her rope. She ran away from a motorbike on the road, and then spun me in circles around the yard just to embarrass me in front of Dave, his wife, a helper, and their farrier too for good measure.

It didn't help that I couldn't give her a rub; her wet, mucky fur was a bit of a barrier to affection. I told Dave she might be the perfect donkey for a second adventure, handed her rope back, and exhaled for the first time in fifteen minutes. Right, we'd done what we came for. Dolly it was, then.

'There is another one,' said Dave, and brought out a gelding. I took him straight off for a walk, and he seemed nervy, jumping at a passing car and some dry leaves scratching along the road. I decided against him instantly, but carried on a little way. He was keen, walking up alongside me at a pretty quick pace. He soon calmed down about the cars, and took his lead from me about where we were going. When we got back to the yard I gave him a good brush down (with the blue My First Grooming Kit I'd got for Christmas, still in its little plastic handbag: always a dead cert for amusing donkey owners), and a bit of carrot, and he began to relax next to me; I started winning him over. He looked indolently past me with his astonishingly beautiful Egyptian eyes, his baby-pink headcollar adding a touch of dandyism. My heart valves popped and gulped like a goldfish's mouth; oxygen flooded through me.

We did a few short circuits from the yard and every time I opened the gate he hurried through. He was clearly saying, 'Come on then!' Mum tried breaking into a jog to see if he would trot alongside, and he did. Trotting! I couldn't imagine Dolly trotting for love nor carrots!

Chico was much younger than I would have liked – only five, just a year older than Mali – and his hooves were lighter-coloured (therefore apparently softer) and thinner-walled than Dolly's. He was quick, but would he be constant? He was skinny and not necessarily even fully grown and had never worked or had any training. His previous owner had eventually given him back to Dave because he was too much for him, and he wouldn't come to the fence, even for Polos.

But I fell for him. I just knew.

SEVEN

A month later we stood adrift at the north end of Aberystwyth prom in the rain, Chico pulling and weaving about, me crying and following him, my phone showing no signal. Two back roads ran up the side of Constitution Hill, parting company as a gulley deepened between them, and ridiculously I didn't know which one to take.

Thankfully Mum and Rhys soon tracked us down. They were due to walk with us, but I'd stalked off without them. The two of them took control with good humour, which could only mean they hadn't grasped the full gravity of the situation. Rhys took Chico's rope and Mum identified the right road and we walked up and out of Aberystwyth. Apart from once or twice for the camera, I didn't lead Chico again that day.

As Mum and Rhys chatted, I looked about the landscape that I'd been born and brought up in, the aspects unfamiliar as we walked on bridleways I'd never noticed before. Rainwater ran off us, washing the strength and dexterity out of my fingers, soaking through Chico's pack pad. I was still holding his salty rain sheet, not feeling firm enough to do anything but keep walking forward; certainly not ready to frighten him with the mac again. Then, during a particularly vigorous downpour, Chico veered off under the trees at the edge of the track and refused to go on. The bare hawthorns offered no shelter but, to Chico, standing in the rain was preferable to walking in the rain. Full of remorse, I put the mac on him, and he didn't complain much; his usual nervous energy had also leached away in the persistent rain. Mum headed back and left us to it.

After five miles we reached the village of Bow Street, and Chico was shivering. We'd survived a stretch of treacherous main road, Rhys leading Chico, and me slowing the cars, searching out eye contact with each driver and mouthing 'thank you'. We paused at Bow Street's Spar, where I had been a thousand times, stopping for milk or bread on the way home to Bontgoch from school in Aberystwyth. The old familiarity collided with the utter strangeness of my current situation. I had an uncanny sense that the stage set of my life was the same, but a new and unrehearsed play was underway, a new reality that was deeply unsettling, and really clammy.

I bought carrots and apples for Chico and flapjack for us, and we stood by the parked cars and ate, for morale, warmth and fuel. People passed us, nipping in for bread and milk. Chico cheered up a bit, and the shivering stopped. Looking after each other, we felt for a moment like a little team, in it together.

Mum's friends Jane and Gerry put us up for the night. We towelled Chico down in their stone barn, removed anything he might try to eat, ran white electric fence tape around the front so that he could come a little way out and eat the grass, and connected it up to the heavy battery I'd been carrying. He stood stiffly in the entrance, looking out and wondering what was going on, and later Gerry admitted that he'd turned the outside light on so Chico wouldn't be alone in the dark. I suspected, being an animal, that the dark was probably the least of his worries.

Jane gave us homemade quiche, salad and wine, hot showers, a feather bed, and warm conversation, but nevertheless an underlying anxiety settled alongside the underlying chill of being cold all day. I perversely held myself back from relaxing, troubled by the feeling that I needed this sanctuary too much. It meant we weren't really coping. Our kit was chaotic and too heavy, everything was wet, we were exhausted; how would we kick the habit of fleeing indoors?

Chico stood reproachfully outside in the electric glow while the rain fell, and at last my body was wrested back from my mind and I slept, profound and fathomless, released from the fear of tomorrow.

Tamlin came to see us on the road the next morning, had a quick look at Chico and said he was fine and we were doing well. I could have kissed her, so vast was the relief of having official sanction, although I didn't believe it. Last night's dark, tired thoughts had been replaced, if not with optimism, at least with action. Chico had survived the night and stayed behind the electric corral and we'd spent hours of the morning in his barn, rationalising kit, leaving lots behind.

As we walked, I called the equine insurers – something that had dropped off the list in the frantic days before departure. We'd already established that my fears were many and varied, as I'd asked them, 'What if… what if I tie him to a fence and he pulls it down?' The woman on the phone had to check with a supervisor. Yes, we'd be covered. 'And if he kicks a car?' She checked again – yes, we'd be fine. 'And someone's dog? A child?' Yes. We'd established that the tack wouldn't be covered unless it was in a locked building with bars on the windows – I explained that it would often be beside me in a tent, just to waste the poor woman's time. And maybe to intrigue her a little. She assured me with delicate tact that they'd pay for removal of carcass.

Rhys led Chico while I read out my bank details, walking along the quiet back road from Bow Street to Talybont, my shoulders lifting a bit as the policy kicked in immediately. A cyclist appeared, heading towards Aberystwyth, having come 'not far', but a distance it would take us another two days to cover. He seemed like us – young, active, outside in the May sunshine – and was delighted by our walk; he gave us an apple for Chico. We were interesting! We were insured! We were dry! We walked on and I ate the apple, leaving a generous core for Chico.

We passed through Talybont, where the Black Lion and White Lion coexist on the village green, and over the river Leri. Five miles further upstream, the Leri runs through my old village, Bontgoch, and alongside the old Welsh longhouse called Llyn Loew where I spent my first 16 years. My parents bought the dilapidated house and renovated it slowly. Some time before we got there it would probably have been thatched, the family living at one end and the livestock at the other, the windows small in the deep stone walls, and the whitewash bright and proud. In my early years we had no running water or electricity, and Mum in her dungarees and headscarf washed my towelling nappies in a bucket with water from the Leri.

Later on, many happy hours were spent holding myself still in the clear, cold flow, breathing through a snorkel and watching fish, their cold, speckled bodies suspended alongside mine in the current. My long-standing childhood campaign for pets never really succeeded – a fairground goldfish died after a week, a stick insect was so boring we eventually released it onto a privet bush in the village, the chickens didn't really count, and Dad didn't like cats. My animal-owning credentials were poor.

In Talybont we passed Richard-the-hairdresser's salon, where I'd got my ears pierced, and had a terrible wet-look mullet cut in 1991; a place that I will forever be transported back to by the smell of surgical spirit, clean hair and cheap gel.

When Tamlin had realised we'd been neighbours, she'd reminded me that we had met once before. 'I put your dreads in,' she said. In 1996 I'd asked Richard-the-hairdresser for dreadlocks to complement my Doc Martens, combat trousers, and enthusiasm for social equality. He said dreads just weren't the sort of thing you got done in a salon and gave me a phone number to call – Tamlin's. I'd walked across the fields to her house, with my sister Naomi for moral support, and spent a long, shy afternoon in her living room, as Tamlin methodically twisted and scuffed my hair into long blonde dreadlocks. They were great. Soon after getting them, I moved into a hazel bender in the garden for the summer. Seventeen years later, and all the help I needed was clearly still on my old doorstep. After casting so wildly around the UK, that seemed significant.

Buoyed now by Tamlin's encouragement, we decided to do things properly and have a lunch break in the corner of a field. Chico was nervous and watchful, tied to the gate, rattling it; he didn't eat or rest. It began to rain lightly, but the stop still felt like a success – the first of what I hoped would become a habit of the road, a routine of self-sufficiency.

In a field across the road was – according to the map – Bedd Taliesin, the grave of the sixth-century bard Taliesin. It's said that those who spend a night there wake as either a poet or a madman, but with the poetry of the bright landscape and the wide-eyed madness of our companion, I didn't feel we needed to invite either element to lodge further; we got into our waterproofs and moved on.

North of Talybont, the back roads climbed high and the temperature dropped. The rain started again in earnest, and the tracks were no longer tarmac. Rhys worried about Chico more than I did; perhaps I had reached the limit of the worry I could hold. Or maybe I was just busy worrying about myself, or happy to let Rhys shoulder the parenting for a while. Also, I thought that Chico would have an animal sense of how to be safe that I couldn't second-guess and needn't try to influence. I was leading him across an old quarry track with a banked surface of bare, wet slate, and Rhys said, 'Don't lead him across the slate – he'll slip.' I held the rope loosely so Chico could choose his own path – some of the surface was gravelly, which was surely grippy enough. But no, his hooves slid on the smooth rock and he fell on his side, caught by the saddlebags.

Shocked, he scrambled to his feet and stood still, the rainwater making a trickling river between his hooves. More heartbreaking remorse. Rhys held his great, wet head and spoke to him gently, but he would go neither forward nor back. The track had high, mossy stone walls on both sides: we were stuck.

'He's lost confidence,' said Rhys, and I was struck by the thought that the donkey might be paralysed by so human an emotion. Taking my cue from Rhys, I joined in, and we gave him some love and sympathy, and possibly a tiny bit of chocolate, before coaxing him across the shining slate; he wouldn't walk through even the half-inch trickle of running water.

We'd been invited to stay at Plas Einion, a huge early-twentieth-century house that looked like a dollshouse and now comprised a number of flats whose residents lived communally in some ways. It occupied a regal, lofty position on a steep hillside, five miles on from Talybont.

Chico had a field to himself, a long and hidden meadow which we dropped down to from above. I checked the periphery, collecting all of the raindrops from the grass into my shoes. I propped up a bit of sagging fence, noted the bluebell patches and decided just to hope he wouldn't eat them (all bulbs being on the bad-for-donkeys list). I blocked up a gap with some oil drums, and returned to find Chico keeping his distance while Rhys assembled a tent for him out of a pile of logs and a tarpaulin. We stashed the bags under it, but Chico opted for a night in the rain instead; guiltily we left him to it.

At the house, we stood like advancing generals in front of a vast picture window, looking out over the misty Dyfi estuary and our passage of the next few days along the far bank. As we dripped wet patches onto the wooden floor, a kind collection of adults and kids gave us towels, hot soup and bread and cheese, then offered us a vintage 1965 Morris campervan to sleep in, parked under a giant rhododendron on the majestic front drive.

Everything was washed clean and bright by the rain: the bright green van with its friendly bright round headlamps, and the bright pink rhododendron. Needy though we still were for hot food, generous people and somewhere to dry our clothes, as I washed my face at the exquisite hot tap in the corner of the garage I felt like the staged advance into the outdoors might be working.

Mum joined us the next day, and the sun came out. She was excited about the trip and delighted to be involved, full of a simple enthusiasm that I wouldn't feel for a long time. Chico seemed to relax in her presence too; he seemed to prefer being a minor member of a crowd, and so did I.

We stayed high, with views over the great sandy spit of Borth on the south side, and the purple knuckles of the Tarrenau ridge across the far side of the estuary. We were walking some way inland, rounding the estuary and avoiding the busy main road connecting Aberystwyth and Machynlleth, but with such a commanding vantage point out to the distant ocean we felt faithful enough to the coast. There used to be a ferry across the mouth of the Dyfi, but now the most westerly crossing is the bridge outside Machynlleth, 10 miles inland from the open sea. A galling three-day detour in the first miles of a long journey, and yet, as my destination was the same as my starting line, what was the point of thinking in terms of detours? It was all one giant detour.

Chico was fired with energy, whether happy energy from being back on the trail with his team after a wet night alone in a huge meadow, or fractious energy from the raw nerves of several days of constant change, I couldn't tell. Would I learn to read him? But then I couldn't tell how I felt either, and I'd spent 33 full-time years on that project. A bit of both, I think.

We were heading for Machynlleth, a pretty market town about 18 miles from Aberystwyth. For weeks, as the inconceivable fact of the walk approached, I'd held Mach in my sights as being some sort of watershed – the end of the very beginning, perhaps. I'd been so blind to anything past the moment of opening Chico's field gate – like expecting to step into the next frame of a film and find it completely devoid of information – but I could imagine walking into Machynlleth, having survived three days. If we could survive three days, we stood a chance, I thought.

We were making good time, Mum so cheerily amenable to Chico's whims that the two of them would walk a long way ahead and then turn around and come back to pick us up, where Rhys and I dawdled, explaining the big idea to dog walkers or taking pictures of the omnipresent Tarrenau hills. And then Chico stopped. Almost hidden by the long dry grasses was a stream, running down the mountainside. It was burbling merrily with the rain of the last few days, but not more than six inches across – the sort of stream a walker would clear without breaking stride.

Chico did not like it, not at all. We all stepped across, but he wasn't convinced. We stood about to give him time to get used to the idea, but it made no difference. We tried slightly higher up, then lower down; we chivvied and crooned; we tried authoritative tones and gentle tones. I'd read about a technique that I was keen to try out, so we dug around in his packs until we found the long rope, tied it to his headcollar, went to sit a few feet away on the far side of the stream, and ignored him. We made a show of having fun, had our lunch break, waved carrots around – sitting on this sunny hillside wasn't so bad. But nothing. He tried to go back, but I held the rope tight enough to keep him near the stream. Half an hour passed and we got bored before he did. Mum went to see if there was another way around, and Rhys tried to tempt him across with crumbs of chocolate, touching them to Chico's pursed, obstinate lips.

'It's *six inches wide*, Chico!' We were losing patience; it was getting less funny. Lunch, which was really just a more concentrated period of the general snacking that took place all day long, had subsided back into the usual rate of snacking and Mum had returned with no alternatives. A cloud covered the sun and the air was instantly chilly, ushering back in my undermining monologue that said, 'What would you do if you were alone with him? Go all the way back? These things will happen… You really don't know what you're doing, do you? One tiny stream!'

Rhys had a theory: perhaps Chico had attributed yesterday's fall to the running water and thought the same would happen here. He suggested covering the water, so we collected armfuls of bracken and laid them across the stream. Then, without conferring, we began a mad dance, the three of us striding past Chico, stomping across the stream, whooping merrily. Then back, around him, giving him a little jostle, and back over the stream again, like some goblin's do-si-do. 'Hooray! We're crossing the stream! Come on, Chico!' It seemed pretty desperate.

But he did it. He summoned his courage and sprang with all four brave hooves, deer-like, clearing the tiny stream with feet to spare. We goblins went wild with congratulation and, poor though I was at reading Chico's moods, the pride came off him in waves.

We made it to Machynlleth and as we approached the main road I put his bridle on him, crouching before his nose and wedging my thumb into the corner of his mouth to get the bit in. Rhys would have done it happily, but with the end of the very beginning in sight, I felt I should do something to feel proud of. Mum and Rhys made me lead Chico into town. I felt like a bit of a fraud.

EIGHT

Chico seemed relaxed in his beer garden, and we camped alongside him, aided by a couple of pints and a shortcrust carbohydrate blow to the belly; the White Lion had invited us to stay. I listened to the populated quiet of Machynlleth at night, watched the patterns of streetlights and ivy, and then noticed that Chico was lying down. We were at peace. In the familiar protocol and architecture of a pub, I'd felt like a fish back in water; many eyes watched the donkey, while the beer took the edge off and made it all feel like derring-do.

The town clock woke us up in the morning, chiming the quarter hours. We left Chico in his corral and went for a fried breakfast, like new parents leaving the baby for the first time. Mach felt different to metropolitan Aberystwyth. It has a proud history: Owain Glyndŵr, a prince of Wales who sustained long and fierce battles against the English and is therefore remembered fondly, was crowned there in the early 1400s. I could hear Welsh everywhere, and with a whole different accent. While we ate I listened to a table of old boys with their high-pitched singsong voices discussing local news, the merits of capital punishment, and what should be done about the regular flooding of the Dyfi Bridge.

I bought soft fabric, needles and thread, safety pins and plastic toggles, and then sat on the grass of the beer garden, with Chico watching over my shoulder, to make some hasty modifications to the packsaddle rigging. Since the disastrous slippage in Aberystwyth town centre, I'd been doing the straps up tighter than necessary, and for three days they'd been chafing with every step, wearing hot, bare patches on Chico's chest. Any animal less stoic would have complained. Now I wrapped the straps in several layers of fleece and daubed Chico's sore patches with Sudocrem – thick, white nappy-rash cream. I was so sorry that I had caused these physical signs of misuse, of coercion. But the tending helped me, at least – it felt good to be taking action, assuming a nursing role, doing the right thing.

The packsaddle itself was a thing of beauty. I'd given up on ordering one from America or France and instead had found Dai, a local harness-maker and carpenter, who set about making one from scratch. It was based on a sawbuck shape, like the trestle that a woodcutter might use. Two shaped planks ran along either side of Chico's spine, attached to each other by a pair of wooden Xs, front and back. It was held on by leather straps under Chico's belly and around his chest and bum. I'd hung a canvas Norwegian army surplus bag off either side. Dai was a meticulous craftsman. The timber had come from an elm he'd felled himself 30 years earlier, just behind Mum's house. He'd tried it out on Chico a dozen times, heading back to his workshop to make modifications with his grandfather's gleaming tools. It was a thoroughly local piece of work and one of the most heartening, humbling parts of the adventure so far.

We set off along the road, me leading at last, holding Chico close with all eyes forward. We crossed the Dyfi Bridge, a 200-year-old narrow five-arch span, and walked out of Powys, the giant landlocked county that we'd meet again on the other side of the waist of Wales, in the borders with England. In theory. In reality it seemed extremely unlikely we'd get that far. Still, passing the 'Croeso i Gwynedd' sign felt significant – Welcome to Gwynedd! We were walking into North Wales after only a few days.

Dad and his partner Christine live in Machynlleth and so the catchment area of their tribe would embrace us for a few more days – that evening we were hoping to make it to a boatyard they knew of that allowed camping. Sure enough, as we turned 90 degrees west and began heading back towards the sea along the Dyfi, a car slowed and a man called out, 'See you at the boatyard! I'll make dinner!'

To get off the main road, we dropped down onto the fertile fields of the floodplain and found ourselves on an old road hewn from the slate. It was clearly so established, I felt we were welcomed by history if not by modern access rules or current landowners. Many donkeys had walked there before; it was a route, a way. Still, it felt a bit like trespass. A farmer in a loud tractor, accompanied by a Land Rover and crazed sheepdogs, came towards us, and leaned out of the window. I put on a submissive, apologetic face. 'Go straight through the barn – it's easier!' he yelled over the engines and the barking, his expression giving so little away that it took long moments to work out that he was being kind, not angry.

We had less luck with the stile – stile number one – but we backtracked around the edge of the field and, sure enough, found a gate that opened onto the old road again. The spirits of all of history's working beasts and ruddy farmhands opened the ways to us. Next obstacle: a field of cows. If I'd been alone with Chico, we wouldn't have gone in, no way. The old road skirted the upper edge of the field so we had a little height advantage, but it curved away out of sight – I couldn't see whether there was safety ahead. But again, brave Rhys made the decision. 'They're dairy cows, I think,' he said, and we both squinted at distant udders. 'Older, more sensible.' So Rhys led the two of us past the disinterested herd. I peeped at the map and worked out how many miles of detour and main road my cowardice and ignorance could have added.

A steep road veered straight up onto the ridge we'd been looking at from across the water the day before. Amongst the peaks up there, we came across a small ford with a slate stepping stone to one side, the first up-close water crossing since yesterday's trial. Rhys forged forward and Chico's spirit followed him, but his body hesitated. We saw the fear and the determination do battle across his features, and then the spirit won – Chico ploughed through the dark water rather than risk the slate bridge. What courage since yesterday!

I was tired – the ford, the road, the cows. The day was hot, my backpack was vast and the strap of my map case rubbed the back of my neck. My choice of walking skirt was a poor one. The cotton was relaxing day after day, and the many things I needed to hand – donkey nuts, snacks, penknife, phone, wallet, bits of bailer twine – weighed the pockets down so they banged against my thighs with every step.

Rhys and Chico, on the other hand, were chipper. Our ridge climbed higher and they got ahead, missing the turn-off and disappearing over the top, all *Swallows and Amazons* and best buddies. I struggled along behind them, fighting with a difficult gate and yelling to them to come back – I was too cross and wretched to climb to the top to call them back down. They reappeared and we paused for some photos, looking out over the astonishing view. Rugged, knobbly hills, lump after lump into the distance, purple by character but lit up by the unstoppable green of the spring, so long restrained, and soaked in the peachy glow of early evening. They were the hills of home, yet I couldn't name one, could barely get my bearings. We were right there, on the frontier. I was sweaty.

Rhys made me pose with Chico, but the donkey and I both knew it was a sham. We weren't in this together: he preferred Rhys and I was scrabbling along behind. My ill-temper fell on deaf ears. Rhys kissed me cheerfully and put an arm around each of us to take a team photo – and Chico reached in and bit me on the belly. A hard, ivory chomp. It hurt.

And as we walked down the hill it hurt more, right in the heart. He's *my* damn donkey! Rhys only just met him! The hot burn of ridiculous jealousy was made so much more abject by Rhys's boundless warmth. He made me lead Chico and we found our way to the Frongoch boatyard and the secret camping bay right by the water, midway along the north side of the estuary.

We had a sunny day off in our leafy camping spot, Chico corralled in the bay next door. After realising it really wasn't warm enough to swim without throat spasms and bellowing, I spent the time sewing fleece sleeves onto the saddle straps. In between I visited Chico for the periodic reapplication of Sudocrem and tentative attempts at picking up his hooves. Now that we were walking, and often on tarmac, it was pretty remiss of me not to be able to lift them. Little stones can work their way up into a hoof and cause grizzly abscesses, lameness and lots of pain so I really needed to be picking them out every day. But I was scared of his hooves, and those eyes that just looked at me with a kind of contempt at my efforts.

I'd tried to get to know him in the month before we left, installing him in a field near Aberystwyth that I'd hastily borrowed from a friend of Mum's. But he just seemed to get further away every time I visited, the white arrow-shape of his nose and ears visible among the trees in the far corner, fixed on me but distant. Mum used to come by with experimental treats from her allotment and get him all excited by running around the field with him. I'd had to stop her from referring to herself as Chico's grandmother – he was a donkey, not a child and I was aiming to be his buddy, not his mother. And yet there was a kind of single-parent fear back in the field days when, for all the advice I sought, the buck for his welfare stopped with me. It was lonely, but the highs as well as the lows were all mine.

Now that we were walking, it was a different story. It would have been pretty much impossible to manage without another pair of hands – to slow traffic, calm Chico while putting the packsaddle on, get the corral made while he was too fizzed up with the newness of it all to be tied to anything. Going into a shop, making a phone call, checking the map – having Rhys there made all that possible.

We were carrying too much stuff, not knowing what we needed. We had a stack of heavy-duty plastic electric fence posts, bundles of electric tape, and the 6kg battery with which to corral Chico. This was the solution I'd settled on during the field month after discovering with alarm that tethering a donkey to a stake really only works with a very sensible donkey and a great deal of training.

We had bin bags of horse nuts, and a molasses and alfalfa mix for calories. We had two collapsible army surplus washing-up bowls for Chico because we didn't know which he'd deign to drink from, and bottles of tap-water to fill them with. We had all sorts of straps and string and tarpaulins, the nappy-rash cream and some tea-tree oil, the blue plastic brushes and the as yet barely used hoofpick. Stuffed into another pocket was the bridle, a spring-balance weighing scale, a dozen carrots from the beer garden locals, plastic bags for picking up poo, and an electric-fence voltage tester. And then camping equipment for two. I couldn't have carried it all without Rhys, and weight-wise we were deliberately going easy on Chico.

Then there were all of the decisions. Was the electric fence up well enough to keep him in? Should we feed him more or less, or something different? Had he got enough grass for the night? Was that a new raw patch? Were the straps too tight or too loose? Was 10 miles too much? Was that path too steep? Was he tired or sore, excited or annoyed, high-spirited or frightened? Without Rhys my nerves would have been much more frayed by the chickens, clouds, engines, distant horses, slippery tarmac, plastic bags, wind, waves, manhole covers, and dozens of other things that made Chico jump, not to mention the non-donkey-related things that crinkled and scuffled and coughed in the distance and kept an out-of-practice camper awake and listening hard from inside the tent.

The day before, as we'd teamed up to get the packsaddle on – one of us crooning and holding him still, the other gently sneaking it on to him and buckling it up with minimum jangling, both of us frowning with concentration and issuing soft instructions and '*good* boy, Chico', 'good *boy*, Chico', 'good boy, *Chico*', back and forth – someone had likened us to new parents figuring out a first nappy.

The camping I was comfortable with, already blissfully scruffy and patchily burned, lifted by the resoundingly, searingly, wildly beautiful country. Every hour the light was different; sometimes the arresting view was a majestic symphony of colours on a hillside, sometimes an achingly idyllic little country scene – a fat lamb by an abandoned hill farm's moss-covered stable door, surrounded by bluebells. Wales was wonderful.

I just wished… I just wished I didn't have this donkey.

Meanwhile, in his small camping bay by the estuary, Chico was getting bored. He was close but he couldn't really see us. My resting relied on not seeing him, blanking him out, but Rhys insisted we take him on a little walk, just around the boatyard. At the edge of the sand, Chico paused. We encouraged him to step onto it, and as he did he became a donkey possessed. He wrenched us on the end of his rope, twisting back and forth, then rolled madly in the sand, then pranced about. And then, adding to the circus, two elastic dogs ran up to him so suddenly that he had no choice but to bray, the first time I'd heard it, high and loud and frantic. Hearts pounding, we struggled to get him back to his bay, and he wasn't keen, not one bit.

The electric fence posts stuck only loosely into the shale ground and I slept fitfully. As I turned off the torch and gingerly arranged my elbows in the tiny tent, Rhys said, in his sleep, 'Oh… I thought you brought him in here…' I smiled into my sleeping bag; so there *were* some anxious thoughts running through his neurons.

NINE

C hico was like a bullet from a gun. I was pulled back up onto the ridge-top, like a person holding onto a rope attached to a bullet from a gun; it was almost useful – I'd certainly never made such a swift 250m ascent before. In my other hand, as I bumped through the tussocks, the wind-up radio chattered in a cheerful Sunday morning way.

This stretch was named the Panorama Walk, and with good reason. The Cambrian mountains were stacked up to the south, beyond the dunes of Borth and Ynyslas, laid out like a dinky railway model. The sea shone ahead of us, and to the north were rolling valleys of soft green fields, like a vision of Welsh countryside too archetypal to be true.

We came across four lots of creatures, three of which were scary. The first was a chain of dirt bikers screaming past Rhys and Chico as they tried to find a way out of the boggy field I had got us all into (after that, I never again, when map-reading, optimistically mistook a riverbed for a road).

All on a nervous high again, we passed a sheep. I'd laughed at Chico for being scared of sheep, but this guy scared me too. 'Bottle-fed,' said Rhys, and I'm sure that's what it was, but the sheep, boxy and tough, with a tightly curled fleece and a skull like a tractor seat, came barging up to my knees with none of the usual timidity. Good grief, what had become of me that I was strung so taut by anxiety as to be scared of a sheep? We hurried on and the very next field had cows. Not dairy, and right in our path.

We devised a plan. I chose a cow-scaring stick and opened the gate, leaving it open in case we needed to beat a hasty retreat. Then Rhys and Chico entered, and walked sedately, taking a long route around the far perimeter of the field. I stayed between them and the cows, one eye on each party, stick at the ready, warning roar in my throat. One cow stood up. And then… no, that was it. Rhys and Chico made it to the far side and I ran back and shut the gate, but it was another 20 minutes of safety before I realised I was still holding the stick.

Our fourth set of creatures were a teenage couple, enjoying some privacy in the greenhouse warmth of their car. I averted my eyes apologetically – they weren't expecting a travelling sideshow to stumble past their lustful eyrie, brandishing a stick.

We dropped down again, to the sweet seaside town of Aberdyfi, far enough west that I could see along the coast to Aberystwyth, five days' walk behind us. We were in a hurry to get there before the Dyfi Donkeys were done for the day, although I soon wished we hadn't managed it. The walk had dissipated none of Chico's energy but sapped all of ours, and when we presented ourselves before Louise, owner of the world's most impeccably behaved donkeys, we were ragged. While I tried to put on a brave face and have a chat, Chico pulled Rhys back and forth all over the dunes, even jumping off the tops like a 200kg toddler, wild with the thrill of the beach. Children came to see, and Louise said, 'Don't go too close to that one – he's not one of mine.' Her two stood side by side under their shelter, chewing on a little hay, offering their velvet noses up for stroking, as related to Chico as a candle is to a volcano.

And yet, when Louise came over to greet Chico, he stood calmly before her, as if she had cast a spell of competence over him. She picked a tick off his chest, then gave him a friendly rub. He bit her on the shoulder and she laughed and said firmly, 'No – we're not doing mutual grooming, Chico!' My foolish heart broke in half, taunted further when I noticed that Chico's ample black willy had put in a hefty appearance. He *loved* Louise. When she drove her two donkeys off home, we were a shattered bunch left behind in the sand.

I tried to lift our spirits by going to fetch fish and chips, but the chip shop opened 'only when they feel like it', and the village shop, on the last Sunday of half-term in a town made up mostly of holiday homes, looked like it had been stripped by locusts. So I bought a curry – a ridiculous choice for eating on the sand, with a donkey so wired we couldn't tie him for fear of him hurting himself. Desperate to get settled somewhere, Rhys and Chico were as cross as each other, and as we walked into the dunes in search of our first wild camp, it was obvious that it was all my stupid fault. Inside my backpack my water carrier chose that moment to leak, bleeding cold water down the backs of my legs. And I had no idea whether an electric fence would work in sand – would the earthing peg function? Would the wild donkey stay in?

The answer, thankfully, was yes. We found a driftwood sculpture, like the prow of a boat, and corralled Chico alongside it for interest, with marram grass to eat overnight. We'd bought bamboo poles to replace the heavy, ugly white electric fence posts, and used them as giant tent pegs in the soft sand. A beer and a little soothing radio, and we felt able to sleep, in between listening to Chico's tireless teeth grinding the driftwood structure just a few feet from our heads.

Restored and triumphant after a successful wild camp, we headed off through the rollercoaster dunes. Dune grass spiked us in the legs as we took the narrow scrubby tracks at speed, assailed by wonderful hot fragrances and wild flowers. Chico, still full of a stroppy sort of energy, dragged me up and down the soft mini-mountains, barging me off the path, nosing about the place with no respect for his feckless muleteer.

We walked on the wide, white sand beach to Tywyn, the next town north, feeling almost in control. But that was to be short-lived. I got a call from Tamlin, who happened to be in

Tywyn, and suggested we meet. As her car pulled into the verge by a housing estate, a wash of relief came over me, to be in the presence of expertise. I started forward to give her a hug, but realised she was angry and stepped back. Chico was eating the roadside grass despite having his bit in his mouth and Tamlin unbuckled it to let him eat more comfortably. Then she asked how I was doing with getting his hooves up. Not really, yet… Not very well… I stuttered.

'You have *got* to work it out, Hannah,' she said. She told me I had to be looking for things I'd not ever heard of before – pinkness, or even blood coming through the soles if the hoof was wearing down too far. 'Then it will be a *welfare issue*,' she said, ominously.

My stomach leaped and my eyes stung; the awful involuntary physical responses to being reprimanded by a teacher gripped me from across the decades – a bad child again. Although I'd started feeling like I was sharing this with Rhys, Tamlin didn't give him a glance – the awful heat was all mine. Chico calmed when Tamlin took his rope, but kept trying to spin me about when I had it; he was hectic and restless. How could I even begin to get his hooves up when my presence made him twist so madly? She showed me how she used her weight against him, leaning into the front of his shoulder to block the motion. But I couldn't even get close with my top-heavy backpack on, and he paid me no heed, knocking me out of his way.

'I don't want to say I told you so…' she said, but I really should have gone with one of her choices, Dolly or Lily. This new reality crashed in on me – I'd had no idea that I had gone against her advice. In that tumult of needy indecision I wouldn't have dared. For two days after meeting Chico I'd pestered Tamlin by text, waiting – in my mind – for her permission to take Chico. I knew she'd met him once before, and that she would tell me whether five years old was just too young. As I'd sat on the stairs in Mum's house, Tamlin had discussed it with me for nearly an hour over the phone. I could tell she was uncertain, a little withdrawn, but I thought it was just that I had come on too strong by asking her to make my decision for me. I misread her concern about Chico as trying to distance herself from me, oh self-centred fool that I am!

I'd really tried not to colour the conversation with my giddy love for Chico. I'd written a list of concerns, first of which was his age, then his hooves. He'd not done much work and had refused to be caught by his previous owner, he had some rubbed areas, and funny black patches on his knees (no, those *are* his knees, said Tamlin)…

But it hadn't really got through to me that it was his character that Tamlin was worried about. 'He's not a lead donkey,' she'd said on the phone, and she said it again now. Well, that's fine, I'd thought. I didn't want a lead donkey. I was going to be the leader.

'But you're not, Hannah. You're not providing leadership. He doesn't want to have to take it on himself, but he is.'

A woman on a mobility scooter tried to get past us on the pavement, giving me ample chance to demonstrate how totally unable I was to control Chico. Shamefully, dangerously so.

'Consider this your bollocking of the day,' said Tamlin, giving Chico a rub goodbye.

I smiled weakly. As she got in the car, I said quietly, 'Tamlin, am I…? Have I…?'

'Bitten off more than you can chew? Yes!'

'No! I know I've done *that*! I mean… am I doing harm?'

'To this donkey? Right now? No.'

Rhys asked if he could get a lift back to his car, parked a few days back along the coast. Tamlin left me with the suggestion that we should get into a routine – if we always started at 8am, we should always have a break at 10am, for example. If I hadn't had hot, shameful tears already spilling over as soon as they pulled away, I might have laughed. We'd not once managed to leave before the afternoon, and kept arriving hours late for our hosts, staggering along with too much stuff and no idea where anything was, batteries dying, strange combinations of food, still using Rhys's classic Volvo Amazon as a mobile storeroom. I had no idea if I could ever bring about the sort of smooth experience that Tamlin thought it should be.

To make matters worse, I was now alone with Chico. And in a town! I wiped my filthy face with my filthy hands, a week in the same clothes, my grubby pride now just stupid ineptitude.

As we walked, I chewed on it all, over and over. Had she really been in Tywyn? That was too much of a coincidence. Maybe Aberdyfi Louise had called her, an SOS to say we really weren't coping. That just deepened the shame, and yet, *good*! They cared about his wellbeing! Which was more than could be said for me.

While I tore myself to sorry shreds, Chico walked well, by my side. Several people made what was to become one of the most regular comments of the walk – 'That's a big dog!' – and I think I mostly smiled back. A girl on a housing estate screeched, 'Donkey! Donkey!' at the top of her voice, summoning all the others in a scary flood of kids pouring over every wall and gate. I waved but walked on quickly – I couldn't quite handle that. Their disappointment followed us like a cloud.

I tied Chico to a fence and he grazed while I ate some wrinkly old apples we'd been given days ago and wrote notes about feeling wretched. A train went by and Chico didn't seem too bothered, then a man on a tricycle and, unconnected, a mother and daughter on a quadracycle stopped to hail Chico. I would happily have swapped him for either silly vehicle.

I felt jealous of passing cats, just for being cats. I felt jealous of farmers, and in fact anyone who knew how to do their jobs. I felt jealous of the people on the train that passed, for having other things to go to, and for being carried away from the exposed and difficult *here*.

Rhys caught us up and left the car in Tywyn. We were heading to a housing co-operative called Chickenshack, and the friendly woman on the phone, Kath, had begged us to come while her granddaughter was there. It was nice to know our arrival was looked forward to; we were nearly there, and only a little bit late.

And then – a cattlegrid. Full width, no side gate, on a private drive that I'd hoped would be a shortcut to a bridleway that skirted a formidable hill called Tal y Garreg ('The End of the Rock'). There was nothing we could do. A second path, climbing halfway up the hill, went straight over a stile and through a working quarry – no good. The third was a bridleway and went right to the top, what a relief! But as we began to climb the hill, the contours got closer and closer – it was too steep, surely it couldn't be right? There was no clear path, just a hillside, but we took comfort from the fresh horse dung along the way; if people rode this bridleway, we could do it.

But it got so steep that we couldn't turn around. Chico can go up a much steeper hill than he can go down, with that huge, front-heavy head. He kept stopping, and began reproachfully to chew the earth ahead of him. With our own lungs thumping, we jollied him on. I worried about what would happen if he took fright. One wrong step and we could tumble the whole way down to the saltmarsh below. People rode up here?

At the top of the field was a high stone wall with clear evening sky behind it, and I could only see a tall ladder-stile crossing it. But we were on a bridleway – there had to be another route. Oh, *cut us some slack*! Then Rhys saw a big black horse, right at the top. He was the source of the dung. People *didn't* ride up here, of course they didn't. We were alone, with an unpredictable donkey, pinned to a hillside on which we could not turn around, with a big black horse above us.

Horses don't really like donkeys. Human beings are quite fixated on there being a correlation between size and hierarchy, but there isn't really, even in human relationships – it's all to do with front and confidence. Whether donkeys are more confident than horses, I couldn't say, but it is the case that a scared horse runs, while a scared donkey faces up to the situation; maybe that's what unnerves the horse. Fight rather than flight. It's handy for a donkey owner in the great outdoors – Chico would often start, but then he'd stop. But a horse can get very jumpy, huffy and stampy, and that did scare Chico. And me. This was the second time we'd been in a field with horses, and I'd still not recovered from the first time. In fact, the first time, which I'd come to refer to as Stalliongeddon, was largely responsible for why I still felt that Chico was a time bomb on the end of a rope.

Of course it had all been my own stupid fault. I'd owned Chico for ten days and he was, despite rain (hence pneumonia) and fresh grass (colic and laminitis), still alive. I pushed my luck by taking him on our first walk.

I had seen how excited Chico was by the giant horses on the other side of the fence, gazing at them like an awed teenager before a red carpet, but still Chico, Mum and I blundered into their field. Perhaps I was encouraged by the fact that the right of way went through there, and that the short path from our corner to the next was symbolically delineated by a row of trees. It made no difference, of course – the moment we were in there, the six giant beasts bore down on us, covering 200m as if they had teleported through my patchy, petrified memory. Mum let Chico go (thankfully, guardian-angel donkey walker Carol had warned me that morning about bolting circumstances and how I shouldn't hang on and risk shoulder injury, except on roads).

One dirty white mare stormed right up to Chico, ribs showing through her great round chest as she made herself extra big, swaggering wildly at him. Chico raced back and forth along the fence, and Mum reports that I said, calmly, 'I don't like this at all.' I don't remember that – I just remember incanting '*fuck!*' over and over again, under my breath, whilst moving through the field with legs of sand, like in a nightmare. Two types of strong animal, both heavier than us, neither of which I knew anything much about, loose in a field. Would the horses kill Chico? I'd heard that one was a stallion and that his owner was worried in case someone rode a horse through the field and got squashed in a horse-sex sandwich. Could the stallion mistake Chico for a girl? Looking at the fearsome difference of scale, I suspected it would just make for the traumatic end of Chico. Raped to death, frankly, to be emotively anthropomorphic about it. Mum would have to agree never to tell anyone how Chico had died on day ten.

I was dazed by my vision of horror, but Mum was an action hero. 'I'll see the horses off. You get Chico!' she called. She's at least a foot shorter than me, but evidently much braver (size not being as important as front, you see). She faced the horses down, right off to the other side of the field and, as she reported later, 'told them off for being big bullies'. I went after Chico, who amazingly let me close enough to catch him by the trailing lead rope.

When Mum turned away from the horses on the other side of the field, they re-inflated themselves, causing terror or excitement in Chico at 200 paces and giving me a good handful of rope burns. My sunglasses flew off with the whiplash, but I clung on and he stopped. The 'don't wrap the rope around your hand' rule, which I was already obeying because I am obedient, really took root. Chico is very strong. Little hand bones could crackle like kindling before a torpid human being even began to lift an eyebrow to the danger. Then there was another bolting attempt when he spotted some superstar dung to smell. But I got him out of there. He didn't seem rattled at all, and neither did Mum, arriving back from the other side of the field and retrieving my sunglasses on the way. My bowels shuddered as the adrenaline coursed through me.

The rest of the walk passed without incident, but I might as well have been walking a tiger for all the calming down I was able to do. 'I think you were in shock,' said Mum later. And then, generously, 'Maybe we polarised each other – one of us had to be the brave one.' I think I *was* in shock for quite a while. Maybe I was still in shock, a month on. That evening I had briefly mourned the inevitable death of my grand solo adventure, and then called up Rhys and asked him to walk with us for the first month, at least.

Back on Tal y Garreg, just below the summit and the big black horse, we were all shaking, even Rhys. A mere few hours since I was promising to be a better donkey owner, and I'd led us into this? The spectre of Tamlin frowned disapprovingly over my shoulder. So as Rhys and Chico climbed in short zigzags, I scrambled straight up and got between them and the horse, bold with guardianship. We all pretended there was no drama here, and none of us more so than the horse, which – not a scenario that had featured anywhere in my list of possible outcomes – wandered off. Rudely disinterested. We found a gate, got it closed behind us, and bathed in the golden evening light of heady, exhausted relief, all the way along the hilltop to Chickenshack.

TEN

I licked my wounds. I've never been a rebel; I don't understand why anyone would deliberately draw fire. My guiding principle has always been to encourage people to like me. It's not very rock 'n' roll, but there it is. But what was I to do with this? No amount of self-effacement, of joking about, of research, could help me. I couldn't make amends to the god of donkeys, and self-flagellation didn't change the situation. I couldn't send Tamlin flowers, couldn't apologise and make everything better. I was a bad person, and I had no idea what to do about it. I think it was a first, in my whole life.

I found brief consolation in remembering that Robert Louis Stevenson, later the author of *Treasure Island*, had battered his poor donkey Modestine until his arm ached when they walked through France in 1878. He hadn't even noticed when her legs ran with blood because of some serious chafing. Her thighs, he wrote, were like raw meat. I'm sure he never checked her hooves. But being less bad than someone else is scant comfort when you are still very bad, and of course Robert didn't have tarmac to worry about.

Eventually, in the open arms and wildflower meadow of Chickenshack, I hit on the only thing that might help. It was the hardest possible option. I was going to have to work out how to pick up his hooves, even though it scared the hell out of me.

Back in the field month, Tamlin had given me a lesson in hoof-lifting. She has a deep empathy for both donkey and human. 'There's no point making it into a fight,' she said. 'You have to work up to it slowly, so that he knows he is safe.' She recommended I buy some riding gloves, so that I could rub

Chico's withers with purchase and vigour. Rather than tie Chico up, as I was accustomed to doing in our daily battles with packsaddle fittings, rain mac conditioning and the rest, she got me to encourage him to want to stay, and to allow him to move away if he wanted to. I held his rope and rubbed his withers – the top of his shoulders, where his mother would have nibbled him for comfort. Apparently this spot actually lowers a donkey's heart rate. So I'd rub, and he'd stay by me – a little suspicious, but liking it. Then I'd begin to rub a little lower, like a nervous suitor trying his luck. Down the legs a little, paying close attention to Chico's reaction. If he began to stiffen, I'd move back up to a safe zone – take the pressure off. If he stepped away altogether, I was to follow him and keep a gentle, still hand on him, to say, 'I'm not going anywhere, but I'm also not threatening.' And it was important to recognise progress. While Tamlin had looked on, I'd managed to stroke all the way down to his front hooves, and halfway down the back legs, and Tamlin had suggested we leave it there. Every day since then I had tried, sometimes getting about that far, but usually, since departure, having much less success when Chico was wired from a day of walking, barging and angry.

At Chickenshack Chico had the perfect set-up – a quiet, calm meadow, plenty to eat but not too much, little enough space to be a bit bored and therefore focused on us. And we settled in next to him, for two long days. Tamlin had said that he wanted to do the right thing by us but needed to know what that was, and so we tried, again and again, to pick up his hooves – cheering and giving him treats when we made any progress, retreating when it all got too much, by turns crushed and elated by the failures and successes.

During breaks, the inhabitants of the community took care of us. Norma gave me an old denim skirt, which I cut short, using the offcuts to make a huge, double-skinned thigh pocket. She told me about the permaculture principles of the

Chickenshack co-op. They lived in four houses set in five acres of land, with a garden, forest, meadows and wetland. Permaculture is a system of agriculture designed to work with natural ecosystems in order to be sustainable, integrated and gentle. It's also come to mean an ethos of living in a more connected way too. Norma was vehement about how much the battered world, and lonely human beings, need to find new approaches to living, getting away from thinking of ourselves as single families defending our small, mortgaged fortresses, and learning to live cooperative and interdependent lives.

Outside, two men worked tirelessly through the hot days, building a new barn for traditional craft workshops. Lively, motherly Kath brought us coffee and encouraged us to come inside and lie underneath the grand piano, which filled the small living room, while her husband Bill played us some poignant, stylish jazz. Seeing my stricken expression at one low point in our hoof efforts, Kath took my arm and said softly, 'It won't always be like this. There will be a time when it's easy, when it's instinctive, and you'll enjoy it.' I heard the first cuckoo for many years, a precious hiccup.

Kneeling back in the green grass – 'Hup! Hoof, Chico! *Good* boy, *good* boy!' – the first success was with his front left. Then we managed to get each back hoof up in turn, scary in their taut potential power. When Chico had had enough, or lost his balance, he'd wrench the hoof from my hands and it'd stamp the ground like some steam-injected industrial process. Oddly though, the front right hoof remained a problem. He'd try, but then drive it down again, unexamined. We came to the conclusion that he must have pulled a muscle on the world's steepest paddock the day before, and couldn't support his weight on three legs. All day we worked at this, the strangest quest of my life.

The hot sun gave way to a chilly evening and Rhys tried the tricky front right again. As Rhys crouched before him like some royal valet, Chico tipped forward and shifted his weight onto Rhys's back, lifting his front left leg too, so that Rhys was holding up the whole front end of a donkey. We'd been trying for that hoof for so long that Rhys was determined to see it through and pick it out, and I tried to take some of the weight, in a half-crouch with my shoulder under Chico's head, and all of us groaning madly, a tableau of muscles being pulled and confused interdependence. A game of Twister of the heart, soul and body. Then Rhys pushed Chico off and rolled, panting, swearing and laughing, into the grass.

Something had changed, and Chico began to relax. He drank water out of his collapsible water bowl while I held it, he came over for nose-strokes or a sniff every time I passed, he even yawned, and his willy came out. He rolled and then lay down in his corral, and we lay nearby, in tentative peace.

The grass in his small corner was flattened and broken from the days of struggle, and I apologised about the stark wreckage in the otherwise untouched meadow. But Norma said that grass can handle being crushed – it thickens it up. It's made to work with animal hooves. 'It'll be interesting to see whether this corner looks different in a year,' she said, a committed, patient witness of natural systems at work.

As we left, very late in the day, with Chico stamping about with excitement despite our breakthroughs, and us struggling with stuff and goodbyes, Kath said, 'You can't know what it has meant to have you here. There have been hard times, and welcoming you in has been important, significant.' I thought we'd just been taking and taking: food and support, space and goodwill. I couldn't really believe it, but it was good to hear.

A month later, as we walked onwards, Kath was diagnosed with lung cancer. As the next spring came, less than a year later, I went back to Chickenshack to see Kath buried beneath that thickened meadow.

ELEVEN

We walked along the high ground as it curved north into the Mawddach estuary. Ahead, the Lleyn Peninsula grew closer, the mountains of Snowdonia hunched at its shoulder and its graceful arm tapering off into the sea to the west, reaching out to Bardsey Island. At last we couldn't make out Aberystwyth behind us any more, but still we'd hardly begun, and the Lleyn looked simultaneously like a giant digression and a hazy promised land. Our bodies were bruised and tired, and my mind scrapped daily with the lack of progress. After looking back at a road sign that showed how many A-road miles we were from Aberystwyth – a mere 40 – I worked out that it would take us 50 weeks to get around Wales at this pace. Something to laugh at, if rather helplessly.

But with Chico, at least, things were going from strength to strength. I *liked* him now. And with that I became a nicer person. I found I was genuinely bothered about his wellbeing rather than just knowing I had to be. I began to sing little walking songs to him ('The hills are alive with the sound of Chico', 'He'll be coming round the mountain', 'Little donkey', and so on) and enjoy his company; I even kissed him once or twice. I found myself getting better at figuring out the causes of his moods. Smoothed by empathy, the whole shebang seemed almost possible. Albeit in only just under a year…

I called the Donkey Sanctuary's expert farrier, Colin Goldsworthy. 'I'll bet you're right-handed, aren't you?' he said. 'Yes, yes – you're pulling the front right hoof out too far, unbalancing the donkey. Get a friend to rest a hand on his rump on the opposite side – that will give him confidence.' It worked, of course. Chico's aching muscle had been a fiction; it was a case of owner error again. Colin also invited me to send him pictures of Chico's hooves, and called back to say that they looked great. 'There should be no problem with four hours of tarmac a day. The walking increases bloodflow to the hooves, which makes them stronger.'

Between the Dyfi estuary and the Mawddach we were walking through the fifth-century kingdom of Meirionnydd, high on the hillside to escape the main road. The rough, majestic landscape reminded me of a poem by the Welsh academic and poet TH Parry-Williams, whose home patch we were approaching:

Ni byddaf yn siwr pwy ydwyf yn iawn
Mewn iseldiroedd bras a di-fawn
Mae cochni fy ngwaed ers canrifoedd hir
Yn gwybod fod rhagor rhwng tir a thir.
Ond gwn pwy wyf, os caf innau fryn
A mawndir a phabwyr a chraig a llyn.

He writes that he doesn't know who he is when he's on a peat-less, rich lowland. Over the centuries the very redness of his blood has come to understand the difference between one sort of land and another. So give him a hill and rushes, bog, rocks and a lake, and he knows just who he is.

I rolled my eyes as we walked. Pull yourself together, Thomas Herbert! Why limit your horizons, confine your sense of belonging? This little blue and green rock in space is *all* yours – why corral off a small corner and persuade yourself, however beautifully, that you only know who you are inside the line?

We walked out of Meirionnydd, north over the railway bridge that crossed the mouth of the Mawddach. But we were still in Wales, still in Britain, and in Europe. I felt something for all of them, and at the same time they were all just lines on maps, drawn by someone else at some other time. But of course I was able to be so flippant because I was free to have it all, to come and go.

Thankfully Chico didn't thwart our progress – if he'd refused to step onto the 820m-long footbridge, less than an arm-span wide, our alternative would have been to round the estuary, 10 miles along the fast main road. We waited for a train to cross first, and then went for it, casting ourselves out over the water. Chico hesitated as the wood resonated under his hooves, but then walked on admirably, keeping away from the edge, so he didn't have to see the drop to the sea below. Holidaymakers coming the other way kindly took the outside line.

As we walked, Rhys and I were fired up with a peculiar, multifaceted energy. It came, in a way, from being very tired, and from always leaving so late – after packing everything onto the donkey, breaking bread with hosts, checking hooves, writing notes, and getting route advice, we raced along with dusk gathering at our heels. But each time, once the logistics had been overcome and we were finally free under our enormous packs, once we had called farewells back over our shoulders as far as the first bend, the liberty of the path was electrifying. We hadn't managed much of a sensible eating routine, and our blood ran thick with sugar: toffee waffles, welshcakes, and salted peanuts. As the adrenaline and fear eased a little, we found ourselves high on living outside. I wore my days of dirt with great pride, changing my clothes rarely, and then often changing them back – unwashed but fresh in comparison – a few days later. I did at least have the grace to recoil a little when I noticed, midway through some task, that I was holding a piece of bailer twine between my teeth that usually sat under Chico's tail.

Rhys looked great. He had been given half a dozen pairs of vintage walking breeches by his tough, octogenarian dad –

thin corduroy ones and thick corduroy ones, moleskin ones and tweed ones, all of them ending just below the knee, some of them with laces. Below his bare calves, his boots were made of buffalo hide. His woollen jumper was a tightly knitted, ribbed grey Swedish army-issue V-neck that had clearly spent decades in a musty attic before being aired on Welsh clifftops. His blonde moustache was getting out of hand.

The bridge deposited us into busy, Saturday afternoon Barmouth and we ploughed on, passing the beach donkeys just as they were being ushered into their trailer. Chico sensed some clearer instruction than mine, and tried to follow them in. Did he think that was enough walking now? Time to go home, wherever that might be?

For long evening hours we walked along the main road, getting gradually worn down by the radiated heat and fast cars. Campsites on either side of the road seemed businesslike and unfriendly so we kept on and on until dusk. We were running out of options and when we got to a village, the second Talybont of the journey, we turned off towards the beach. But here it was even less welcoming – a neon clubhouse bleated out the evening's entertainment, and little groups of skinny teenage girls managed to heehaw at us with more dull-eyed sarcastic venom than I was ever to come across again. At the sea dozens of people had gathered to watch the sun set with a hot, surly restlessness, and we cut away from them, heading north along the beach. Up ahead were some big dunes we could surely hide amongst.

But our promising dunes were not to be – just minutes from the holiday village was a river, too deep to cross. We fought through the pebbles, Chico getting crotchety with our lack of clear direction. I twisted an ankle; the weight of my backpack was very unforgiving as my tired feet stumbled on the stones. And then Chico trod on my twisted foot, right on a blister that had grown in the hot tarmac hours. I howled and cursed, and cried for exactly one minute, bringing Rhys running back from his recce along the beach to see what was wrong. We camped where we fell, right there in the curve of the river, hemmed in by the holiday village. But thankfully lacklustre teenagers don't like to stray from the glowing embers of the fruit machines, so we were safe.

The morning brought a new feat of bravery from Chico. The tide was out and the river, as I had hoped, ran in plaits and sheets and channels across the beach. Rhys took Chico for an acclimatisation walk on the sand, moving him closer and further away from pools of water before we finally went for it and walked across the rivulets, boots hanging from our hooked fingers. Chico made it – another triumph for the wonderdonkey, determined to conquer his fears.

We walked on like a team; the beach was wide and yellow and beautiful. June crowds were out and Chico weathered the sand buggies and kites, footballs and nudists. There were far more nudists than footballs; I'd never realised they had a patch there. They looked happy and defiant in the hot sunshine, and I found it funny that they should be corralled away from covered people – their tiny, distant penises couldn't have been less offensive. 'I can't help but notice that you are completely naked too, Chico,' I commented to him.

As we walked I told Rhys about my memories of Shell Island, the campsite that we were heading for. It's not actually an island, but road access is via a causeway that floods at high tide. We were approaching from the beach and were looking forward to stopping by for an hour or two. Having slept wild the previous night, we wanted to fill up with water for Chico, and maybe find a patch of green grass. Rhys and I dreamed of a nice lunch under some shade, followed by an ice-cream and a snooze, and perhaps the shop would be happy to charge our phones.

I'd spent many long holidays there. With 300 acres of camping space set amongst another 150 acres of dunes it was apparently the biggest campsite in the UK. The fields near the toilets and shop were manicured and organised, but the furthest reaches were wild, and we used to stay for weeks, with friends coming and going. Someone had a tipi, and children and adults alike turned feral in the scrub and sand. We played long, breathless pursuit games, found tiny frogs, taped shells and flowers into scrapbooks, learned to do face-painting and fell asleep by the bonfire in the evening. I had birthdays there and brought schoolfriends along – I remember unwrapping a pair of Bermuda shorts, no less. My first very own tent, bought with money from my Saturday job, debuted there.

But I'd never approached from the beach before, or been back as an adult. I felt like a prodigal daughter, returning after decades spent away, the fond memories and lessons of a childhood spent there leading directly to the journey we were now engaged on.

'*WHERE HAVE YOU COME FROM?*' The words were shot in our direction from between pursed hot-pink lips, with astonishing viciousness. The woman drew herself up before us, in a tight white mini-skirt and heels. We couldn't have been less prepared, and faltered. I reached for friendliness, which generally serves me well.

'YOU HAVE TO STAY ON THE FOOTPATH!'

'I'm sorry – where is it?'

'Well, it's NOT HERE! And it's not for me to tell you.' The woman was in a blind rage. I was worried for her trussed-up heart as her chest heaved in inappropriate, synthetic clothing, and taken aback by the gulf between our transgression and her reaction.

'We will not have horses here. Or *donkeys!*' Oh, the disdain!

A man cowered by her side and interjected in a simpering Birmingham accent, 'It's rules and regulations, you see… Private property, the beach, you see…'

Rhys began to explain, coldly, that almost all foreshore belongs to the Crown, but he'd overestimated the level of the argument. 'If I came into your living room on a horse, you'd tell me to leave, wouldn't you?' was the woman's furious logic.

'Well, I… I think I'd probably ask you what you were doing there first. I would be quite surprised…' I floundered further, the sun-baked daydream of longed-for ice-cream, water and shade only just fading. If, instead of firefighting against this crazed assault, I'd carved out a long enough moment to recheck the map and see that we *were* on the right of way, *actually*, we might have fought longer, but it would probably have made little difference.

'*GET OUT!*' She stalked away, and I gathered my thoughts and my donkey, and followed. At the reception hut I stopped and said to the little Brummie, in a high and wavery voice, 'I've been coming here for 33 years! And I'm a travel writer and I've written lots of articles about how great it is here! And…' He pointed silently to the woman, so I turned to her and carried on. 'And I'm very upset by your attitude!'

'Well,' she said, 'I'm very upset by *your* attitude!' It was not one of history's great exchanges.

I'm fairly certain I'd never done this before, but as I walked away, I gave her the finger over my shoulder; a last gesture where words had failed. It was at least raw and genuine and, much though I later wished I had, I don't think I'd have been able to pull off the words 'Kiss my dusty ass!'

Rhys walked ahead with Chico. As we trailed, thirsty, shocked, sunburnt, wronged and wounded, across the causeway, he called over his shoulder, '… probably just tired and fed up…'

'Yes,' I said. 'I think she's just one of those people who's really excited to have something to be angry about.' How very forgiving of him. And it was true. With our lives on our sweaty backs we were free to leave her far behind, but she would always be stuck with her horrible self, and her besieged version of reality. I mustered pity and soothed myself with it.

'No!' said Rhys. '*Chico's* tired and fed up.'

We corralled him into the scrubby silage-bag corner of a field, where there was at least a little shade, grass and a hawthorn for afters. Rhys and I made the executive decision to drink the warm bottle of beer left over from the night before, our only liquid. 'It doesn't change all the birthdays...' said Rhys, having a bash at salvaging my poisoned memories.

No ice-cream in Llanbedr, but water, sweet water from the pub's tap, fed to Chico on the pavement. He wasn't that bothered; I suppose an animal built for the desert doesn't fret about a four-mile walk on a beach. We headed up into the foothills of the Rhinog mountains, on an uncertain route that ended up being really, soul-soothingly beautiful.

We seemed to be in estate farmland – it was deserted, there were ruined barns and farmhouses, open gates and fallow fields brim-full with wildflowers and edged with tall stone walls. I heard a cuckoo – cuckoo number five, then six, then seven. Two tracks didn't quite meet, but with just a single field between them I risked it, emboldened by the way the land there seemed to stand open. We let ourselves through a gate and our linking field turned out to have an old path of sorts. Deep, cow-trodden ruts in the baked earth wound upwards through a grove of low old oaks standing about among vast boulders covered with mustard-coloured lichen, the rough purple of the bare Rhinog mountains as a backdrop, and Snowdon ahead. Amongst the oaks a few heavy black cows ignored us, thankfully.

Back on the wide estate tracks, two children on a mini quadbike shot out through a gap in the wall, paying us no heed. They passed us a few more times, sometimes pursued by yipping dogs, before stopping to ask what we were doing. They wore shorts, T-shirts and flip-flops, not a helmet between them, and screamed about the gravelly tracks, filling the air with dust and a mood of pre-pubescent worldliness.

We walked past their homestead shortly after, a graveyard of vehicle parts, wrecked plastic play equipment and disintegrating mobile homes, all leaning up against a low, peeling farm building. Two enormous grain silos stood empty, and the quadbikes were discarded on the track outside. There wasn't an adult in sight.

We'd phoned ahead, seeking a haven after the Shell Island shock, and so were drawn onwards through this endless hot day by the promise of a warm welcome at Merthyr Farm campsite. But of course Chico couldn't know that. As we left the estate land and walked up the brow of a bare, sheep-occupied hill soaked in evening sun, Chico began to seek out nuggets of sheep shit to eat. They were as black and baked as lumps of coal and he crunched them up. In protest, we wondered?

He did well out of Merthyr Farm's Lizzie though. She was 100 per cent pure mother, although actually quite new to it, with bright-faced little Nia, less than a year old, sitting on her hip, and two school-age stepchildren. Chico was introduced to his vast field, a galaxy of buttercups and daisies, with two tall cairns of rocks piled up high in the centre. And then Lizzie turned to us. 'I'll bet you need a paned?' I melted. Paned literally means a cup in Welsh, but emblematically it is a hug, an arrival, a welcome, even warmer than a cuppa.

TWELVE

Another estuary – the third since Aberystwyth – stood in our way. This one was a kind of double estuary of the rivers Dwyryd and Glaslyn. There was an island in the middle, and beyond the sand flats, salt marsh and shining ribbons of water was the beginning of the Lleyn Peninsula. The peninsula jutted out to the west at a right angle to the coastline we'd been following ever since Aberystwyth, forming the northern edge of Cardigan Bay.

The Briwet Bridge ran across the mouth of the first estuary, a listed 150-year-old wooden toll bridge that carried a single lane of traffic, the train line and a footpath. The old thing was getting shaky, built with just the occasional donkey in mind rather than the daily rush of schoolchildren, shoppers, commuters and tourists looking in Harlech for what they couldn't find in Porthmadog, and in Porthmadog for what had sold out in Harlech. Shore-shaking work on a replacement bridge was destabilising it further. In short, it was closed until the end of the week, and so we turned inland to begin the day's walk to the next bridge upriver, at Maentwrog. This part of the world was new to me, and very beautiful from our vantage point in the foothills, so I couldn't feel aggrieved. If you didn't know where you were heading anyway, it wasn't a detour. With no plans, there were no plans to change.

And so we had got to Felinrhyd Stables, a tatty, wonderful place. It was 10pm when we finally came panting, exhausted, up their path and parked Chico in a gap between gates – not the finest paddock, but easy and grassy. Still, Chico *hated* us! It had been a tough day, thanks to a new adversary that was significantly worse than yesterday's Shell Island sentry.

Things had begun well, though. Lizzie Roberts, it turned out, was a vet, and that morning had pared out Chico's soles, the thick skin that sits inside the hoof walls. This is living tissue and could get sore if the hooves wore down to the point where he was walking on the sole rather than the hoof. With quiet, matter-of-fact generosity, Lizzie refused payment for the hoof-paring or the camping, and as we were readying to leave brought out three bags of packed lunch, one of which contained a carrot and an apple and had a sticker marked 'Chico's lunch', with a smiley face. 'And fill up your egg box from the chicken coop on your way past!' she called after us. I did, picking warm eggs out of the hay as the hens pecked my ankles.

Chico didn't want to go – he stopped before we'd even made it off the sheep-poo-hill. Well, fair enough, nor did I. I wanted to lie in the daisies like a fat cuckoo, taking food and kindness and veterinary reassurance all day long. Chico took some coaxing. Was he tired? He'd walk a little way and then stop completely, and we'd pull and push and wheedle. Rhys's buffalo-skin boots had given him a couple of giant blisters and he was grumpy with the terrible stinging pain. I was fractious too, just to make up a full house. We all had a great fight in a lane of oaks, where Chico got really naughty, pulling away and running, stepping on the trailing rope and jerking himself, and then planting and refusing to move. Was he in pain? Was it the leadership thing? Although the sun was warm, a few midges loitered in the shady damp air under the oaks and Chico refused to walk on and away from the tiny, sucking dots.

Mum texted to ask how things were going and then texted back to say, 'Just finished Rob Louis Stev Cevennes book – he only did 12 days, maybe C knows Modestine had it easy.' We were on day thirteen.

At the very top of the hill was Llandecwyn church, clearly a halfway stop to heaven, and surrounded at that moment by silver sunbeams, unfolding through the firm white clouds. The land was piebald with patches of sunshine and dappled with sheep and the frothy white blooms of the spindly ash trees that grew through the drystone walls, themselves all speckled with grey lichen. The bellcote of the church, and its single bell, made a plain, bold silhouette stamped westwards above the mottled landscape.

For us, however, things got worse. We missed the path to heaven and instead plunged into forestry so full of midges that it became clear that it was they who'd been winding Chico up all day. Rhys and I behaved just as he had been all along, charging about, frantic. Every time we stopped, the midges would descend in a mist of panic, biting and crawling along our hairlines, finding our fleshy earlobes, lips and eyelids or choosing bony bits – ankles, jawbones and ear-rims. Argh! Madness! It was like being pursued by zombies. We fled wildly on, all three of us deranged.

I had the map – I always had the map. I was pinning memories to the contour lines and shapes of lakes, forests and crossroads, and refused to give it up. But that evening I failed in my duty. Amongst the trees there was nothing to navigate by; paths twisted without being noted, time passed independent of distance. The trees were identical in the gloom. I couldn't study the map very well while stumbling along, and I certainly couldn't stop and suffer the tickle and sting of midges in crannies. I had to refold it, and yelled like a banshee while I did, the map flapping a metre square against my legs, my hands swiping and scratching at my face, wrists and legs. Those midges must have been getting in under Chico's hair, diving unseen for his sensitive skin, taking tickly bites of his much greater surface area. Our blood was hot and wild, three intoxicating courses in the mossy shadows.

We went too far. A whole mile too far and an even worse doghouse mile back to the invisible path. By the time we got to Felinrhyd Stables – at 10pm – the midges were finally abating, but we kept our torches turned off nonetheless. The stables were run by a woman called Eurliw, a beautiful made-up name that means 'the colour of gold'. She offered us her mobile home so we wouldn't have to put up the tent, and brought us both a restorative paned. She and her four children were all still up, having driven around trying to find us. 'Bechod!' she said, stroking Chico's neck sweetly. I was pretty sure that meant 'sin' – was she accusing us? It would have been fair enough.

I cooked the strangest meal from our last supplies – rice, Lizzie's eggs, wilting leaves of wild garlic I'd collected in the oak lane, a bendy old carrot of Chico's, and a glutinous sauce of golden vegetable cuppasoup, all unevenly scorched and broiled by the inconsistent stove.

And now it was midnight, and therefore my birthday. I'd been about to announce it to Rhys, but he'd managed to fall asleep just in time, breathing heavily beside me, the poor, sore man. Sneaky! An alarm peeped in the darkness, and I got back up onto aching feet, tracked it down behind a pile of old furniture, and took the batteries out. How were the symptoms of carbon-monoxide poisoning different from the deep exhaustion of walking with Chico, I wondered? I switched off the headtorch and fell asleep.

THIRTEEN

Interesting things always happen where geography creates confluences of people and journeys – bridges and fords most of all. We crossed the Dwyryd river on the old stone bridge that ran alongside the new concrete bridge and joined up to a Roman road. The footsteps of history rang out. The village of Maentwrog was named after Twrog, a giant who picked up a rock (a 'maen' in Welsh) on a nearby mountain, and threw it down there, where it destroyed a pagan altar. It also marked the grave, apparently, of Pryderi, a character from the beloved Welsh medieval legends of the Mabinogi. There's a stone shaped like a huge bar of soap in the churchyard of St Twrog's and if you rub it you will be fated to return, so they say. I had nothing against the village, but having crossed the river and got back on track by turning west again, I passed the old stone by, unrubbed.

In honour of my birthday we stopped at the Oakeley Arms and had a pint of ale and at least half a dozen packets of crisps – welcome junk food after a snack drought. Thus mellowed we walked on, back into forestry thankfully free of midges but crossed by the twists and turns of the Ffestiniog railway. The railway runs from the mining town of Blaenau Ffestiniog at 220m, down the 13 miles to Porthmadog on the coast; these days it carries tourists, but once it transported slate to waiting ships. In its early years it ran downhill on gravity and was pulled up by horses, who would ride down again in wagons. Steam took over in the 1860s.

We walked through the woods, chancing it, and were unlucky. A footpath crossed the tracks, with tatty old stiles on either side, and full-width gates that were chained shut. It turned out that Rhys was as stubborn as Chico: he used the spanner and pliers we were carrying to deconstruct the stiles, bit by bit. He was spurred on by irritation that a right of way should be locked – there were ancient signs saying, 'Please shut the gate', so it had been fully accessible in the past and had no doubt seen plenty of passing donkey carts. It was now designated as a footpath though, and it annoyed him that routes were, these days, so dictatorial. The landscape belonged to either walkers or vehicles.

Going back to the main road couldn't have taken more time than the wholesale dismantling and diligent refurbishment of two stiles, but I enjoyed watching him succeed. He was going to leave us the next day to go back to work, and the ale had barely taken the edge off my heartsick, nagging worry.

The phoop! of a distant steam whistle through the woods gave us some warning – by the time the train passed our stretch, its passengers would only have seen the strange sight of a donkey accompanied by two sheepish people holding a broken stile in place and trying too hard to look innocent.

My long-legged father strode towards us and remarkably managed to find us in the tangle of forestry tracks, across a felled hillside of red stumps. We handed him Chico's rope, glad of a break from the fidgety animal. Within moments they'd disappeared ahead of us, and reappeared half an hour later at a crossways. Dad handed the rope back, saying, 'He really does what he wants, doesn't he? I don't know how to make him slow down! It's not my job.'

When we got to the campsite I'd chosen in Penrhyndeudraeth, Mum and her boyfriend Harry were there too. While we made Chico comfortable in his corral, Mum and Dad assembled a feast, on gas stoves and in Dad's campervan: cheeses and salami, salmon, boiled potatoes and eggs, a salad – a salad! – and cakes, fruit and chocolate. Harry gave me a bottle of wine, which was swiftly decanted into camping mugs. As we piled our plates high, the midges descended on the damp campsite and we ended up eating on the run, the five of us leaping up and dashing to a new picnic table every so often. Chico, this time, wasn't so bothered – Mum, donkey grandmother, had sought advice at the Aberystwyth farmers' co-op and had brought a plant-spray bottle with a homemade mixture of vinegar, lemon juice and citronella oil. She sprayed it on the donkey, and on the salad.

FOURTEEN

Mum took over from Rhys – I still didn't have strong enough arms or nerves to be the sole muleteer. The three of us walked through the rain, alongside the steam railway, across the Cob to Porthmadog, observed by two motionless swans sitting on the dun-coloured, severed water. The Cob is a sea wall that was built across the mouth of the Glaslyn estuary in the early nineteenth century by the MP William Madocks, to reclaim the land for agriculture. As the river was diverted, it dug out a harbour, and around the harbour grew Porthmadog – Madocks' port.

The town gave way to suburbs, which gave way to dunes, deserted playgrounds and shuttered ice-cream kiosks. All three of us were wet through. We'd been passed along to a couple called Iain and Lindsay, friends of Chickenshack Kath, who lived in a solitary white house on the headland at the far end of the beach called Black Rock Sands. We'd seen the house from the other end of the beach and struggled towards it, heads down in the salty squall. Almost there, with shelter in sight, Chico decided he'd had enough, and stopped. No amount of nudging or small pieces of carrot could convey that he should walk now for shelter in ten minutes, and so there was no choice but to stand together with imposed patience in the pouring rain for an extra half hour, until Chico deigned to walk on.

Lindsay and Iain are horse people. On passion, donations, and occasional funding, they run a charity that brings together young people with behavioural and confidence problems, and rescued horses with their own histories to overcome. As we arrived, they met us on the road, took us straight to the stable and gave Chico a wonderful welcome, with hay and love. When he was comfortable and enjoying a panoramic view of the beach below, they looked after Mum and me too, hoisting our every item of sodden clothing up on the drying rack alongside dozens of horse blankets.

Horses, they told us, are very truthful animals. Their actions and their emotions are always the same – if they look scared, they are scared. They are very quick to see when another creature's actions and intentions do not tally, for example if a predator is pretending to be sidling on by but is actually preparing to pounce. If a horse senses mixed messages from a person, they'll react by becoming less cooperative, or frightened, or distracted. Working closely with a horse, a person has to learn to be clear about their emotions and intentions – they have to be very honest, often for the first time in their lives. In return, they can find a simple, powerful connection.

'Horses have enormous, all-encompassing hearts,' said Lindsay. 'They accept people for who they really are. And they are very forgiving.'

In the morning they introduced Chico to their young New Forest pony, Leia. She had been terrified when she'd first arrived, and covered in lice, having been abruptly removed from her mother in the annual New Forest round-up and sold at auction for £3.50. Iain and Lindsay were gently increasing her experiences of the world, building her confidence. Chico is a determined donkey, genuinely keen to overcome what scares him, and meeting Leia was sure to be good for him too. I meant to watch, but slept right through.

We headed off on what turned out to be our shortest and most relaxed day so far. Were my own emotions and intentions a little more in line perhaps? We certainly weren't short of concerns: there was no on-going road from the end of Black Rock Sands, so we tried our luck along the railway line, through a field of cows, onto the rocky beach. Chico followed us, skittering over a mile of hard-going, rounded stones, occasionally eating crinkly white blooms of dried seaweed. Signposts warned us of adders in the grass, and a train passed close by, beeping and making us all jump. I cursed the driver's bad timing, and then realised with a laugh that it was a friendly greeting. I'd never been greeted by a train before.

We hit Criccieth, and stalled, blissfully, between a grounded rowing boat full of municipal flowers, and a beach cafe. Chico siphoned up the whole of a cafe's dog-water trough while Mum siphoned up a cup of tea. Then people began to come up and say hi. A woman leaned out of her car to tell us that her grandfather had walked a long way with a pony after returning from the first world war. He'd been a gas warden, and walked his pony as therapy, to recover from what he'd seen.

Next came Ken, a gentle old man who fell for Chico in a big way and spent ages chatting until his wife came to collect him, saying, 'Wrong end of the donkey, Ken! You'll get kicked!' I felt obliged to stick up for Chico, pointing out he'd not yet kicked anyone and was unlikely to start with dear Ken. 'He's just had both hips done!' barked the woman. 'It was expensive – he'd better not take any chances.'

Eventually we wandered on a few hundred yards, and then retired under a beach shelter for a bit while it rained. Chico ate around the daisies and allowed himself to be stroked by a family of Spanish tourists. A few hundred yards after that, we found a chip shop. Chico looked lovely, tied to a beautiful pink flowering hawthorn on the lawn beneath Criccieth's thirteenth-century Welsh castle, and was soon surrounded by admirers. We ate our early fish supper between rain showers, admiring the flashes of sunshine on distant beaches and the ever-changing cloudscapes. It was just the sort of day that might mistakenly have been thought of as bad, if we'd been looking at it from inside a house.

And then we wandered off, through the town and onto the coast path. Mum was completely relaxed about where we'd spend the night, and therefore so was I. Infectious calm really worked.

We camped right on the coast path, by the curve of a river, with Chico making himself at home in a tiny, empty corrugated-iron shed. The sky blazed, its towering orange sunset reflected in the river. Mum folded herself up in the tent like a little doll and fell asleep, and I burrowed down next to her and made her a scruffy birthday card on lined paper – a biro-and-highlighter picture of a donkey in a shed under a wild sky.

Mum – 61 today! – was already up when I woke; she'd collected twigs and made a little fire on the path, and the saucepan was boiling for tea. Every time she went anywhere, she'd return with something for Chico – she announced today's breakfast as 'hawthorn with goose grass on the side, garnished with a single laboriously harvested thistle'. Chico ate it in his shed with great satisfaction.

When we were walking, I was generally annoyed by Chico's verge munching. He'd stop whenever he felt like it, often wrenching my arms or catching me off balance, mid-stride, as he whipped me to a standstill at the end of his rope. He'd be hungry at annoying times, like for the first hour of the day's walk, when he'd surely had a long night of grazing in his field, and I – usually having started embarrassingly late – was keen to make progress. He'd reach for tiny bites every few steps when we went uphill, which looked distinctly like delaying tactics to me. When we walked along busy roads, he'd speed up or slow down suddenly in order to lunge past me, mouth-first into the hedgerow. But if I directed him towards the hedge to get him out of the way of a car, or in order to stop for a moment to chat to someone, he suddenly wasn't interested. Like this we made slow, mal-coordinated progress, like very bad country dancers or reluctant entrants in a three-legged race.

But Mum, keen self-taught botanist that she is, was delighted by his browsing. 'Yesterday he really wanted woody ash branches,' she'd report, 'but today it's all about these delicate fronds.' Chico's tendency to graze at right angles to the verge went unchecked, his great rear sticking out into the road. I gave Mum a grumpy telling-off but she bounced back, pointing out things for me too. 'Elderflower's coming!' and 'Time for pignuts!'

We spotted a campsite on the map and Harry came to meet us for a birthday celebration. I borrowed the car and drove to the supermarket in Pwllheli to buy a feast. The speed of locomotion was alarming: I went three times around the one-way system. The range of food on offer in the shop was even more of a challenge. In clothes I'd been wearing for weeks, a patchy tan, wind-blown knots in my unwashed hair, hands dark with dirt, I stood in the softly humming refrigerator aisle and felt overwhelmed. The cashier asked me for ID, which I didn't have, but was still delighted. 'I was 34 on Tuesday!' My grin must have creased up my dirt-filled wrinkles as she let me have the bottle of wine and agreed that living outside was evidently good for the aging process.

We ate the feast in Mum and Harry's dome tent. Outside, the sky was very dark – a great shell of low cloud stretched all the way to the far horizon, where a distant band of light suggested that we really were at the centre of the weather, singled out for an exciting night. The wind was vigorous, and the tent bucked and convulsed, battering us inside as we laughed and gorged. I crawled back into my own tent, a much calmer wedge-shape that sloughed off the wind. It felt cavernous; I was alone in there for the first time since departure. Chico stood next to me in his corral, his mac on, stalwart against the wind and lit up by a campsite spotlight. A few hours later the hail began, flung horizontally at the tent and the donkey. I unzipped the door and looked out at Chico and he looked back at me, his expression surprisingly stoic.

By the morning the sun shone, Chico was dry and grazing happily, and the other campers, all of whom had enormous multi-roomed dome tents that housed more than one branch of a family tree, wandered about with the cheerful camaraderie of a field of survivors, bound to each other by common experience and the lending and borrowing of mallets.

I had another reason to greet this new day: it was going to be my first alone with Chico. Mum and Harry were going home, Dad would join me soon, but in between the two I was going to see if we could make it on our own. I sat on the grass and prevaricated – I parcelled up birthday food to take, sewed new lambswool sleeves to the straps of the packsaddle, planned the day's route, wrote up my diary, handwashed my clothes, and had a shower. With only one detergent for washing-up, clothes, body and hair, I ran out of things to do in the shower, but stood under the hot spray for an extra five minutes, dawdling. Chico lay down on the grass for some well-earned rest after the night he'd had.

We finally set off at two. I hefted the saddlebags onto Chico and then discovered that the path to the beach was too narrow, and hefted them off again. Chico, full of energy as he often was when first released from his night's confinement, barged through the narrow gateway, knocking me into the sand, and ran up the dune with me scrabbling behind at the end of the rope. At the top, the full-bellied wind off the sea blew a plastic pot over the dune and into our faces, my hair whipped in my eyes and blinded me, and a family ran up the narrow path to see him, alarming us both even more. Our hearts were already pounding, all alone together, the flinty sea choppy and glinting in the distance under bright sun and dark clouds, roaring and foaming close up. We had the longest day of the walk so far ahead of us, and we'd set off at 2pm – what a fool I was.

It was an inauspicious start, but as Chico fell into step with me on the beach, I looked back at him, and he looked up at me, and I grinned.

FIFTEEN

At Natasha's house I discovered that my enormous capacity for eating did have its limits. I stayed for a rest day, Chico outside in his very own field, and Natasha fed me a roast dinner, banoffee pie, elderflower wine, bacon rolls, a takeaway curry fetched from Pwllheli, gammon sandwiches, and homemade bara brith (Welsh fruitcake made with tea). That, it turned out, was all a human being could handle. Natasha also washed and tumble-dried all of my clothes as I lounged about naked under my waterproofs, bouncing on the trampoline with little Ela and Tomos. Twelve-year-old Iona had sewn me a brilliant mascot – a mini Chico, winking, for which one of her own grey socks had been sacrificed. Harri, Natasha's husband, wasn't interested in donkeys. But we discovered later that he, like Gerry way back on the first night, had snuck out to put the outside light on for him.

Natasha had extended her very warm welcome through Facebook, and on the phone had offered me the rest day. As Chico and I had walked, exhausted and late, into the village of Sarn Meyllteyrn, Natasha's shrill neighbour Lowri had pulled over to get the gossip, asking where we were going. 'Oh, the Gwyn Joneses'! Just tonight?' Two nights, I said, and by the time I got to Natasha's, Lowri had already dropped by to flaunt her knowledge to Natasha's mother-in-law, who had called up Natasha, and all rather embarrassingly before I had officially taken her up on her offer of a two-night stay. From the hill you could see the sea on both sides of the patchwork land, and it was glorious. But I suddenly understood that it might also feel a bit claustrophobic out there, towards the narrow end of the Lleyn Peninsula, amongst thick, deep hedgerows and with aged spectacles peering from every terraced window.

After the rest day, I managed to leave at 5pm – a new late record. At first I was waiting for Dad, who was coming to continue the assistance. Then he arrived, and I went to get Chico from the field, only for him to run away from me – a first, and funny and worrying in equal measure. He usually played a little hard to get, swinging his great head away and giving me the slip a couple of times, just to remind me who was boss, but this was different. He'd been in the field for nearly two days – perhaps he just really liked it there. He didn't want to get back on the road, he'd had it with me? Or maybe he was playing? If it hadn't been so embarrassing – walking after him with the headcollar in my hands while he waited for me to approach, only to race away kicking his hooves in the air – it might have been a fun game. Dad and the Gwyn Joneses suggested I might corral off some of the field, or trap him in a corner. I felt it wasn't right, though, and once they'd left me to it, I eventually made progress, following him quietly, arms down, eyes averted, calm and silent but refusing to go away, finally getting close enough to stroke him into submission. He was all fizzed up and upset, not playing after all. While I'd been trying to catch him, he'd run up to the far corner and stared down a tiny, bold, ginger calf in a neighbouring field; I wondered if it was interspecies disquiet.

A couple of women appeared, having followed our progress on Facebook. Cracker Dawn and Val were live wires – delightful and a bit alarming at once. Cracker Dawn had brought a huge carrot, which she insisted on offering to Chico from her mouth to his, grinning sideways at the camera, in a peculiar pornographic sort of way. Then she found her way to my heart by handing over a whole homemade cake – a marbled peanut and chocolate one because at some point I'd written online that I was eating a Snickers bar. I felt a heady dash of celebrity, incongruous for a woman who didn't seem to be succeeding very well at her chosen activity, struggling to catch a donkey in the early evening.

Thankfully, Dad, Chico and I didn't have too far to go – the next place we'd been invited to stay was close by. We walked there along the 300m-high hog-back ridge of Mynydd Rhiw, Rhiw mountain, as the sun sank low in the sky, unrolling long red shadows of a man and a donkey across the hilltop. We passed a Neolithic axe factory, where, five or six thousand years ago, men and women found just the right fine-grained shale to make tools, and quarried it in open-cast hollows. Molten rock had forced its way up, searing the local rock and forming this rare and useful seam. The factory made and traded big axes for cutting down trees, but they also made smaller ones for their own use, including finer woodworking tools for shipbuilding and domestic scrapers and knives. The traded tools have been found right across Wales, passed from person to person from this end-of-the-road headland.

We strode off the mountain and back into the deep hedgerows, speckled with flowers. A van came towards us and I wrestled Chico into the side as usual, but the driver stopped and leaned out of the open window with a broad, boyish smile. 'Elm, is it?' He was admiring the wooden part of Chico's packsaddle. He gestured into the van. 'We've been making this, me and my son.' The young man in the passenger seat said hi, and passed a beautifully made wooden stool through the window, the seat lovingly shaped to suit a grateful bottom. 'It's elm too.'

'We're heading for Felin Uchaf, near here somewhere, I think?' I said, and the man nodded. 'Ah, yes – that way, not far, nice place,' he said, pointing back the way they had come.

Felin Uchaf was some sort of centre where people made buildings – that was all I knew. A carpenter called Alice, the younger sister of a girl I went to school with, worked there, and I'd spoken to her on the phone a few times. She'd been worryingly blasé about our arrival time and whether bringing a donkey would be okay. I'd tried and failed to get to the bottom of who was in charge.

The place turned out to be an old mill surrounded by the towering ribcages of several raw, half-built wooden structures. It was deserted when we arrived, except for a young woman called Adela from the Czech Republic. She helped me corral Chico into the corner of a field, running off to the garden to get some more bamboo canes while I moved a pile of rotting cut reeds that Chico was keen to eat but shouldn't. I was already thinking about my dinner; would I have a packet of couscous and a tin of mackerel? 'Would you like food?' asked Adela. 'The others will be back soon – we can make some for them.'

I confess, my selfish heart sank.

For several weeks I'd been cared for, fed and sheltered by kind strangers, often turning up late and dishevelled, sometimes soaked through, always with a catalogue of needs. Before the walk began I had become totally accustomed to my own fortress. Visiting someone else's fortress was fairly difficult in ordinary life – I'd turn up with a bottle of wine or flowers or pudding, say thank you too much and 'only if you're having one' a lot, wander about awkwardly admiring ornaments and feeling out of place, in someone else's space. I had worried about being a perpetual guest on this walk, but as with so many worries, the reality when it came left no room for that. In the first weeks we'd been so needy, these little concerns were banished. I arrived exhausted every time, feet hot and sore, donkey fractious and desperate to know where he could rest. Wet things just had to be dried, tools borrowed. If food or a bed was offered, my animal-self just reached out faster than my sluggish, weary manners and snatched the comforts.

I hadn't even done the washing-up, not at Natasha's or Lindsay and Iain's, or Chickenshack. I was almost getting used to arriving empty handed. Occasionally I'd think perhaps

I could offer something from the saddlebag pantry, but in the surrounds of a nice house, the crummy, greasy, battered supplies looked a bit dingy for sharing.

But at the same time, I was also under the spell of the self-sufficiency of the road. I could look after myself and Chico, camp at a moment's notice. So when Adela suggested we cater for a dozen, I was taken aback. I just wanted to fill my belly as fast and single-mindedly as Chico filled his when I gave him his two handfuls of alfalfa.

Offended by my own greedy instincts, I pulled myself together and headed for the tiny kitchen, where somehow between us and a few other people who appeared, we made a simple and lovely meal in moments, with little coordination or planning. A giant saucepan of couscous with lemon juice and pepper, a tomato sauce with vegetables and spices, some salad; when everyone came back from an evening spent surfing, piling sleepily and saltily out of the van, we all ate and were satisfied, without a raised heart rate or caterer in the place. People appeared, found a bowl, filled it and emptied it, had a chat, got some seconds, disappeared again. Some people sat outside, read books, talked softly, everyone said hi to me. Most were in their early twenties, and they came from all over the world.

Dad had retrieved his van and slept in it, and I was invited to sleep in one of the roundhouses. The cone-shaped thatched wooden building was on stilts, 15 feet across, with a wooden floor, a single window, and a sleeping platform around the inside edge, dotted with foam mattresses. In the middle was a lantern and an extension cable with a few mobile phones charging. I joined three guys, and laid out my sleeping bag on the unoccupied mattress. Each man had a bag alongside him, some handwashed socks drying or a book open on the floor, but not much stuff – our needs were few and with simple tiredness we all went straight to sleep.

In the morning everyone got up and started building without fuss. There was a complete lack of bells or foremen. I wandered about and found people quietly but enthusiastically at their work all over the place. Dafydd, the man who the day before had waved the stool at us from the van window, showed us around. It turned out he was the founder of Felin Uchaf, though he hadn't admitted that to us on the road. In his energetic company, with his eyes full of dancing sparks and his curly blonde hair sticking up all over his head, the world became a brilliant, breathtaking, enchanted place. His great excitement for architecture and philosophy, history and biodiversity, the global and the local, all holistically treated as one, was irresistibly infectious. He believed that architecture should be drawn from the people and the land, not assembled from bits shipped in from all over the world and foisted on the landscape. At Felin Uchaf the buildings had grown from the ground.

It had been nine years since Dafydd and some friends had launched an appeal, bought their patch of windswept land, planted hedgerows and begun to grow thousands of trees. First had come the meeting house, which they'd built using the materials at hand: earth, short timbers, reeds for the roof. It was no coincidence that the finished building looked a lot like a Bronze or Iron Age meeting house; with the same requirements, the same resources, and the same elements to withstand, the finished result was similar.

Inside, the meeting house was cool and quiet and smelled of old wood smoke. The earth floor was well swept and a single bee hummed through the beams of light from the long, hemispherical window in the thatched roof. Around the perimeter were sitting cubbies behind clay arches, then space for benches and seats, the storyteller in the centre and the enclosed fireplace at one side. I could feel the presence of years of people, listening to tales, resting their heads on each other's laps, being together in the flickering gloom. Here was a space that had its priorities right – time, people, community.

A new building was underway, attached to the mill – a green-oak-framed barn that would become a visitors' centre. The enormous frames had been raised by hand in the way they had been for a thousand years, with ropes and blocks and tackle, and a great deal of sweat and teamwork. On the other side of the road was an even bigger structure, at a later stage of construction. The woodwork was finished, including a huge oak cruck carved with the 32 nationalities of the volunteers who'd had a hand in it, from South Africa to Sweden and everywhere in between. Now the roof was being thatched with local reeds and the walls were being filled with local sheep's fleeces.

Such beautiful work, undertaken for its own sake, is a rarity in these times of miserly housing and cheap, almost disposable chipboard furniture. The structures at Felin Uchaf embodied hours and hours of creative endeavour by countless hands; a vast amount of learning and teaching, with people contributing weeks or months of their valuable labour.

Felin Uchaf was founded on a brave vision and it seemed to me a wonderful success: the conviction that people could be trusted to come together and care for each other, to have their work valued and shaped without being harried or pressured. They looked after each other, and needed little. It was a simple, healthy place.

On a table in the meeting house I had found a verse attributed to the poet Goethe. Mum had been trying to remember it as we'd walked together, set to music, but hadn't managed.

Whatever you can do or dream you can do – begin it!
Boldness has genius, power and magic in it.

There, in that cool, calm, enveloping space at the end of the land, I cried a bit. Perhaps there was some magic in having begun this walk, even though I was now so tired and wrecked and lost in the point of it. People had started asking if I was doing the walk for charity, and when I said no, several had come back with, 'What are you doing it for then?' I'd pause, uncertain. 'Fun?' I sometimes said, without conviction. This wasn't fun. I wasn't at all sure Chico wanted to be doing it, I didn't know a thing about him really. The responsibility for him weighed heavily on me, the shame of being so barely in control, the neediness as a guest, the hefty backpack, and most of all, the haunting presence of the nine-tenths – the 900 miles – still to go. This was hard. And why? What was it for?

But at last our stretch on the map was beginning to look a bit healthier – it could probably be seen from space by really sharp-eyed astronauts. We were getting to the tip of the Lleyn Peninsula, marking daily progress along the cliffs and bays. As if walking along the inside edge of a boomerang, I could look back across Cardigan Bay to where Aberystwyth lay and, between there and here, the route of the 20 days so far. It might feel a lot like a strange folly, but just by doing it, something was being created.

Boldness – yes, it really was bold. Goethe's little verse lifted me right up; it said it was okay to do something for boldness alone. It was justifiable to begin a dream, just to see how it would go. Perhaps there was magic being made. Perhaps I'd find power in all of this powerlessness, and maybe even moments of genius in the wearying naivety.

This page, above: Moments after swapping £375 for a donkey. *Below left:* Dai Evans making the packsaddle. *Below right:* Chico was deeply suspicious of everything during the field month.

Overleaf, above right: Aberystwyth's Victorian promenade. *Middle left:* Wild camping on the Lleyn. *Middle right:* Tywyn beach. *Below:* The wilds above the Dyfi estuary. *Opposite:* Bryn and baby Nia at Merthyr Farm.

PART TWO

ANGLESEY AND THE NORTH COAST

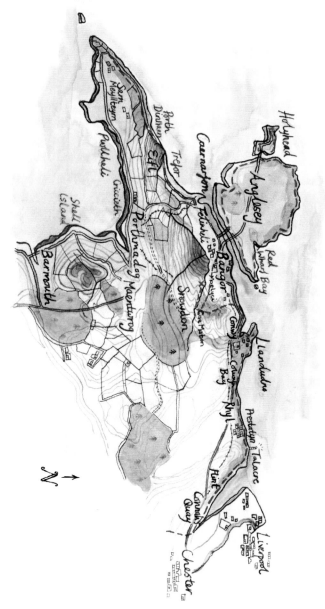

SIXTEEN

With the simple wisdom of a deep thinker, Dafydd at Felin Uchaf had completely changed my perception of the Lleyn Peninsula. It's not the end of the earth, out on a limb, he'd said. Far from it. In ancient times, when the world travelled by boat, the sea was the global highway, and this limb of land reached out and drew people in. The Neolithic axe-makers of Mynydd Rhiw were boat-builders and this peninsula was their centre, not the periphery. The thick, wooded hinterland, the woolly interior, was much harder to get to. We weren't at the end of the line but at the edge of the rest of the world.

I insisted that we go right to the tip of the peninsula and camp there, in order to have 'done' the Lleyn. Chico wasn't impressed. He dragged his hooves on the tiny distance from the Mynydd Mawr campsite to the top of the lookout mound. Was he worried by the sheep that stood about, skinny, shorn and white in the black, burnt gorse? Or was it just that he could see that our path led nowhere, with sea to left, right and straight ahead? 'Quick, Chico,' Dad said. 'The sheep will bite you!'

Then we turned away from the rest of the world and changed our bearing from west-by-southwest to north-by-northeast – almost a full 180. Almost as soon as we turned course, Chico turned bad. Were he a creature with a nomad's internal compass, I might have suspected that he was angry at this obviously whimsical direction setting. I tried to take him up Mynydd Anelog, a 192m hill on the north coast of the peninsula. This would give us a fine view of our turning point and the cliffs ahead, and would avoid us having to retrace the exact same steps we'd taken to get to the land's end. But Chico would not. I tried three routes, twice each, and each time he refused. We returned to the road, me defeated, frustrated and only just into the morning's walk, Chico a wretched mystery to me. Was he triumphant at the win? Tired? Sore? Was it random or highly significant?

Dad left us, and without him to make light of it, I picked through the various bad possibilities, obsessively shredding the situation into fragments in my mind. My rolling programme of escorts had come to an end. It was just me and the donkey, and neither of us was feeling very good about it.

As we walked between tall, exultant hedgerows, wild with life like overgrown mohicans, crowned with cow parsley and pink campion, Chico suddenly thrust his face through the long grass and into the roadside ditch. This was unusual – generally it was the verge at mouth level that he went for. I lurched into self-flagellation – the poor creature must have heard the water trickling in the ditch, he must be parched, did I not give him enough water last night? Oh, Chico! Mea culpa! Drink freely, please forgive me!

But when he lifted his head, there was a whole cheese sandwich in his mouth. A perfect fresh triangle of white bread and cheddar, sticking out either side of his great lips. For once his expression was unmistakeable – utter delight, with an edge of defiance. I lunged forward to wrest it from him – bread was not good for donkeys, and who knew about dairy products? – but he was ready. He swallowed it with a single smack of triumph, turned and walked on.

We were not harmonious travel companions. Chico was beginning to show a preference for not doing whatever I wanted to do – contrariness for the sake of it. Donkeys always have a touch of this, I think. They may be perfectly happy to go left or right, but if you make the mistake of pulling them one way, they immediately take against it. The body language was so familiar from storybooks that it almost made me laugh. Chico would plant his hooves firmly, and the frame of his bony legs and strong shoulders became an immutable structure with a living strength as steadfast as roots or rocks; trying to move him by might was as fruitless as trying to pull Stonehenge along on a string. I might manage to pull his head forward a little, but this would just result in him jutting out his jaw and fixing me with his great, hard eyes. Never did body language say 'NO' so very clearly. 'Whatever it is you want of me, just NO.'

The Lleyn Peninsula was all new to me, and I'd never even heard of the towns coming up. The place names were different too – lots of hamlets called 'tyddyn', a word meaning cottage that I'd rarely seen down south. Lots of villages and terraces were called 'Tai'n Lon' – another North Walian name, meaning 'houses on the lane'. Everyone automatically spoke Welsh to me, with the calm certainty with which someone in France would speak French – the assumption being that everyone did.

My Welsh was fifteen-years rusty, and in Aberystwyth speaking Welsh always felt like a test. People there rarely began a conversation with a stranger in Welsh, and would quite often end one having switched to English. Perhaps they were hoping to be kind, but it always felt like a snub to me. That, along with the fear of bumping into old teachers who'd speak to me so shamingly slowly and clearly with their singsong nursery-school voices and searching bright eyes, had caused me to stop speaking Welsh, pretty much, over the years. I could understand almost anything in Welsh – I'd spoken it daily at school for 14 years – but in Aberystwyth it wasn't about communication but about belonging. I could make myself understood, but could I do it with enough relaxed fluency and colloquialisms to pass as real Cymru-Cymraeg? Sometimes I could, but often I couldn't, and I'd hear every one of my mumbles and hesitations as a defeat.

'Cymru-Cymraeg' means Welsh-Welsh – a Welsh person who speaks Welsh. Welshness is almost exclusively defined by the language, which is a peculiar situation – in a strange way both very open and very closed. On a day-to-day basis there's no need to prove generations of Welsh blood, or to have the right skull shape, hair colour or surname. All you need is a perfect grasp of the language. And a perfect grasp of the language is something that can at least be learned – you just have to live there, study very hard, and speak it every day. It is ethnicity by merit and effort, in a way.

The week before, a woman had leaned out of a car window and, after talking about the donkey for a few minutes, had asked if I was Welsh, or a 'dysgwraig' – a learner. I was stumped – there had to be more options.

I'd thought that North Wales, where the language is more widely spoken, would be an even harder place to be rusty. But the opposite was true, and I babbled Welsh at every opportunity. Gone was the familiar flicker of judgement as the other person weighed up my level of Welsh and assigned me a level of Welshness. Was it just the particular people I met? Was it that they felt their Welshness to be less under threat and therefore didn't feel like gatekeepers? Or was it that I just spoke happily, with the have-a-go boldness of a person on holiday? Sai'n gwybod!

We arrived for the night at the Penrallt campsite, which belonged to Pete and Sue. They organised beach clean-ups, and their buildings were covered all over with brightly coloured buoys, rope, nets and other flotsam and jetsam, plastic jewels that looked great, having been changed back from rubbish to objects of worth. Pete helped the clean-up kids get in touch with the companies behind some of the most prevalent litter and ask them to do something about it.

They had extended a welcome via Facebook. Pete had helped with the beach donkeys in Blackpool when he was a kid, and when they'd taken on this campsite, he'd had a dream that they could provide accommodation for pilgrims, with stabling for the donkeys. He was pleased and tickled that his vision had come true. They had a wooden camping cabin that they called a pilgrim pod, but Sue offered me the luxury yurt instead, full of little Buddhas, floor cushions to meditate on, and a kettle for tea. Chico lay down outside.

We were walking along an old pilgrims' trail. It had all begun in the fifth century, when Celtic monks went looking for quiet places to become hermits. Some of them found their way to Bardsey Island, off the far western tip of the Lleyn Peninsula, and soon many others followed. The island became a holy destination – making three pilgrimages to Bardsey the equivalent of doing one to Rome – and many ancient churches and holy wells of North Wales became important points on the route. By the Middle Ages it was a highway of the faithful. It's said there are 20,000 saints buried on Bardsey, which isn't even a mile square.

Pete and Sue gave me several scallop shells – the symbol of the pilgrim. The big ones, bigger than my palm, would have been used as a bowl or a scoop, held out in hope as pilgrims sought food and shelter from the locals. The way would have been hard, with no guarantee of hospitality, and highwaymen lying in wait. The idea of doing this without warm welcomes or pockets full of snacks chilled me – a better seat in heaven would be the bare minimum incentive to make it worthwhile. Growth through adversity, the transcendence of the journey, the motivation of a higher purpose... With a shell bobbing on a thread around my neck, I tried to ponder these profound things on the road the next day, but that godforsaken donkey kept stopping, wrenching my arms and interrupting my spiritual development.

I posted a picture of Chico in classic plant pose to Facebook. In no time, Tamlin, Aberdyfi Louise and a few other kind donkey people had all responded with: 'Listen to your donkey.' I ground my teeth.

'He's trying to tell you something,' they wrote. I'm sure he was, but to me it sounded like this: 'Are we nearly *there* yet? You didn't tell me we were just going to keep going, and going, and going. I don't *like* walking. This is a stupid idea for an adventure. Can I have an ice-cream? Ay caramba – a lamb! Let's go back this way. Grass, grass, ash, hawthorn, grass…' And so on.

I'd checked all over for packsaddle rubs and pinches, I was feeding him more than before, we'd had two short days and two rest days in the last five days. It hadn't been too warm, he seemed relaxed at night, his hooves were in decent condition. There were a few things that I thought it could be. One: general tiredness, compounded by walking fully laden again after a few days of slinging lots of the stuff in Dad's camper. But he never showed signs of physical tiredness – in fact his naughtiness took more energy, not less. And it wasn't consistent; suddenly he'd find his walking mojo and stride along brilliantly for half an hour.

So two, then: it could have been that he was just better at walking with two people. Two people chat, stride, provide forward momentum, and Chico followed along willingly. When it was just me there wasn't the same distraction. I faked momentum by singing marching songs, talking out loud, making phone calls, ignoring Chico, and it did work a bit. If anyone caught me up on the road, Chico got moving.

Or perhaps it was number three: my new zero-tolerance policy on verge chomping. He was doing it a lot more now, always looking for an excuse to stop. We were having regular grazing breaks, including a long, unladen lunch break, so he wasn't wasting away. I'd tried not to let him graze at will, and it was getting better, but sometimes he'd look at me as if to say: 'No chomp, no walk. How do you like *that*, you irritating woman?'

One other thing it could have been: perhaps he knew something about Porth Dinllaen that I didn't. I had been looking forward to this stop since Norma at Chickenshack had told me about it – an early-nineteenth-century fishing village in a cove with crystal-clear water, no road access, and a pub. The kindest, most warm-hearted pub, with dear, friendly staff, nice locals, and Welsh ale. Chico took against Porth Dinllaen in exact inverse proportion to how much I liked it.

As we approached across a golf course, Chico got really disinclined, until finally some other walkers caught us up, and then he was fine. It was a golden evening and we descended the cliff and rounded the bend onto the beach to find people snorkelling in the cove while a few dozen others were sitting on the wall outside the pub, drinking, chatting and awaiting the late arrival of a donkey.

We walked up and I began to take his saddle off, but he took fright and had a great wet fear-poo all over the beach, the first since Aberystwyth on day one. Then he took off, in any direction he could, with the super strength that fear gives him. Leaving luggage and poo all over the beach, I followed him down to a spot where we were away from people, and tied him next to some grass. We sat together and began to calm down. Golden ale was waiting for me a few hundred yards away, but I practised patience.

After a while Chico pawed the ground, ready to roll in the sand. I untied the rope to make him more comfy and, instantly, rolling forgotten, he took off again, round the headland and down the next beach. 'Can my daughter come and stroke your donkey?' called a woman from a window of the house on the headland as I was dragged off at the end of his rope, his hooves clattering on the stones and the whites of his eyes showing as he broke into a wild gallop. I discouraged her over my retreating shoulder and she looked cheesed off.

I got him back to the calm place, tied him again and soothed us both. After another long while I thought I might risk moving him towards the spot where I hoped to corral him for the night, past the bar, in a sheltered corner between cottages, away from too many people and out of sight of the sea. We'd have to pass the pub audience – I'd get the chance to offer some explanation for my total lack of control over my skittish creature. I got up to untie him, and at just that moment two high-energy spaniels rounded the bend at top speed, saw the last thing they expected with only 10 feet of reaction time, and opted for mad yapping. Chico took his only option, opened his throat and brayed. And brayed, and brayed, and brayed. Thirty long seconds of hoarse, wheezing, bay-rattling decibels, that were probably heard in the Wicklow hills across the sea in Ireland, and certainly jangled the pints of ale in the hands of the ever more amused pub-goers. It was a sound like mooing and sawing, with a treble of air horns and a giant's fingernails on a blackboard, and a bass line of banshees and baboons. It was incredibly loud, and sort of hilarious. The dogs were dragged away, donkey soothing began again, a kindly delegation appeared from the pub with carrots.

Things got better. I got Chico to his spot, assembled the corral, fed and watered and brushed him, put up my tent on a tent-sized terrace garden above the village, and finally joined the few remaining pub folk. The kind landlord Stuart made me a bowl of chilli and rice, despite not doing evening meals in the pub. I drank two pints of elderflower-flavoured ale when my body craved water and became a classic drunkard, first complaining about Chico to anyone who'd listen, and then returning to put the waterproof rug on him and giving him a sort of pissed snuggle. 'I fuckin' *love* you, I do…'

Stuart, Gary-the-barman, John-the-local and their drunk friend Alec gave me the blissful opportunity to be vulgar – a glorious tawdry delight after all of the philosophy and spirituality of late. We laughed until the small hours about selling Chico for parts, the potential market for donkey salami, his impressively pliable suede anus that opened to a diameter of at least four inches when he pooed, and creative ways of sabotaging the golf course out the back. I climbed happily into my tent, stuffing chocolate chip cookies into my mouth, my torso aching from all the verge fights, but my mind happy with friendship. Even the slug in my sleeping bag didn't dent my mood.

I decided we'd stay at Porth Dinllaen for a rest day. Chico might not like it there, but I did, and I was in charge. The farm and campsite I'd passed on the way in, with a granddaughter who had taken to Chico, said I could take him up there for the day and night, to get him away from the beach and onto some fresher grass. As we started off across the beach, past the pub, now surrounded by people enjoying a Friday lunch, I whispered, 'Please walk nicely, Chico. At least past the pub. Don't show us up again.' We managed three quarters of the short distance before Chico executed an impressive move. He stuck out a front hoof, tripping me up, just as he put on a sudden gallop forwards. Holding onto the end of the rope, but with my feet no longer touching the ground, I did a moment of perfect donkey-towed horizontal Superman flight, before hitting the sand, hard. The full pub audience looked on. Still holding the rope, I got dragged a little way along the beach before having the sense to let go. The big double pocket on the front of my skirt was always full – horse nuts, phone, wallet, penknife, pen, raisins, and on this occasion a poop-scooping plastic bag and a mini Babybel – and I landed on it hard, thumping my thigh muscle thoroughly. I was spared hanging about to soak up the shame, as Chico pretty much dashed in fits and starts right back across the golf course, in front of a golfing audience, all of us holding our breath as he veered towards the meticulous green, and away again.

I shed a few quiet tears as I put up his corral in the grassy field, my dead leg and whiplash like external signs of the relentless wrenching and bruising of my self-esteem. 'Beer?' said a man, leaning out of his caravan. He was called Barney, and over the course of two cans we discussed euthanasia, Wimbledon, and his grim accident. He'd fallen out of a train in 1971 and been unconscious for two weeks. His jeans had been torn away, leaving only the pocket with a letter inside it by which the medical staff had tried to identify him. He ended up losing the use of his right arm at the age of 18. My leg ache and self-pity faded.

As I walked back to the beach I tried to figure out what Chico didn't like about Porth Dinllaen, but it beat me. It seemed perpetually clear that I didn't know anything about the inner workings of this animal.

SEVENTEEN

Mum came back. I don't think I asked her to, but she came anyway, as if she'd seen a Batman signal in the sky above Aberystwyth, a summoning searchlight in the shape of a galloping donkey and a woman in flight. The little silver-haired superhero arrived and took a look at the impressive Eifl on the horizon. The triple-peaked mountain had been psyching me out for days – a great towering rock in my future. It dropped into the sea in sheer cliffs and its three horns were continually crowned in purple rainclouds, even when the rest of the coast was baby blue. Our route, and that of the countless pilgrims, was the high pass between the peaks, and our next night's sleep was to be with Andi, who lived on the far slopes. 'Pah,' said Mum, 'I've walked through Nepal,' and we set off. Of course, I'm not scared of a 560m hill either, I thought. But then I'm not scared of donkeys, and look how that's working out…

In the event, we walked uphill all day long, spreading the altitude rise over the 10 or so miles, and finding ourselves above the treeline amongst the bilberries and larks without too much trouble. Oh, except for the several occasions when Chico refused to move, one of which was on the fast main road. It was an S-shaped bend that went fairly steeply uphill at the same time, and Chico came to a halt, sideways on, in the path of oncoming traffic. I ran up to the corner to wave my arms around – thankfully we were past the evening rush hour and the cars crawled by with grins of amusement through the windscreens. Eventually, after a sweaty 10 minutes, he began to move on slowly, encouraged with handfuls of grass. The only people we saw all day were the members of a very glitzy and somewhat overweight hen party which made the Nefyn town bus pull over so they could reel across the road in their incredible heels to pose with the non-compliant donkey.

On the high pass, as with all high ground, we ascended out of ordinary time and into eternal time. As the last telegraph poles faded into the mist behind us and signal ceased trying to reach our mobile phones, there was no litter, language or fashion to pin us to an era. There were only old stones, rolling very slowly over each other, obeying gravity. The occasional sheep loitered; it could have been its own grandchild or grandparent – who was there to mark their ovine generations? Who begat who? The lichen grew, moss gathered. With the breathing of seasons, bilberries swelled, fell and shrivelled, went adventuring in the guts of rabbits. The birds flirted over the bare landscape but only needed to fly a little west before the rock disappeared and they were half a kilometre above the licking, living waves.

The twin thrill and chill of even this brief remoteness ran through me. If we'd stayed long enough perhaps we'd have found ourselves guests of the Iron Age people who lived there once, in the hilltop forts, piling the stones up again. Far below us, on cliffs above the waves, was Nant Gwrtheyrn. From up there we couldn't see that it was now a beautifully restored language centre – it could still have been the frenetic quarrying village where Irishmen made granite cobblestones for the streets of Liverpool and Manchester in the 1860s. It could have been the trashed commune of the 1960s, or the abandoned ghost village of the following years.

On the other side of the mountain was another quarry, great slides of rock around dead-eyed old buildings, now two dimensional, and too high for the softening clutches of weeds. As we walked down through it I realised that time had gone marching on in its conventional way; the sun was setting and the lights were coming on in the town of Trefor below us. Dusk in June is late – we were going to be bad guests again, and Chico was not for hurrying.

Andi found us in the gloom, coming from the wrong direction after an extra few miles' accidental diversion, and I put the corral up by the light of my headtorch. Luckily Andi and Will were unfazed, claimed to be evening people anyway, and fed us Will's delicious chicken casserole at midnight. Will's delicious chicken casserole went straight into the league tables as one of the best things I had ever eaten, ever. And beds! I slept for many years, and outside the world turned.

Andi and Will had just taken early retirement and moved from the suburbs of Nottingham to this 400-year-old cottage where the mushrooms, cobwebs and neighbourhood long-horned goats had been taking over. They were planning one day to provide specialist holiday accommodation for families with autistic children. They were in love with their little town of Trefor and had countless tales of great kindness, which I'm sure they were attracting by radiating out their own good energy and copious laughter. They sent us off with warm hearts and pockets full of flapjack.

The hills of the Lleyn stuck up from the low ground like giant molehills, and we skirted the slopes of one and then another, like a country dance. From our elevated position we could see across the plain to some hills to the south, and sea beyond – with a shock I realised we were looking at Criccieth and Pwllheli, where we'd been ten days before. We were done with the peninsula, and from the other side of the final hill the next great detour was visible – the vast isle of Anglesey, 124 miles around.

EIGHTEEN

We were inching towards the bigger roads and faster life of the north coast of Wales, along a disused railway – the line that previously joined the North Wales railway to the Mid Wales railway and was now a cycle path. Although Chico did undertake the occasional stretch of superb strolling, head down, undistracted by verges for whole dozens of minutes at a time, he was still tricky, and a thought had taken root in my mind: perhaps we needed a little time apart.

Mum had gone home, and an air of passive aggression had settled between Chico and me, congealing at times into out-and-out active aggression. As is generally the way when relationships falter, and with nothing to distract us on the straight, flat cycle route, I began to catalogue his sins, his classic moves, guaranteed to press my fury buttons: nudging me into brambles, twisting me off balance, running back the way we'd come, bracing himself against me by treading on the side of my foot. These things made me wild, and fairly often I would be driven almost to violence. On one occasion, shocked by the sudden pain of hoof-on-foot, I even drew back my boot, ready to kick him. Thankfully I had just enough time to realise that with so little flesh on his leg, the impact of my boot on his bone would be awful, and I put my foot back on the ground.

The worst thing of all was his slow-motion condescending snub, often just when I thought we were having a companionable moment. He'd pivot that great neck and swing his head away from me, closing an eye with a sigh of weary disdain, and then opening it again to gaze into the middle distance – a look that asked, 'What does she *want* from me?'

Yes, I needed a little me time, and he needed a little him time. I decided to find a place that would care for him for a week, while I raced around Anglesey alone. What better timing? Anglesey is an Area of Outstanding Natural Beauty, but only around the coast. The coastal path was full of stiles, so Chico and I would have had to retreat to the interior often, which was, by all accounts, fairly boring. There were two bridges off the island and they were next to each other, so I could drop Chico off somewhere like a toddler at nursery, give him a thorough rest, and pick him up at the end.

It was a plan of genius. I would take off like a speedboat untethered from its anchor! I'd leap stiles in a single bound! I'd go into shops and pubs! Best of all, I'd make some serious progress.

The vast city walls, towers and battlements of Caernarfon's thirteenth-century castle presented a cold shoulder to the sea beyond the north end of the Lleyn. Behind the walls rose Snowdonia, and this vantage point out over the Menai Strait and Anglesey beyond had over the centuries been the site of a Celtic hill fort, the long-standing Roman fort of Segontium, and a Norman motte before Edward I built his intimidating castle, to subjugate the Welsh.

We rounded the city walls on the outside – immaculate and deserted. I tied Chico at a petrol station and picked up a copy of the *Daily Post* with us in it. The fortnight-old picture clearly showed Rhys hiding unsuccessfully and suspiciously in the bushes behind us. Without me noticing, Chico dropped off a great pile of Chico chocs on the Caernarfon pavement – later on someone sent a message on Facebook saying they'd spotted the poo and guessed we'd passed that way. Then S4C, the Welsh TV channel, called and asked if I'd talk to their evening magazine show *Heno* ('Tonight'), on the side of the road – they'd seen me from their office as we wandered through their car park. 'Something tells me we're not on the sleepy old Lleyn any more, Chico.'

I asked them to bring a hairbrush, and stopped in a layby to remind myself of the Welsh for words like challenging, inaccessible and stubborn. The film crew arrived and everything went alright. I decided not to use the hairbrush – I wasn't sure if I could get it through the thatch, especially with an audience, or that it would look any better afterwards in any case. The interview was brief, and they edited it together so that Chico and I were walking at double-speed, like a Chaplinesque slapstick routine.

We walked on through the evening sun, and reached the village of Felinheli on the banks of the strait. Across the narrow water was Anglesey. Felinheli has a wide strip of grass between the beach and the first houses, which the locals consider their communal garden, and a bunch of people were playing football on it with bottles of beer in their hands. Near the pub more people had brought their pints out and were chatting with their neighbours. I tied Chico to a lamppost and cleared the cut grass out of his radius. Two sweet women brought him a bucket of water and me a bottle of beer and a packet of prawn cocktail crisps, and we chatted in Welsh, soaking up the festival atmosphere, while their children busied themselves bringing the cut grass back to Chico until I noticed.

I had no desire to leave that lovely place, possibly ever, so I asked around to see if anyone would mind us camping on their village green. No one did, including the landlord of the pub, who I figured was probably the unofficial village elder. So I corralled, de-rigged and fed Chico, and sat on the sea wall watching him and chatting to the curious.

Even a scary dog fight didn't quite spoil the mood. A liver-coloured, short-haired pointer ran into Chico's corral and decided to fight him. Never is dog ownership less appealing than when two fight wildly in a public place, their humans forced to wrestle them apart as everyone gasps in alarm at the spectacle of sudden savagery. Now I was that owner, and my donkey was giving as good as he got. Better, in fact, according to the post-fight analysis – a few onlookers swore quietly that they'd seen Chico land at least one punch. Both beasts had spun together like a hairy Waltzer, the dog trying to bite the donkey's back legs, the donkey trying to whack the dog with his front hooves. I'd heard that donkeys could be swift and lethal and I didn't want to see it. We tore them apart and the dog owner chastised her dog. I tutted at Chico, but only for show – I knew he'd have no understanding of having done wrong by me. And it *was* self-defence.

When the sun went down and the townsfolk retired to bed, I put the tent up, slept well, and set my alarm early so as to be packed up before the first dog-walking shift. I still didn't have any desire to leave, and swung my legs on the wall some more. A woman called Kay brought me a mug of tea and a buttered scone for breakfast, and a packed lunch too, and took a plastic bag full of Chico fertiliser in return.

We departed at last, and as soon as we crossed the village boundary it began to rain. We were taking a sneaky route through a National Trust property in order to avoid a tangle of heavy A roads, but a few hundred yards along it, Chico stopped. The road went very slightly uphill through dark overhanging trees – perhaps that was the problem. I tied him to a fence and walked until I was out of sight to show him that all was well, but he was unmoved, and unmoving. Eventually we tried another path, acceptable to the señor, until it was halted by a cattlegrid. I fought my way into the thicket around the adjoining gate – not just thorny undergrowth but whole tree branches. The gate, when I'd crawled right into it, was padlocked fast, and rusted solid for good measure. Two hours after leaving Felinheli we were back, wet, jaded and setting out along the A roads. He didn't like it much, but damn him – he'd seen the preferable option. When he chose to play dead lions at a thunderous intersection of the A55 and the A487, heavy rain falling on our heads and fast cars flinging filthy puddles our way, I had a moment of illicit sympathy with those despicable people who maltreat donkeys in distant countries. These sullen beasts really didn't go out of their way to cool the boiling hearts of frustrated muleteers. Robert Louis Stevenson was given a goad – a pin attached to a stick with which to prick the recalcitrant rump into action. If a travelling goad vendor had passed my way, and the spirit of the age had condoned it, I'm sure I'd have been first in the queue, with a side order of spurs.

Chico acquiesced to keep walking across a couple of terrifying roundabouts, but then made the mistake of dawdling right by a roadside cafe. So I figured I was well deserving of my own graze, tied him under a tree in the car park for shelter and went inside for chips, coffee, and a little restorative time apart. It was the first time I'd left him alone like that, and I told myself that he didn't think of it as abandonment. It was a fair while before I noticed that he could see me through the window from 60 feet away – 30 inside and 30 outside. His big round eye was fixed on me and my chips, and he wasn't grazing any more, just staring at me, a picture of wet reproach and loneliness.

When I went back he wouldn't move, wouldn't eat, wouldn't look at me. The cafe cook had taken him some potato peelings which lay untouched – they'd added insult to injury, I think. Only some really high-level bribery could unravel this cold war, and thankfully the cafe owner brought out some Maltesers. Even then Chico was indifferent at first, refusing to sniff one, or part his great wounded pout. Finally he took a step out from under the tree, and we walked on in an uneasy armistice, the final hard-won mile to Chico's week-long pit stop.

Moelyci is a community hill farm that includes a much-loved mountain, bought by the surrounding farmers to rescue it from becoming a caravan park. There are market gardens and a veg-box scheme, pick-your-own berry fields, allotments, courses and community events. And now they found themselves the very kind babysitters of a donkey badly in need of a rest. As we'd come into their catchment area, several people had told me about them, so I'd called with my unusual request and they, thankfully, had said yes. We put Chico in a field with good shelter, a stream, lots of thistles, and a border with the shop and gardens so he'd be greeted by all the visitors. I handed his rain jacket, brush, horse nuts and nappy-rash cream to Shan and Paul, stashed anything I could do without under a bench in their potting shed, hauled on my now rather heavier backpack, and departed alone, with many, many backward glances.

NINETEEN

Crossing a stile, it turned out, wasn't all that exciting after all. Walking into a shop was pretty good, although the newsagent's was dire – I bought a kilo of longlife cake, wrinkly apples and cheap cheese anyway. Then it began to rain so I tried out strolling into a pub for a coffee, and slung a measure of brandy into it. The pub was on the mainland side of the Menai Bridge, next to the sign that said 'Môn: Mam Cymru', which means 'Anglesey: Mother of Wales'. The excitement of the freedom soon passed, and I just sat, alone, in the light of a blinking fruit machine, looking at Anglesey and waiting for the rain to pass.

On the other side of Menai Bridge was a Waitrose, and with disproportionate excitement I bought another kilo of much more exciting food. My bag was getting really heavy, but walking along pulling long Polish kabanos sausages from my backpack like arrows from a quiver made it worthwhile.

People in Llanfairpwllgwyngyllgogerychwyrndrobwllllan-tysiliogogogoch answered my Welsh with English, which was annoying and disappointing after the Lleyn, especially since I could say their wretched place name, since having taught myself as a teenager, for a party piece. In the next pub I was shamefully told off for putting my bare, sore feet on the seat, and then a bus-load of people looked at me strangely as I crouched for shelter behind a wall while eating my fish and chips. There was nothing interesting about me without my donkey. I was just a lonely fool with a big backpack, in the clammy wind.

I read the local information plaques I would usually just have tied Chico to, listened to my wind-up radio that I didn't usually have enough hands to deal with, chased a few thoughts that rattled in my under-occupied mind. What was I doing there? A donkey walker without a donkey. I was completely free, and yet almost instantly I discovered that Chico had provided a kind of momentum, even when resolutely stationary. I was forced to run around him thinking of reasons, solutions, treats and alternative routes. Without him I was just plodding on. I saw pretty Felinheli across the water, and felt nostalgic for the day before.

Thankfully it got sunny, and plodding in the sun provided its own momentum. I was at least the master of my own stamina and timetable for a change, and it was just after midsummer so the days were long. I could pack up in 20 minutes and once I'd got over the initial excitement of shopping, my needs were few.

Moelyci was having an open day the following weekend so I set that as a target. Anglesey is 124 miles around, and once I was finished with it I'd be almost a third of the way around Wales. I found pieces of poetry on my phone and learned them by heart as I walked.

At Newborough Warren, a vast 23-kilometre-square dune system and beach, I tried walking with my eyes closed, aiming for 500 footsteps, but after 268 I'd veered 90 degrees to the left and walked into the sea, got my shoes wet, and spent a little while worrying that my anatomy was out of alignment. I hid my backpack behind a hummock and went around Llanddwyn Island, the island of the Welsh patron saint of lovers. Hers was a pretty miserable lot – she fell in love but then rejected the advances of the prince in question, who either raped her or was just not favoured by her father. Then she turned him into ice with a potion from a fairy and went to live on this island as a hermit for the rest of her fifth-century days. Love's never easy, but that's ridiculous. She's also the patron saint of sick animals… I thought of my worn-out steed across the water and hoped he was well.

I walked through the village where Prince William and Kate lived, incubating the baby George who'd be born a few weeks later. William's RAF base made its presence felt, like a great and busy nest of metal wasps.

Holyhead was the biggest town since Aberystwyth, run-down and rough, but with the resigned efficiency of a port – a place that most people didn't stop at, a grubby forest of road signs and ferry logos, lorry lanes and winches, surrounded by foothills of rolling council estates. But in the middle of it all, as a huge ferry pulled slowly out of the hot harbour with Dublin on its charts, dozens of teenagers were leaping off a high concrete jetty into the sea. Further on, a couple of families poked their beach barbeques and shouted at their children, some sea kayakers slid into the water, and on a grassy bank a pressgang of young men were doing some sort of vigorous circuit training, pulling heavy ropes up and down and hammering out the squat thrusts.

I strode onwards to the remote northwest corner of Anglesey. I stopped in Church Bay to find the cafe was closed on Wednesdays and the pub closed from 1.30 to 6pm. It was 1.40 on a Wednesday and the pub was surrounded by people drinking white wine in the sun, but they wouldn't serve me. One wine drinker asked where I was going. 'Ah! This next bit of coast is *sauvage*!' she said, with a posh purr. Another disappointed woman complained angrily, but I couldn't help but admire the pub's attitude, in a way. They were refusing to have their whole lives dictated by their work, even if the demand was still there, and grumpy. Instead, I snoozed on the 570-million-year-old rocks on the beach, had a swim and ate a tin of mackerel and an orange, breaking up what would be a 12-hour, 23-mile walk.

Sauvage it was. The path scaled the cliffs through yellow grass and crunchy heather, accompanied by the hot smell of pine sap. It was little more than a foot's width in places, and the precipices plunged into the sea below. There wasn't a soul around. The mobile had been off for days, my radio had ceased to pick up anything, I spoke to no one.

It was strange without Chico – I had nothing to offer people. I'm sure the pub would have poured forth the white wine if I'd had my travelling sideshow. There was no purpose but to 'tick off' Anglesey; when I'd last had reception, a text from Mum had said, 'That north-coast stretch of the island is beautiful, but I guess that's not what you're doing it for?', which seemed strange, but almost true. I had to make an effort not to think of 'doing' Anglesey at all. I was skirting the landmass, hardly scratching the surface, certainly not completing anything but a quick loop. Walking sans-donkey was faster and much less involved, passing through invisibly, eating up miles for miles' sake. By the end of that longest day I was 83 miles down with 41 to go, lying on a campsite trampoline with my aching feet in the air, eating strawberries as the bones painfully rearranged themselves. The last push had come when I reached the Wylfa nuclear power station and realised I didn't want to camp in audible range of the sinister hum.

I paid for my longest day the next morning, too tired to get going until late, and when I did I blundered about, making navigational errors all the way around three sides of a giant and confusingly shaped field. As I trudged through the thick waist-high grass, my boots filled with prickly grass seeds; the unused stiles were covered in nettles tall enough to sting my arms. Horseflies stalked me, often landing heavily enough to be slapped off, but one got me on a bare buttock while I crouched for a pee – a cruel and unusual injury. Thankfully the landscape drew me on, foxgloves, pink campion and purple heather edging the clear blue sea which faded without a horizon into the hazy sky.

At Bull's Bay, to celebrate a new view of the coast ahead, I decided to have lunch with my feet in the shallows. But the reality was far from idyllic. My feet, freed from my shoes, hurt with a kind of frantic ache – I ground them desperately into the slimy, gritty pebbles, trying to itch the bones themselves, pleasure and pain together, and watched by a full and bemused beer garden.

I stopped for the night in Porth Eilian, nowhere near as far as I'd hoped to get, but my feet wouldn't take me another step. I lay outside my tent feeling angry with everyone – the man who'd said there were three campsites by the church, the church for being hard to find and having no campsites near it, a driver for giving me new directions so very slowly as I stood on my burning stumps, and the kind campsite owners for saying, 'Ah, we wondered if you were looking for us when you passed this way an hour ago!' Then I ate a cheese sandwich – almost the last of my supplies, rolled into my tent and fell asleep with my headtorch on; the night before it'd been my glasses.

'Is it true, about the donkey?' said the campsite owner – he'd called my mobile when I was staggering around the church, and heard the answerphone message that said I was walking around Wales with a donkey. When I explained, he waived the fee and told me to buy a bag of carrots instead – the power of Chico worked remotely, it seemed. I was cheered.

'You've got your world on your back,' said a man as he passed my tent. 'I admire that. I've got to the age now where I need a combustion engine...' I felt noble. Although my feet hurt, my legs were like pistons. Good! Fast! I'd never thought I could happily walk with a backpack, but here I was doing it. I could walk anywhere!

I ate a tomato and a Curly Wurly for breakfast – the very last two items in the pantry. My bag was noticeably lighter, at least, but I'd have to plan my route to include meals. Luckily I was into the last quarter of the island, and there were well-spaced villages and beauty spots. A narrow path through thick growth twice my height led me on a treasure hunt to Lligwy beach, with soft white sand underfoot and elderflower and honeysuckle fragrancing the air above. Sections of the route felt French – more sticky sap, gnarled roots and dusty tracks. The Welsh sections were less romantic; I spent a long time meditating on it before deciding that hot bracken smelled like cardboard. Somewhere a donkey brayed in the distance.

At the next refuelling opportunity I sat in the shade by a snack hut and ate a 50p cake from the 'Past its best' basket on the counter. A couple sat down with three ice-creams, one of which they put on the floor for their dog, an annoying mutt with a bark like a rubber shoe being scuffed on the floor of a gym. I wondered what flavour they'd chosen for him. When they'd finished they got up to go, and the man picked up the dog bowl and poured it over the dog's head.

My phone picked up Manx mobile reception and the radio tuned into BBC Radio Lancashire. I'd walked into a new part of the world. Ahead of me was the north coast of Wales, an unknown quantity. I was exhausted but desperate to get there and start making progress along it.

I arrived at the holiday town of Benllech at 8.30 on Friday evening to find that hundreds of other people had too. Big groups of friends and families from Liverpool and Manchester had leaped in their cars after work, hit the North Wales Expressway, put up their enormous tents or unlocked their mobile homes, had a shower, and presented themselves ready to party, cackling loudly in the evening sun in crisp white shirts and summer dresses. I asked a small family if they'd keep an eye on my backpack while I went to look for the reception.

'Do we know that lady?' said the young daughter loudly as I walked away.

'No, we're just looking after her bag,' said the father.

'Why?' said the daughter.

'It's called being nice.'

I found myself tying back my hair and tucking my pilgrim's shell inside my T-shirt in an effort to look less feral. '£25 per tent, per night,' said the friendly, corporate young staff in the fiercely air-conditioned reception. I thanked them and left, retrieved my backpack and walked back onto the beach.

I'd erred towards campsites on Anglesey. I liked the idea of camping wild but each day, as the evening drew in and I got tired, it was a welcome that I craved much more than the facilities. A human voice, someone to report my mileage to and discuss the area with. A small patch of sanctioned grass where I could sleep without keeping one ear open. Far from finding other people menacing, I felt safer with the herd. I'd camped wild on the other side of the island, and had chosen a patch right by a hotel. I was invisible to them behind a tiny dune and a frothy elderflower bush, but was comforted by the sound of the non-residents leaving the bar at the end of the night. But £25 a tent was enough to send me off into the unknown at dusk.

Beyond Benllech is a vast corner of sand flats called Red Wharf Bay. The path ran above the high-tide mark, but right now the tide was out and I could save myself nearly three miles if I walked straight across the sand. Even so, it was a long way, a mile of sand. I ate a preparatory serving of fish and chips at the pub on the beach and asked if I could fill my water bottle and buy a few slices of bread. The landlady brought them out, wrapped in foil, and I told her my plan, in case anyone needed to find my body in a few days.

Rhys texted, 'Low tide: 8.55pm' – exactly the time it was, so I picked up my backpack and walked out onto the open sand; hard wrinkles as far as the eye could see. There was a mast across the bay, so I aimed for that – I'd reach the far side just near a car park. The wrinkles got deeper and full of water, and I thought about sinking sand. Halfway across I saw a second mast that hadn't been visible through the salty heat haze, and changed my trajectory, but a bit too late – when I reached the bank it was all hummocks, and the light was fading fast. I balanced across the knobbles, avoiding the pools of water. One was full of writhing crabs, which made me jump. After the hummocks came a band of tall reeds; I launched myself through, reached a high breakwater with a slatted footpath on top, threw my backpack onto it and climbed up. Every so often along the footpath there was a little collection of stones, shells, seaweed and feathers, arranged in a corner, on the path and hanging from the handrails. 'Don't think about Blair Witch!' I instructed myself. It was too dark for my map now, and I almost trod on a toad that was crossing the boardwalk where it descended to the beach level.

Up ahead was the car park; the human things were comforting – flagpoles, bins and a locked toilet block. As I looked for a place to put up the tent, I came across several more people with the same idea – an old bus with people watching TV inside; a motorbike and campervan; and then a big group sitting around a bonfire with the kids still up and playing, a spent barbeque and a gas lamp casting a gentle light. I declared my intention to camp nearby, and a woman called Tammy came to invite me to their hearth for a cup of wine.

I felt like I'd come home. This friendly crew only lived in the nearest village, but gingerly drove their caravan down the very steep hill on sunny weekends. 'We call it a mini adventure – this is our third weekend in a row!' Friends had joined them with their tents, and we sat around chatting as the stars came out and the night got cold. Tammy made us all laugh about Kate Middleton getting in her way in Waitrose: 'She was dithering between the swedes and the carrots!'

In the morning I unwrapped my slices of bread to discover that the landlady had put a few wrapped rectangles of butter in there too. Real butter! Then the couple with the camper and motorbike combo gave me a cup of coffee – real coffee! – and a bottle of Skin So Soft, the Avon moisturiser that has the added benefit of deterring midges. 'You don't know about the Llanddona witches?' they said, when I mentioned the little shrines along the walkway. Some time in the early seventeenth century, witches were supposed to have washed up on the beach right there, having been cast away in a boat with no oars or sails. Those ones were a bad lot, the men were smugglers and the women begged and stole, and around their necks they wore red neckties with a fly kept in the knot that could be released to blind their opponents. Bad people did bring trouble from the sea – the Vikings, Normans and Irish for a start. Witches with magic accessories can't have been too much of a stretch of the imagination. I was glad I hadn't known about them the night before.

It was 18 miles along the coast back to Menai Bridge, and the Moelyci open day was tomorrow. I could do it! The day began mercilessly with a climb so steep I had to do shifts walking backwards to unfold my ankles. 'Walkers!' said a sign stuck to a water butt in a meticulous garden by the path. 'Please feel free to fill your bottles from the tap on the wall. Enjoy your walk!' After a particularly unfriendly bristling of 'Private! No entry! Strictly no access! Residents only!' signs along the path the day before, not to mention a faintly ridiculous 'Please use this bench at your own risk', I fell instantly in love with those kind water providers.

I'd rounded the last corner and was back on the shore of the Menai Strait, where four tides a day wash up and down the narrow channel and Snowdonia towers purple beyond the water. I swam in the sea, clear and calm as a lake, with long strings of bladderwrack and tiny jellyfish for company, while a Russian family set happily about building an ambitious sand castle nearby. Striding on through Beaumaris, I barely glanced at Edward I's exquisite thirteenth-century castle, but set my sights instead on a posh ice-cream, realising for the first time that I could legitimately enjoy Anglesey as an achievement, and see a finish line ahead.

I asked a bunch of passing boys, off out for a Saturday night and smelling of aftershave, to take a victory photo of me on the bridge, then headed into the Bridge Tavern for a pint of something cold. I ordered some food and was shown to a table for nine. After a bit of confusion it became clear that I wasn't the party of nine – I'd never felt less like one of nine in my life. I was a woman who walked by herself, saying little, swimming often, sleeping and waking and walking on. When the pub closed, the staff let me put my tent up in the tiny overgrown beer garden. Tomorrow I'd walk the few remaining miles across the bridge and back to Chico, where Rhys would be joining us too. Would Chico be rested and willing? Would he recognise me? I fervently hoped so. Next up, the uncharted north.

TWENTY

I'm not good with failure; who is? But on this occasion it looked like we were going to have to admit defeat. Chico, Rhys and I were almost halfway up Snowdon, and it was very clear that we were not going to manage another step of elevation. Desperate for some sort of summit, I left the two of them by the path and walked the last hundred yards to the midpoint cafe, where I bought enormous fruity ice-lollies to mark the semi-success and lift our spirits.

'Hey, that's cheating!' said some joker on the path, nodding at Chico. None of us responded.

Snowdon isn't on the coast, of course, but we'd been in its presence since before my birthday – over a month – and it seemed to summon us. The easiest path to the top is really very easy, and designated a bridleway, plus Rhys was with us and game. Chico had a week's rest behind him and was looking sleek and healthy, having lost so much more of his winter coat in our time apart. And I was fresh from such bionic mileage that Snowdon would be a mere stroll for me. We began confidently.

But it was not to be. For starters we were late setting off – we'd stayed at Cae Mabon, a magical wooded dell full of beautiful cob houses, hobbit holes and a roundhouse, an eco retreat for creative and spiritual courses and events. Cae Mabon's owner, Eric Maddern, was an old friend of the family. He was a musician and storyteller, and I used to have his picture books and story tapes as a child, all about the love of trees and the story of evolution. He had led us out of the bottom of his land, but we'd come to a halt by a foot-high stretch of fence that Chico wouldn't step over. Eric had anticipated this and brought wire cutters, which he used to cut a strand, and then another, but Chico was resolute. In the end poor Eric had completely demolished his own fence, pulled the wire clear, carried away the stones that had stood about and uprooted the foliage. All that remained was a gap of bare earth. But still Chico would not cross it, held as if by magnetism or magic on the other side. We tied him to a tree and walked away down the path, and luckily as soon as we were out of sight he brayed with dismay. Rhys went back to get him, and he walked right through the gap.

Eric piloted us to the bottom of Snowdon, and there we got enjoyably held up by Steffan, the very camp and enthusiastic host of an inn. He stopped us on the road with a tray of divine ice-cold homemade lemonade, a glass for each of us and one for the postman. Steffan was the self-appointed host of the whole mountain too. 'I've had postcards sent to "Steffan, Snowdon, UK" that have got to me!' he said proudly. Dogs, muddy boots, base-camp parties, walkers' own picnics – everything was welcome there, as was Chico. Steffan insisted that I walk Chico through the inn. 'Your pony – bring her this way.'

The converted eighteenth-century cottage was small and cool, as Welsh cottages are – more stone wall than space between them. Inside were all manner of precious-looking knick-knacks, Welsh dressers with china balanced all over them, original paintings by Anglesey artist Kyffin Williams, and antiques that Steffan introduced one after another without drawing breath. It was no place for a donkey, but Steffan would not take no for an answer – in fact he seemed puzzled that I thought it odd.

Thankfully there were two doors, so Chico and I, as bemused as each other, walked in one, through the hall, the gallery and a living room, past the kitchen and out of the front door. There was a moment of triumph at having pulled it off with no breakages, and then we stood around slightly awkwardly for a minute, before bidding each other farewell.

It was well after midday by now, which meant that the majority of Snowdon summiteers were on the way back down. Perhaps that's what put Chico off – group after group passing us, all going down. The week's rest had clearly not caused him to be any less suspicious when it came to my navigational skills, and I don't suppose a detour through a cottage had done me any favours. Chico could no doubt also see the bright and rocky path heading straight up the mountain, already above the treeline, with no discernable purpose or destination. Voting with his hooves, Chico said no.

'Wow! I bet he cost a million pounds!' said a sweaty family man, panting by.

'Where were you four hours ago when we needed you?' said another man on his way down. Standing by a gap in a fence, I thought, glumly.

The little Snowdon Mountain Railway train heaved noisily alongside the track, an echo of the previous industrial life of the area. Engrossed in their own exertions, no one seemed to notice that we weren't moving, at all.

'Did you rent him? For the climb?' asked a walker overtaking us on the way up.

'No, he's mine,' I said. 'He's no help. I'll give him to you for a tenner.'

'I'll give you £20!'

I held out the rope for him, but the man had gone.

When I had got back with the ice-lollies, Rhys and Chico were both a bit shaken. It turned out that Rhys had tied Chico's rope around a boulder a little way from the path, but Chico had pulled it hard enough to shift the boulder, making him jump, which in turn made the boulder bounce, and the donkey had taken off across the hillside, towing the boulder behind him. Thankfully the rope had come free, Chico had stopped and no legs had been broken. I sympathised cursorily, distracted by my lolly. A few weeks later we'd all be sorry I hadn't paid more attention to their close shave.

It took 20 minutes to walk back down – we'd come hardly any distance at all. But as soon as we were facing downhill, who was to know where we'd got to? In fact, who was to know where we'd been aiming for? Rhys thought about trying again tomorrow, but I was already busy reframing our failure. We got halfway up Snowdon! Wow! What a feat!

TWENTY-ONE

We retraced our steps and headed back towards the coast, the hot weather holding for day after day. Snowdonia is a landscape usually found brooding under thick cloud, mountains all the colours of the lifecycle of a bruise, purple quarries left strewn across hillsides. Yellow moorland, green forestry, grey cloud, all smudged together and misty with rain from the clouds that file up there from the sea to dump their cargo. But in that searing heatwave, the mysterious, damp old Druid had been laid bare, his sombre frock torn off, naked and spread-eagled. Shocked and burning in the long midsummer days of sunshine, with only a heat haze for modesty and a few cold, clear hours of night between the hot sunset and hot sunrise.

Here and there rows of whitewashed miners' houses shone like capped Hollywood teeth. The hills had bleached out just as Chico's hair had during our time apart – both donkey and mountains were now the colour of driftwood. In that part of the world, fences were made of slabs of slate stuck into the ground and held together with twists of wire – a precious resource anywhere else, but in the land of quarries the quickest fence to hand. Each slab was a different shade of blue, purple, grey and black, matching the rectangles of roofs in the distance.

The tarmac melted and blistered like molasses under our feet and hooves. Horseflies prowled the air, a centimetre long and speckled brown and black. They're not clever creatures: they landed heavily and pierced our skin with a sharp jab. All three of us walked along swishing and slapping like clumsy marionettes. Their favourite feasting site was just between the arm and shoulder blade, in a gap behind the backpack – a section of relatively still flesh when all four limbs were swinging. Those thirsty bastards could pierce through clothing, and my thin vest disguised their landing feet; it was a tough place to reach for scratching purposes too.

We walked back around the community-owned mountain of Moelyci again, this time anticlockwise. Snowdon had been a diversion, directly inland and back the same way. Anglesey had been a giant circuit. The Lleyn had been a freaking peninsula! And before that were those estuaries! I'd chosen to walk around Wales clockwise based on nothing except a vague, unexamined feeling that I wanted to, but here I still was, stumbling slowly through all of this geographical debris. Now, at last, we had ahead of us a long, straight line. Sixty miles, more or less due east along the north coast of Wales, until the coast ran itself into the Dee estuary, on the other side of which was England. We didn't know anyone on the north coast, there were no family friends, no Facebook invitations, no personal recommendations. There was just a string of place names that were a bit alien to me: Penmaenmawr, Conwy, Llandudno, Prestatyn, Flint, and running between them the thunderous A55 and a train line. 'We'll just have to camp wild,' we told a few people, and several times we got the answer, 'Well, just don't try camping wild in Rhyl, will you?'

We had reached Mynydd Llandygai, a miners' village halfway between Snowdon and the coast. To our right was the vast and noisy scar of the mile-long Penrhyn quarry, once the biggest slate quarry in the world, and still going. It hammered and boomed in the still, hot air. Our feet stuck to the road, but we were free! Free to go east at speed! A car pulled over and a woman got out.

'I've found you! I read about you in the Donkey Breeds newsletter! I don't suppose you want to stop for a cup of tea?' I declined, but we took photos and swapped emails – her name was Jan. It was about 4pm and I had no idea where we would stay that night. There was time to get many more hours done, but if we sat down we might never get up. And… tea? I was so hot that my tongue was pasted onto my teeth. Chico had taken against a footpath and come to a stop a little while before, the altercation leading to Rhys and me sitting on the scorched verge in hot defeat and Rhys suddenly squirting Chico in the face with his water bottle. We'd all jumped, and none of us knew whether it had been a squirt of refreshing kindness or aggression. We were all too hot to communicate, even with ourselves.

As we walked on, I realised my error. If Jan had offered anything colder than tea, I'd have probably licked her with enthusiasm. We paced along in silence. And then – praise be! – she appeared again, this time with Steve. 'Really, my house is just there. I have three donkeys. And a separate field for Chico. You can camp. I'll make dinner.' This really was hospitality overkill – we submitted immediately with sleepy delight, and the half-mile to her house felt as long as any of the whole walk. We lay about in the daisies on her neatly mown lawn, while Chico dismissed Jan's three beautiful, compact, dark-eyed donkeys and kept an eye on us instead.

Emboldened by being welcomed as one bona fide donkey owner by another, I went over to Chico to do the twice-daily comedy nappy-rash-cream application. We'd noticed two days before with much hooting that poor Chico had a bite at the base of his willy. A horsefly probably started it off by drawing blood, and ordinary flies had then made it worse, clustering on the matte black skin, heads jostling into the dark red sore like animals at a watering hole. I'd been covering it with thick white goop so it could heal in peace. Keeping me on my nursing toes, the sore was always in a slightly different place, migrating around depending on how relaxed his little feller was.

Chico didn't seem to be offended, and I talked to him and smoothed his downy white belly so as not to catch him rudely unawares, finger to genital. But this time I was too brash. The flies were bad, and Chico was already feeling pestered, constantly swishing his tail and flicking his ears. One more creature around his undercarriage was all it took to push him over the edge, and that creature happened to be me. I leaned under and dabbed the sore and he lifted a hoof in warning. I put on a second scoop – it needed a little more. He lifted the hoof again, ever so gently. The cream wasn't quite central on the target, and without thinking, I reached in a third time to smear it over. This time that rear hoof lifted and came down with the speed and power of some steam-driven, cast-iron stamping machine, making perfect contact with his irritant. He caught me on the lower thigh, on the muscle only just above the knee, dead on. It was a single, calculated kick, with no malice or anger, no messiness or fight, but still administered really hard.

I had a moment of shock in which my body assessed the damage. It was a kick hard enough to break something, I was sure, but no – nothing was broken. An inch lower and he'd have caught my knee and all of the complicated and delicate game-over goings-on in there: ligaments, tendons and moving parts. Instead I just had a bruise, a sore muscle, and a firm reminder of our boundaries. Chico grazed nonchalantly, and I couldn't really hold it against him. I'll never know for sure, but I suspect that his aim was exactly as he intended – putting me out of action wouldn't have done him any good.

Jan and Steve fed us and told us about the history of Penrhyn quarry, which had been founded in the 1770s by Richard Pennant, Baron Penrhyn, who also owned six sugar plantations and 600 slaves in Jamaica and was an enthusiastic anti-abolitionist and member of parliament. Richard Pennant's successor, George Hay Dawkins-Pennant, built himself a fantasy mock-Norman castle, doing little for the dynasty's local reputation. By the end of the nineteenth century the quarry was the largest in the world, employed 3000 quarrymen, and had become the site of terrible hardship during two strikes, one of which lasted three years.

Jan and Steve talked about the deprivation and injustice as if it still contaminated the ground they lived on, and perhaps it did. We asked about the strange marks on my map – an odd rectangle that looked like a matchbook, with 30 dead-straight strips, long and thin, just where we'd met Jan the first time. They had once been miners' houses, each with an acre of land with which to support the family. It was poor quality land, rocky and swampy, but, as Jan said, 'It would have been beautiful – bog cotton and snipe! The Penrhyn estate didn't own the land anyway – it was common land.' The estate allowed the quarrymen to build their own houses, working hard with bad tools until midnight after a long day at the quarry. Once the houses were built, the miners had to pay rent, further tying their lives into the control of their employer.

The housing was overseen by the quarry manager; their conduct as tenants could lose them their jobs and the terms of their leases forbade political gatherings. Even worse, a quarryman's wages depended on what he produced, and that depended on the quality of the seam he had been allocated. Meanwhile their employers were making a great deal of money.

'The Penrhyns sound like real pirates,' we said.

'They were BASTARDS!' said Jan with passion, and then clapped her hand over her mouth in surprise.

It was a clean, clear night, cold as a desert on our bare hillside, but we were woken by sudden and incredible heat as the sun interrogated the tent at 7am. The quarry had already commenced its chugging. We fumbled with the tent zip and fell out into the grass, panting and sweating. My horsefly bites itched and swelled in the heat, the sleeping bag stuck to my legs, my breasts stuck to each other, my breath was hot in my throat, and after a moment of relief it became apparent that outside wasn't actually much cooler than inside.

We walked on, step by weary step, down a hill and up a hill to a village called Rachub. I found an L-plate on the road and stuck it to Chico's bum, where it was more poignant and less funny than I'd intended. It was the 19th of July and we'd left on the 28th of May. Would I ever stop feeling like a novice? My tender hoof-shaped bruise jiggled with every step.

'Siwgr aur!' shouted a woman as she ran across the street. Golden sugar, it means, although I'd never heard it as a term of endearment before. 'Here!' She caught up with us and handed us a big bottle of Vimto squash, incredibly welcome. We sat outside the closed pub waiting for the closed shop to open, and a man sidled up and laughed very hard and not very kindly when I said I was walking around Wales with Chico. In the heat it admittedly seemed far wiser to be the one waiting for the pub to open at 2pm on a Friday… When it did and he was furnished with his usual, the landlady got quite carried away with the task she'd taken on herself – smashing up ice cubes and posting them into the Vimto bottle for us.

When the shop opened, we stocked up and walked on, eating ice-lollies. I fed the last daub to Chico, who ate the stick as well. Rhys saw and was furious: 'That's just not *responsible!*' He went on to remind me of the time I let a nice cat called Arnie eat chicken bones at a dinner party, resulting in a tableful of friends and flatmates growing silent with horror as Arnie began to choke, his yellow eyes wide and his legs stiff. He was fine, and we're all still friends, but the reminder of my poor animal husbandry wasn't welcome. We walked in silence, and the L-plate fell off into the dust.

We reached Abergwyngregyn where we hoped to find somewhere to camp, and at the last house I knocked on the door to ask for water to see us through. A man answered with a very big smile and a very small towel – he'd been in the shower, but filled my bottles happily. Meanwhile Chico had a big, hot, green poo in the gateway of the church next door. We'd have cleared it up except that, fixing us with eyes full of concentration, he then peed on it – a jet of fierce yellow ammonia, opaque towards the end. He stayed in position – legs splayed, tail raised – for ages, and when he was done, we grabbed his rope and ran away from the scene of the crime. Good parishioners of St Bodfan's, please accept my apologies, and Chico's potent fertiliser…

Lavan Sands was a spectacle – huge sand flats that, at low tide, stretched for four miles across the Menai Strait to within a few hundred yards of Beaumaris. The tide was up as we made camp, covering the miles of mud and dissolving its salty crust. Seabirds gathered and scattered, banking and turning above the wrinkled skin of shining sea. When it retreated, thousands of skinny green succulents were left behind, standing straight like tiny cacti, each casting a perfect shadow. As the mud dried and cracked, an inch-high cowboy and horse would have felt right at home, riding into the sunset.

In the early seventeenth century a king's postman managed to get stakes erected every quarter mile across the treacherous sands – I ventured a few feet into the slimy sand and wouldn't dare go further. In the postman's day people used the sand flats to travel along the coast too, in order to avoid the twin promontories of Penmaenmawr (Big Stone Headland: 380m) and Penmaenbach (Little Stone Headland: 245m). These great rocks shove themselves right up to the waterline, and were very visibly in our way.

Over the centuries the routes had been worked on until it was the A55 that reigned supreme as a conduit to other places, claiming the prime seaside land in the name of restless movement. Between the headlands was the town of Penmaenmawr, with the dual carriageway a fast and formidable hem, backed up by the train line. Thankfully for us, a new cycle route had been built, for a time running alongside the road, then crossing it on a ramped footbridge to run alongside oncoming traffic. The train line crossed back and forth too, accompanying the eastbound traffic around the mountain and above the sea, as the westbound traffic plunged through a long tunnel. It was like a maypole dance of transport options, ducts full of busy people weaving around each other.

Our little band – two slow people and a donkey – followed our chute; there was nothing else to be done. Then we fell below it, passing underneath the road and rails, and waving to a couple leaning out of their house – a crazy spot to set up home. How could a person retain their humanity in the middle of all that noise and exhaust, all that reinforced concrete, metal legs and fresh tarmac, the sun diced up as it shone through barriers. They lived on the hard shoulder, while everyone else shot by.

They saw us admiring an action man attached to the top of a cycle route sign, one plastic arm up in a salute. 'We put him there!' they yelled. 'And we've got more to do! We're going to make zip wires for them!' And there it was – joy in the eye of madness. We smiled right through town and out the other side.

Wild camping was a bit like musical statues; we'd keep going and going, and start looking for perfect places, and eventually the sun would get lower and so would our standards, and finally it would be dark and we'd just stop wherever we were. No matter how good the spot, by the time we found it all three of us would be tired and angry, and we'd make camp with hostile resignation.

On this occasion we'd found dunes to camp in, but only just. We were in a corner behind a broken fence, alongside a caravan park. It wasn't ideal. We sawed down a tent-sized patch of thistles, scouted for dog turds with the dimming headtorch, and strung up Chico's fence. I'd worried that there wouldn't be enough for him to eat, so when we'd come across some planted roadside trees I'd harvested some branches – hawthorn, ash and hazel – and tied them to the top of his packsaddle. He'd looked like a pantomime character disguising himself as a bush and didn't seem to mind the indignity one bit.

With nothing to do but pack up and go in the morning, we got on the road unusually early, walking on through Conwy's dunes, then past its marina and through the medieval town walls, coming to settle under a tree right by the formidable castle. In its time, the town would have been populated by Edward I's English citizens, the Welsh only allowed to come in during the day, frisked of arms and not permitted to trade. I went shopping and returned with full Welsh breakfasts in polystyrene boxes. We took our shoes off and made ourselves at home while a string of interested people – every one with a northern English accent – stopped to stroke Chico.

In an unprecedented move, Chico was so relaxed that he had a public snooze despite the Sunday crowds. It's always a bit hard to tell – he stays standing and his eyes don't close, but they droop to half-mast and he keeps still, resting one back hoof at a time. He didn't even stir when a coach hit a kerb and gave itself a loud flat tyre – I suspect the driver might have been craning his neck at us, having seen the castle plenty of times before.

One Liverpudlian woman screeched, 'Ee! Has he been a good boy?' Not really, I said, out of habit. But actually he was being very good. Almost worryingly. Was he alright?

We walked on, over the bridge and out of Conwy, up the wide seaside path past Deganwy and Llandudno's west beach. We drew attention wherever we went, but walking across the wide beach of a Victorian seaside resort was, surprisingly, about as hidden as we ever were – we must have looked like we belonged. Only a few people came over, and each one was a father despatched across the sand by his family to enquire about donkey rides, then sent back to report with disappointment that Chico wasn't that sort of donkey.

We passed a small group of men sunbathing on the beach. They had black beards and white skin, made more so by heavy zinc suncream, and alongside them was a huge catering saucepan full of something boiled and white – beans or potatoes? I wondered if they were the off-duty staff of some takeaway, but couldn't guess at the nationality. Somewhere Middle Eastern perhaps? One of them leaped up and gestured at Chico.

'Ah! I know him!'

You do?

'Seriously! Yes! He's my... he's my supreme leader!'

We grinned and walked on. Chico, you dark horse. You didn't tell me you were a guru! Although with that taciturn poise, those knowing eyes, and the gruelling spiritual journey that he seemed to be leading me on, I shouldn't have been altogether surprised.

TWENTY-TWO

He seemed happy, for a change. Rhys had gone off by train to track down the car and I was leading Chico onto the Great Orme, a 200m-high headland with sheer cliffs that sticks out into the water on the far side of the sea-level town of Llandudno. We were approaching from the town's west beach and would descend onto its north beach, but couldn't miss a trip up the impressive Orme, with its name derived from the Old Norse for sea serpent. We trudged up the steep, rocky footpath. 'Igam ogam' – Welsh for zigzag – warned the sign, helpfully. I realised quickly that Chico might physiologically not be able to get down – he could manage wide steps, or shallow steps, or just a few steps, but these were uneven, narrow, steep and numerous. I was worried he'd charge off the path – the slope around it was unstable and even steeper. We jostled for balance on the stones, and being attached to a strong, wayward animal was scary. At one point, Chico pulled me down and spun me in the dusty gorse; my heart leaped with fear: it could have been a lot worse. There was nothing for it but to keep going, eyes up. The vertiginous views of Llandudno right below us were breathtaking, and changed with each igam ogam. He did it brilliantly, I was so pleased with him, and he was good to me in return.

Something was changing. Rhys said Chico had brayed while I'd been off looking for our boxed breakfasts in Conwy – braying to me, he thought. Now we stood on the top of the Great Orme, looking back the way we'd come, past walled Conwy, the big and little stone heads, and across the hazy water to Anglesey, and Chico brayed again. He'd found his voice, it seemed. I still didn't know what he was saying, but he did seem to be saying it to me.

Then *I* had cause to bray – there was a locked gate at the top, with a kissing gate next to it. We were sunk. We couldn't go on and we couldn't go down again. There were houses up there, and people appeared from everywhere and began making phone calls, looking for other people who might possibly have the key. The land, it turned out, belonged to the man whose farm zoo we were hoping to stay at that evening. Chico kept up the braying, every time I went out of sight and sometimes when I didn't. He made two babies cry. I felt honoured.

A blind granddad was brought out to meet Chico, and someone's little dog climbed the high gatepost and tried to launch himself at us, yapping. Men fiddled with the gate's hinges, but that and the phone calls came to nothing, and after a while everyone faded away again. I got out my own little emergency tools and managed to undo one screw, which swung the catch away from the bolt – a stroke of luck. I opened the gate, led the bemused donkey through and screwed the catch back on. It looked and felt like a magic trick.

And then I heard another distant bray on the hot evening air. I hadn't realised, but the Llandudno beach donkeys lived up there. Chico brayed again, bit me, and took off along the steep road down the other side of the Orme. I was struggling to keep hold of him, and in a stroke of bad luck his rain mac, rolled up and tied to his packsaddle, came unrolled. Still tied on, it billowed out behind him. Chico careered down the hill in the middle of the terraced road with the mac flying behind him like a wizard's cape.

I caught him and held him close all along the lengthy, busy promenade. Llandudno is a Victorian resort, like an undiluted Aberystwyth – the old hotels bigger and more regal, the vintage air more intact. Punch and Judy battered each other while kids seemed a bit disconcerted. A brass band played the Welsh national anthem to an octogenarian crowd, and then moved on to 'God Save the Queen'. I flinched, but the old folk all stood by their deckchairs, chins up, dabbing their eyes, as the enormous red sun sank behind the Great Orme without cooling a degree.

We found the farm park, completely deserted but for the animals, and with all of the doors open. The man on the phone had said we could camp by the kids' play area, so, feeling a little strange, we set the tent up by the swings and corralled Chico next to us. He looked intently across the path at a paddock containing a few horses, a yellow Shetland and a little donkey. A crazy bird cry came from somewhere – a kookaburra, perhaps? Some deer bounced about in the next field, goats in the field beyond and llamas opposite them, and Chico's expression seemed to say wearily, 'Oh, you people, what's this now?'

With an absence of people who minded, we had a day off, taking the tent down during the daytime. It was a shonky, wonderful place, with barbecues every night and a band on Thursdays – a perfect antidote to the buttoned-up seafront.

Next up was Colwyn Bay, half a dozen settlements all merging into each other, starting with Rhos-on-Sea – God's waiting room, apparently. It was eerily empty, on a Tuesday evening, and the heat had turned into a heavy pressure, cooler, and with even a few spits of rain. In Colwyn itself some teenagers rolled cigarettes and stood around on the beach. A gang of girls with painted-on eyebrows ran up to us in their socks and crowded around, screaming and flapping. Chico trod on a socked toe and when the girl made a fuss, I said, 'Well, that *will* happen, won't it?' As we got away from them I felt a bit remorseful – that really must have hurt.

Colwyn Bay, like Penmaenmawr, has the A55 and the train line running between the town and the sea, with only a few underpasses, and that evening even the A55 was quiet. The beach was brand new: they were halfway through the process of bringing in sand dredged up a kilometre out to sea and redistributing it along the shore, with sea defences to keep it there. It felt new – unsure of its role in the life of the bay, not yet settled in. The pristine beach furniture was shiny and over-designed, while the pier, from an earlier period, was dying, skeletal and patched up but still the most beautiful thing for miles, brittle under the foreboding sky.

The sun was low, already setting half an hour earlier than it had at midsummer. We reached the last underpass and decided to head inland and uphill, in hope of finding a campsite that was marked on the map but that no one, including the internet, had heard of. In any case, options were few on the unforgiving mineral expanses of promenade, cycle path and beach. And then there, on a steep road of big semi-detached houses, were Angie and Paul and little dog Toto, leaning over their garden gate.

'Where are you going with your donkey?'

'We're not sure…'

'Stay in the garden?'

The art of giving rolled effortlessly off Angie and Paul. They handed out beers and we stayed up late, and then in the morning came a tray of scrambled eggs for breakfast, eaten al fresco all together as we chatted easily. Out came provisions from their cupboards, toilet rolls, and *Wild Wales*, a book by George Borrow, the nineteenth-century walker and polyglot who wandered the country talking to people on the side of the road and showing off his Welsh. They both left for work, advising us not to camp wild when we got to Rhyl, and giving us the house keys to lock up when we were done showering and taking photos of Angie's Olympic torch. While he waited for us, Chico strolled round to the handkerchief-sized front lawn, lay down with a view of the street, and went to sleep. It was our first shower since we'd had a wash in a river pool four long hot days before, and it was a bit like heaven. 'Showers are a really good invention, aren't they?' we agreed, and let ourselves out of the front door just as Paul arrived back for lunch.

TWENTY-THREE

I t was a shock, after the enveloping greenness of the Lleyn, and the raw, rough crags of Anglesey coastscapes. Here was a land of perfect horizontal lines, the sea on our left, broken only by offshore wind turbines that looked randomly placed until, as we continued, they assembled themselves very slowly into perfect rows, like forestry plantations. Closer was the horizontal line of the shore, and then a tract of flat sand, lightly wrinkled like the sea. We walked along promenades, horizontal feats of concrete, laid down and left. We felt very small, but a creature in the distance could be seen approaching perhaps for days before we finally passed each other, like wagons on a prairie or awkward partygoers in an empty hall, too far apart to converse.

The blankness of the surroundings discouraged conversation, although a few people paid no heed to that and veered all the way over anyway, bravely. There were no accidental meetings here, no cosying into small talk or foliage. Just the occasional wilful buddleia curling its roots around the concrete and casting its purple cone flowers into the salty air, and once or twice a staunch teazle, taller than me, hollow and papery, but spiked and ready. Chico took a bite, but just the one.

There was, now and then, a long car park, some signs prohibiting things, a bench or two, and once a shack selling cakes and buckets. There was a stretch of clean concrete shapes, stubby three-dimensional stars the size of cars, scattered like a game of jacks to baffle the sea and dissipate its energy. Each one was identical and fresh from the giant mould, even more contrary to nature than the endless flatness.

I felt menaced by the barren landscape; I was the wrong scale, interminably slow, unwelcomed, nostalgic for the snug hedgerows and friendly horseflies. I went into the shop because it was there, and emerged with a custard slice – itself a cake of unmanageable horizontal structure.

'Isn't it beautiful here?' said the young woman in the shop, catching me completely by surprise. I hashed together a flimsy answer and then thought about it for hours while trailing along. If you'd come from Liverpool or Manchester for your precious week's freedom, why wouldn't you keep going another half hour on the road and find a little green nest to snuggle into? A friendly, human place? Somewhere with geography and wildlife and irregular shapes? Was I a terrible snob? On our inland side was mile after mile of mobile homes, themselves coming into alignment as we passed, uncluttered by people.

But this place wasn't just the holiday compromise of people without the money or imagination to move on – the shop woman had said it was beautiful. Maybe it was. Maybe if your life was spent in a busy inner city, toiling through claustrophobic vertical lines, full of urban fuss and noise... maybe what you really craved was just a massive space, a vast and distant horizontal line. Maybe it was a Grand Canyon experience, the thrill of being inconsequential, the delight of the kids running free, safe in the knowledge that they'd get tired long before they reached anything at all. Maybe if life usually imposed, it felt good to be exposed. If life was messy and dirty, this sterility would be a relief. If there were a million things to worry about in ordinary life, here there was just sea, sky and promenade.

Or maybe there was a really good pub on the far side of the caravan park.

'It's certainly... striking,' I'd said, and it was. It wasn't a landscape to ignore or forget, or confuse with anywhere else. We'd had a little chat, ending with her advice, 'Don't camp wild in Rhyl though, will you?' I assured her we wouldn't.

It was hard to work out the scale – we seemed to make no progress for hours and then leap forward several kilometre-squares of map. When the sand came up to meet the sea wall we chose the beach for a change.

And then, by mistake, despite the warnings, we were pretty much in Rhyl. And it was evening. We stalled in Sandy Cove, a suburb of busy little prefabs built on sand. A couple brought Chico a bucket of water and declared their desire, if they won the lottery, to open a donkey sanctuary and call it the Donktuary. 'Good, eh?'

A man with a baby under his thick, tattooed bicep came to ask what was going on with the donkey. He didn't like the idea of camping, not one bit. 'And what do you *eat*?' he said, incredulously. We buy food, I said. In shops! He shook his head disparagingly, one of the few people on the whole walk to fail to see the attraction of the idea. Perhaps the state of the Sandy Cove shops held the answer – we went to three, with not a vegetable between them. Rhys came back with Desperados and Doritos: beer flavoured with tequila, and high-vis crisps. A pretty good haul, under the circumstances. As we crossed the bridge into Rhyl, we were rushed at by a bunch of boys on bikes – a threatening move to make us flinch. Clouds had muscled in and spat a little, darkening the sky with an early dusk. Damn it! Where were we going to camp?

'Don't camp here,' said a young couple who we interrupted in a corner of the park. Too close to the road – the police will probably find you, they said. I thought the police sounded far preferable to most of the other people who might find us. There was a tent peg on the ground, a sign that we ignored. On the other side of the railway line was a reclaimed brownfield site – flat, stony ground now covered in gorse bushes and scrub, with a path around the outside and signs marking it out as a wildlife area. Dog walkers had gone back to nature by letting their dogs' turds sit naked, rather than tying them up in little plastic bags before slinging them in the verge, as had been the case for the last 20 miles.

It was pretty much dark – we had no other choice. We walked gingerly into the middle of the space, visible from every direction, and put the tent up between some skinny gorse bushes for low-level moral support. Tall lights from an industrial estate shone across the tent, and a siren passed in the distance. The tent was small, with a space under the flysheet on either side of the inner tent where we stashed the packsaddle, panniers, bin bags of donkey food, plastic bags of human food, and the assembled stove, boots, donkey mac and waterproofs. Inside was just big enough for two human beings – the width of two collarbones, with a few inches less headroom than would be needed to sit up straight. Generally we'd get in, planning to listen to the wind-up radio, chat a little, or work out tomorrow's route, but would fall asleep within seconds; being forced to lie down was the main reason, but the shortage of oxygen probably helped see us swiftly off.

In the brief moment between switching off the headtorch and closing my eyes, I saw a faint gleam of light pass across the tent. I clutched Rhys's arm and we lay silent, listening so hard that all we could hear was the pressure of suspense in our own skulls. We were lying on the ground, with faith in this thinnest of membranes. The torch beam crossed again, and rain began to fall, rumbling loudly on the tent and robbing us of our only useful sense. I reached up to touch my penknife in the tent pocket, and Rhys whispered in the dark, 'What on earth are you going to do with *that*?' He's right, I thought. Even in Rhyl, with its bad reputation, what were the chances of an opportunist murderer hanging out in an underused municipal wasteland, just where we happened to be lying, wide-eyed and soft-bellied, gift-wrapped in polyester? After dark, in the rain? Even in Rhyl there probably weren't *that* many murderers, per head of the population. It would be a stroke of bad luck. I put the penknife back.

'Use *this*!' whispered Rhys, and put an empty Desperado bottle in my hand.

The torchlight didn't come again, but we waited a long time, imagining the dead-eyed recluse approaching across the scrub, crunchy footsteps masked by the rattling rain. He was standing right above us, the rainwater running unheeded over his face and shining on his greasy forehead and weak chin in the cold light of the industrial estate as he thought through his options. He'd always liked the idea of a little local massacre, and now here was the opportunity... Should he? Nah, he couldn't be bothered. But then, it would be so easy...

Perhaps Chico looked him in the eye and persuaded him out of it. Human beings – they're dispensable, but donkeys? Everyone loves a donkey. You couldn't go on living undercover in Rhyl as a donkey murderer.

I woke up with the bottle stuck to the side of my face, the leftover dribbles of tequila-flavoured beer warming and escaping as stale fumes. We always meant to leave at dawn, whenever we had to camp somewhere indiscreet, but somehow as the sky lightened and the sinister threat of night-time faded, we felt less urgent, more brave. The world belonged to us again, and we snoozed on like innocent babes while Chico chewed patiently outside.

TWENTY-FOUR

Part of the reason for finding ourselves camping in Rhyl was that we hadn't wanted to push on through – we had business there. Chico's donkey passport had his birth details on it, including an address in Rhyl. I'd been phoning around but no one knew anything, so we'd decided to walk to the address anyway.

Rhyl is the land that social responsibility forgot. Another Victorian seaside town, but this time seriously down at heel and gathering horrible statistics on shoplifting, inadequate housing, obesity, underage pregnancy, debt, heroin use and alcoholism. As we passed, West Rhyl was just about to make the national news for being named a 'welfare ghetto' by the Centre for Social Justice following the announcement that 67 per cent of its working-age population was on benefits.

Some people attributed this to large-scale migration from the cities of the north after the second world war; others blamed a landlord who'd bought up lots of the bed and breakfasts in the 1980s, turned them into cheap shared houses and advertised (depending on the rumour monger) either in prisons or the run-down areas of those northern cities. The cities also brought the drugs. The seaside attractions closed down one by one, and the tourists who did still come were poor.

Our own favourite seaside attraction, the beach donkeys, had ceased operations when the donkey man, Kenneth Edward Jones, had died at the age of 80 the year before. His family had been known as the 'cockers', because his dad had been famous for being able to ride a cock horse – a high-spirited stallion – until it was tame.

We found the road named in Chico's passport, a long one leading inland from the beach. People were friendly, in as much as they yelled the usual few greetings. In top spot was 'You don't see that every day!', to which I sometimes answered, 'I do!' Often it came out with more of a weary or caustic edge than I meant, and I'd follow up with lots of grinning and jollity to smooth things over. Better was just to smile nicely and carry on. In second place for Rhyl was the ever popular 'That's a big dog!', sometimes directed to the person's own dog ('Ooh, that's a big dog, isn't it, Maisie!'). Maisie was usually of the same mind as me in thinking, 'It's not a dog. I'm not an idiot.' In third place was 'Don-KEH!', yelled in a Scottish accent, thanks to the film *Shrek*. There were also a good few 'Bethlehem's that way!', and one young man pointed at Chico's face and then mine, and said, 'Not being funny, but you look just like him!'

And then came a cry of 'Chico?' Between the tyre garages and the tanning parlours a lean young woman with a chubby baby under her arm had just come out of a terraced house, and recognised Chico instantly. Her name was Janette, and it turned out that she had worked for donkey man Ken for ten years.

I had wondered if it was foolishly sentimental, looking out the place where Chico was born and raised, but as soon as I got talking to Janette it became clear that it was actually weirder to spend so much time with a living being and *not* know a little about his past.

Chico's papa was a stud. Literally. Chico had many, many siblings, including Janette's all-time favourite donkey, Chico's sister Dixie. His papa, called Rocky, was ginger and spotty, but still the top jack in the stable. Janette emailed me some pictures, and it was clear the genes had come through strong: Chico had Rocky's nose and fuzzy brow. Chico's mama, Bonny, gave him his kohl eyes – she was a classic dark looker. Photos of baby Chico show a tiny, skinny foal standing primly by his mother, with a bright white nose and two back hooves, and a great fuzzy bouffant on his forehead, like we all had when we were young.

And what did Chico give her, his poor mama, in return? Janette said he used to kick her for milk. He was up and chasing dogs when he was 25 minutes old. He was naughty and timid at once – he'd demand attention, but then run away when he got it.

There had been beach donkeys in Rhyl since 1848, and Kenneth Edward Jones had 42 of them. When it was work time, Janette said, they used to open the gate and the donkeys would run through the Rhyl streets to the beach, pursued by the crew on bicycles. The new donkey on the block would be sent along to learn the ropes from the others, but when Chico's turn came he refused to put his hooves on the sand. So they sold the wayward little beast to the neighbouring Llandudno beach-donkey set-up. Did they confess that he was sandphobic? I didn't ask. In any case, Llandudno's wide sands must have remained untouched by the hoof of Chico because he didn't stay long – he was sold on twice more, and thus came to be in a stable in Shropshire, waiting to make an impression on me as I came on by, one day in April. Rocky now lived on the Great Orme – could Chico have been braying at him, that evening before he bit me and flew down the hill? His sister Dixie, his nieces Kelly and Gem, and his mother Bonny all worked the Barmouth beach – might that be why Chico had tried to follow the beach donkeys into their trailer, all that time ago?

And might his sand aversion explain his wild antics that very first time we encountered sand in the boatyard at the Dyfi estuary? Not to mention the debacle at Porth Dinllaen…

Or was that all sentimental speculation? Janette crouched down in front of Chico, took his rubbery, whiskery chin in her hands and looked him gently in the eyes. He stayed still and held her gaze, with his ears pinned back. People passed on the busy pavement, buses inched their way round parked cars on the busy street, and the two of them shared a moment of sweet quiet.

When the baby needed feeding, and Chico began to get restless on the pavement, we said goodbye and moved on down the road. There was no one around at the passport address except for a few chickens, but we walked around the yard and the stable, and watched Chico for signs of recognition. He looked at his old home, sniffed a few things, took a drink from a saucepan under a drainpipe, and left again without any great signs of excitement or distress.

Every now and again, passers-by would ask whether Chico had any say in the journey – especially if it was raining and he looked sorry for himself. I'd say a defensive yes, and now even more so. Quite apart from the fact that he'd been so keen to walk out of his yard when I met him, and had responded flatteringly well to my novice attempt at winning him over with a little grooming, he'd also brought the whole situation on himself. Ironically, if he'd have just behaved his silly little self and followed some older sibling onto the sand in Rhyl in the first place, he would never have begun his side of the chain of events that led to his role in this most peculiar team event. So there, Chico.

We went on, our new knowledge about our donkey giving him new depth, fragments of his history, suggestions of his psychology and character, other people who had been fond of him. We felt a bit honoured to have him along, small but active in the face of the winding paths of chance and circumstance.

This leg of the journey was not suffused in spirituality. There were no enclaves of hippies, no sense of the old pilgrims, little Welshness, wildlife or architecture. It was about moving on, journeying through the landscape, our little family of adventurers moving across the map. We felt like a team, camping wild night after night and surviving, eating grapefruits in the car park of Asda, filling up with water when we needed it, finding patches of grazing in an urban churchyard, washing very rarely, getting strong – just the three of us on this hot and heavy-duty coast.

And we'd managed many hours in a town! It was a relief to get back in sight of the sea, the grey-blue expanse covered all over in little white waves, flicked up by the onshore wind. As we stepped back onto Rhyl's promenade, something banged, and banged again, making Chico and me jump. It was bangers! Those old-school wraps of explosive in tissue paper that bang on contact. Were we stepping on them, or was someone throwing them at us? I looked around furtively, with a smile on my face so I wouldn't give anyone the satisfaction of looking like a grumpy grown-up, but there was no one there. That was Rhyl all over – a sense of foreboding, but without knowing if it was real or rumour, conspiracy or just neglect. Were sinister children hiding in the shadows and watching us flinch? Were murderers waiting in the bushes? Crimestoppers notices on the beach threatened serial foulers with surveillance, inviting people to grass on dog walkers that let their dogs crap on the sand. Last night's teenagers had been worried about the police – was this town compensating for years of abandonment with a heavy hand?

Everyone seemed to be having fun on the beach, though. If it was true that the population of Rhyl had been encouraged to come and claim the dole at the seaside rather than the inner cities, it did still seem preferable. 'Costa del Dole', the tabloids called Rhyl in the 80s. One of the saddest of a bunch of sad old statistics was that Rhyl had a quarter of its population in long-term bed-and-breakfast accommodation. Not living it up at the seaside, but bunking in holiday accommodation forever. Clearly, being on holiday is only good if it's a break from ordinary life, with all of the certainty and integration of real life just on hold, not discarded forever. Dreaming about the eternal holiday after the lottery win is all very well, but if that woman a few miles back really did set up the Donktuary, would she not be disappointed to find that it involved a lot of shovelling shit?

It's a fine line between being footloose and being rootless, being free and being lost. Imagine if we were just walking with Chico from one place to another, penniless, directionless, everything we owned on our backs. We wouldn't be much fun. We'd be needy.

For us and for the holiday bed-and-breakfast visitors of Rhyl, the enjoyment depended on the knowledge that in the end we could stop and go home. We were not really nomads at heart, and living without foundations would be harder than it looked.

TWENTY-FIVE

Sand makes Chico want to roll. Once he gets the idea, he puts his nose to the ground and walks along, snuffling his nostrils in the soft, warm sand. Then he paws the ground with a hoof, scattering a fresh patch, lowers himself down onto his front knees and then one side, and rolls. Sometimes he manages to get all the way over, and then looks pleased with himself.

Miles and miles of sandy promenade was too much for him. He and I walked fast, me holding him close and not letting him roll. Rhys was ahead of us and then behind, walking in his flip-flops and in so much pain with huge, stinging blisters on his heels and under his toes that he couldn't stop or talk. Eventually we gave in and took Chico's packsaddle right off so that he could really go for it, which he did.

He's not an animal who shows a great deal of delight, opting instead for a grumpy sort of catch-all resignation, but he sure does love to roll. And we sure do love to watch him roll. Kicking sand around the place, his giant eyelids closed in rapture, bony little legs in the air and hooves tucked under, snowy white belly all round and taut, he wriggles his spine into the ground. Then he heaves himself upright, and gives a little snort of satisfaction at an upside-down job well done.

We gave our own little snorts of satisfaction at the prospect of a pint of shandy on the grass at Prestatyn, the next town along. Even better, they were bought for us by a man called Garfield who had seen roughly where we were on Facebook, and cycled along the front from Colwyn Bay, looking for us. He said he found our walk inspiring, but then let on that he regularly did 100-mile runs, over 36 sleep-free hours. He advised Rhys on his woeful feet, suggesting lubricating them with Vaseline and shea butter. 'You wear two pairs of socks, of course?' Rhys shook his head, but dug around in the saddlebags for another pair, and double-socked for the rest of the walk.

Prestatyn is where the Offa's Dyke Path begins, named after and often running along the momentous eighth-century earthwork thought to have been built by the Anglo Saxon king Offa, probably to keep the Welsh out of his Kingdom of Mercia, or at least to stand on top of and keep an eye on them. The dyke runs pretty much all the way along the border of Wales to the Severn estuary. After so much blazing coastal heat, I was really looking forward to turning south too: bidding farewell to the sea for a few weeks, plunging into the green and pleasant land, making some serious progress, and swapping this anonymous rough-and-ready population for some of the well-behaved old guard – horsey people who'd lived there for generations.

But it wasn't time to head inland yet. The coast of Wales ran for a further 30 miles, through the rest of Denbighshire and Flintshire, stopping just short of Chester. I couldn't imagine it would be pretty – I was expecting industry and deprivation. But I decided to see it through for two reasons. Firstly, my outline of Wales would be the wrong shape if I sliced off this top corner. I had a responsibility to the yellow highlighter line I was drawing: it really ought to be more or less the shape of the country.

The other reason was a lighthouse. Tom and Anneke, next-door narrowboat neighbours of ours in London, had bought a leaning lighthouse. They were letting us stay, and we couldn't wait to get there.

Apart from Rhys's blisters, all was well in the world. In fact, after the shandies, I was startled to discover that I was enjoying myself, walking through the Gronant dunes, making up a song about bags of dog poo hanging on the fence to the tune of 'Ten

Green Bottles'. We'd reach the lighthouse tomorrow morning, which was exciting. We'd survived Rhyl, we weren't far off the end of the north coast. We were probably 400 miles through the walk, and nearly two months – a decent total, inching up daily. We were doing it! I was warm and drunk and proud, in the light of the low evening sun.

And then, as comes just after pride: the fall. Rhys was a little way behind and I was leading Chico. I thought I'd have a quick pee – that shandy draining swiftly through my perennially dehydrated body, no doubt. I dumped my backpack in the sand. There was nothing to tie Chico onto up there, and I couldn't risk holding his rope and peeing – he'd have wandered away and dragged me, crab-like, pants down. So I clipped the carabiner on the end of the rope to the strap of my discarded backpack. That, I thought, would give him a little resistance, and he'd stay there. He wasn't being wild or strong, just munching dune grass. And even if he dragged it a few feet, it wouldn't matter.

Wrong, wrong, wrong! Disaster took a mere heartbeat to descend, draining the woozy, hazy warmth from the world in a horrifying instant. Chico had pulled the bag, very gently; a tiny twitch. But a dark shape twitching at his heel of its own accord is pretty much exactly what Chico's whole physique and psychology is geared up to respond to. And he responded faster than I could comprehend, taking off with the acceleration of pure terror, his hooves kicked up high and bucking, and the backpack bounding behind him through the dunes in pursuit.

Donkeys stop running when the danger abates, and look around themselves sheepishly. But now we would find out what happens if the fear doesn't stop. My backpack chased Chico *for hours*. The sun set and the moon rose.

'He fell!' yelled Rhys, who could see further than I could, before running after him. And then they were both gone, into a vast dunescape the exact same shades as a brown donkey at dusk.

'RHYS! RHYS!' I yelled, and stopped, swivelling my ears around, away from the wind. 'RHYS? RHYS!' Oh god, oh shit. Oh, what an idiot I am, what an *idiot*!

The dunes up there were a mile long and half a mile wide, running in three parallel rolling ridges. To the north was the sea, to the south was a golf course. We'd come from the west and the outskirts of Prestatyn. There were roads back there; what if he scrambled into traffic in the evening half-light? I ran across the ridges and at last saw Rhys, and beyond him Chico. Relief numbed my mind, but as I got closer I could see that it wasn't all over yet. Rhys had managed to take Chico's packsaddle off, but the bag was still attached to his headcollar, and he was out of range again. As I reached them, the wide-eyed donkey got a new burst of energy and fear, and despite the two of us calling to him, trying our hardest to dampen our own panic so as to sound reassuring, he galloped past us, back the way we'd come, picking up speed. And then he was gone again.

Rhys threw his camera bag into my arms and tore after him.

It got darker – it must have been 9.30. I ran to one side of the dunes and looked out over the beach, then to the other and out onto the golf course. I looked through the camera, using the zoom to spot distant bushes that weren't a runaway donkey, and shadows that weren't Rhys. There was so much space, and I raced around it, senseless, panting and cursing myself, full of self-loathing, taking dozens of minutes to get anywhere with each change of direction.

From the far southeast corner of the golf course, by the hidden, overgrown, ankle-breaking Prestatyn gutter, I saw Rhys, standing on the top of a dune, back to the north. I sprinted towards him, and then found it wasn't Rhys but a man with binoculars shouting, 'Donkey's over there, by the road!' and pointing west.

It took ages to get there. As I ran I kept hearing distant screams; I was sure it must by Chico, his thin, brittle leg bones snapped in a gully, or lying on the side of the road, thrashing around wildly, still trying to get away from the stupid, stupid bag, screaming in pain. But it was just seagulls, aloof, gliding in the last evening thermals, unfussed by our silly all-consuming drama.

And then I heard Rhys calling softly; I couldn't see anything in the dark – stupid eyesight. Stupid me. He was holding Chico's head, walking around slowly, Chico's body still in a spasm of fear and soaked in sweat. I felt shy and guilty, and didn't go too close. Rhys pointed at a nearby bunker, and at the edge of it was my backpack, dark and still, slumped in the sand. I looked it over. It was very sorry for itself, wet and gritty. The top pocket had come open and was empty, and the whole thing smelled pungent.

Don't come near us!' said Rhys. 'I don't think he wants to see that backpack!' Chico flinched. The disgraced backpack and I went ahead to look for the rest of the bags, scattered across the dark mounds half a mile away, and for a while I lost them again, as they made their slow progress across the dunes, Rhys singing reassuringly to Chico all the way. I found the man with the binoculars, though. Adrian was the warden, keeping an eye on the tern colony, and he'd brought one heavy pannier all the way over to me. I had to be grateful, but it was the one bag that Rhys had had the foresight to leave by the path, as the marker for where all the rest of the stuff might be. I carried it all the way back.

After a few hours we'd found the packsaddle and Rhys's backpack; the only critical thing we were missing was the white tape from the lost pannier. Without it we couldn't make Chico a corral, and without a corral he couldn't relax, although he seemed to have gone into some sort of catatonic state, eyes locked on the horizon, keeping watch for the beast that had chased him.

We'd have to take it in turns – one of us sitting up to hold his rope while the other slept. When dawn came we'd be able to look for the missing bag.

And then on a last-ditch scouting mission Rhys fell over the pannier, and on the way back stepped on the wind-up radio from the top pocket of my bag. He pulled up some handfuls of dune grass and laid them across the nearest path so we'd be able to go back and look for the other lost bits in the morning. We did, and found everything, except for two bottles of beer and four tomatoes, gone, mercifully, without trace, except for that damp, yeasty smell.

We slept where we'd found the packsaddle, brazenly out in the open dunes. Adrian had said it would be alright – we probably wouldn't be singlehandedly responsible for wiping out the dune system. I sat in the sand, and in every direction the billion tips of dune grass filled the world at my eye height, shivering like the scales of a fish, silver and blonde and green, and painted pink with the dawn. The blades crushed by our wild and directionless tramplings were already picking themselves up, filling in the disturbed hollows, reaching for the clouds again.

I watched Chico watching the horizon. His sweat had crystallised and he was strong, salty and coarse; there was something very kangaroo-like about his sinewy back legs – ready, taut, almighty. We were all ragged, but I marvelled at the restorative power of another day. Here came that wondrous sun again, with forgiveness and unequivocal life.

I wound the radio, its winding mechanism all crunchy with sand, and into the morning burst the voices of other people, the world forging on, with news and conjecture, politics and arguments and jokes. 'Time and the hour runs through the roughest day,' I comforted myself, in Macbeth's words; both of us pretty reproachable human beings.

TWENTY-SIX

Conservation officers are not all created equal – we were about to meet one who really liked toads, and one who was surprisingly keen on humans. We didn't see Adrian again, as we left the Gronant dunes with our tails tucked under, but I felt the gaze of omnipresent binoculars. The previous night Adrian and I had talked about abandoned tents and disposable barbeques, those many thousand little bags of dog poo, and quadbikers that had taken down a fence and killed a whole tern colony. It must be hard, in your hide in the middle of that rippling plain, not to take a dim view of your fellow human beings.

Next we met Mandy, a conservation officer employed by the county but working from a cabin in a holiday park, surrounded by classificatory posters of fish and seaweed. Mandy had four little Welsh Mountain Ponies, borrowed from the mountains for the summer. Their task was conservation grazing, keeping down the plants that would otherwise cover the dunes. All my life I'd had a nagging sense of guilt about playing in dunes, from early days spent leaping off the tops, to the previous day's bashing about. I had the impression that dunes needed plants to grow on them, roots to hold the sand together. Stabilisation was good, I thought.

'That's not the case,' said Mandy, and explained dunes to me, as we stood watching Chico spurn the water from her outside tap, despite all the sweating of the night before. By definition dunes are a landscape in flux, and to keep a dune system alive it has to be always in a state of change. A dune ceases to be a dune when it turns back to sand and blows away, or is washed away by the sea, but it also ceases to be a dune when so much vegetation grows that it becomes a woodland or scrubland. Between those two fates dunes live and move, fluctuating between bare sand, pioneer vegetation, and more established fauna.

Conservation of something in flux sounded counterintuitive. Wasn't conservation – and, ooh, conservatism too – about keeping things the same, as they always were? What if the way things always were was in a state of change? My mind rolled this nugget around, and inarticulately I tried to ask a bad question.

'So, um, what's the point of trying to save sand dunes? I mean, what's the *value*?'

There was a moment's silence as I realised that this was not a good question to ask a conservationist. Dunes shifted quietly past, along the concrete holiday park road.

'I mean, are dunes of importance to *people*, say?' I made things worse.

Natterjack toads were where Mandy's own passions lay. They're endangered and had died out completely in Wales in the 1960s, but reintroduction had been successful, and Mandy was taking good care of them. She showed us some of the scrapes she'd made for them to breed in. Natterjacks have a yellow stripe down their backs and a very loud croak to help them find scarce mates, and they walk about on their four short legs like babies who are through with crawling but not quite ready to walk.

Mandy was also pretty fond of the horses, and Chico was going to have to be too – they'd be neighbours for the night, while Rhys and I stayed in the lighthouse. We took Chico to their holding pen, and hung around while they all got used to each other, Chico pretty cool in a 'Oh, the things I've seen' sort of way, and the horses jumpy in a 'What the hell is that? This isn't an ordinary Tuesday!' sort of way.

The lighthouse was a beautiful thing: five stories high, a white column with a black base, a light room and gallery walkway at the top, and a red domed roof. Exactly what you'd come up with if someone asked you to draw them a lighthouse. I could see just why Anneke and Tom had fallen for it, but as we got the two very serious padlocks off the very serious metal door and stepped into the round, damp interior, we immediately felt glad we didn't own it. There was a lot of work to be done.

It had a portfolio of complex and urgent engineering demands. The sand was being unevenly scoured out from underneath, the wrong sort of render was eating away at it from the inside, and the wrong sort of paint was causing trouble to the render on the outside. It used to be on the edge of the land but the dunes had retreated and it was now way out on the sand flats, under siege from the waves at high tide, and from holidaymakers all the rest of the time. The lighthouse called to people, a beacon of interest, and they trekked across the beach to see it, climb the steps, rattle the door.

'There's no padlocks!' shouted an excited, high-pitched voice on the other side of the door. 'Help me get it open! Come on!' We froze, unsure of how to protect this fortress that wasn't ours. 'You can't come in! It's not ours! It's a building site!' we shouted back through the door. They clanged off down the stairs in disappointment, and moments later the next hopefuls arrived. Eventually we realised it wouldn't end, and decided to trust the bolt on the inside of the door, and go exploring, up.

The staircase wound around the inside of the five-metre-wide lighthouse, from the entrance room (chemical toilet, buckets and spades, serious looking engineering equipment), up to the well-swept bedroom (bed), then the kitchen (a jerry can of water, a camping gas stove, and a basket of miscellaneous liquors), then a room with nothing at all in it except for dead flies on the windowsill, and then the lightroom – a conservatory, 18m above the sand. From up there we were like Rapunzels, refusing to let down our hair but issuing friendly waves. We were high up above the northernmost tip of mainland Wales, at the Point of Ayr, the poetically named spit of land at the mouth of the Dee estuary. The evening sun turned the sand blood red, and our enormous proprietorial shadow stretched off into the east, pointing across the sea to Liverpool.

We stayed up in the lightroom and cooked some laverbread – a can of squishy black Welsh seaweed that we mixed together with oats and fried up with bacon. Laverbread is a South Walian thing, and as we ate the delicious mess I felt the pull of the south. I always seemed to wish that I was two or three weeks ahead; two or three weeks ago I'd thought I would be happy if only I was at the lighthouse, but now we were there I was using the vantage point to look away to the next thing. The curse and the thrill of the long-term traveller.

There was no electricity or running water in the lighthouse. Clouds had closed in, and a few drops of rain spattered on the glass. We picked our way down the stairs by the light of one headtorch, which just intensified the darkness. Each round floor was made out of chipboard, soggy in places, and there were chunks of brick missing here and there. A few people had mentioned the famous ghosts, but I'd resisted the temptation to find out about them – I'm sensible in the daytime, but very susceptible to the spooky rogues in the dark. A round building, it turned out, could still be full of dark corners.

A few hours later we both woke up at the same time, and lay in the dark wondering what had called us to the surface. Then came a deep thumping, booming sound from the windward side, as much a feeling as a noise. We opened the window, and outside was the sea, churning and glinting in the darkness. It was raining hard, and the squally wind was flicking the raindrops and the sea spray into a brackish blizzard. We ran up and down, leaning out to look at the storm from the door and every window, and crawling onto the lantern's walkway to scare ourselves, high up but small, powerful and powerless at once, like Neptune, or Jack and Rose on the bow of the *Titanic*.

We couldn't see the shore, and it was like being on a ship at sea, except that we weren't moving with the waves but standing fast against them. It was no small feat for the old beacon, which had witnessed this twice a day since 1776.

Apart from the test of time and tides, there seemed no guarantee the old thing would stand firm, but I was so grateful to it for trying. When we got back into our sleeping bags and tried to think of sleep, I realised there were no dark corners left – this impressive building was looking after us. Guardian of the open water! Custodian of plucky human endeavour! Protector of us, clueless and overexcited cuckoos! There was nothing to fear in here, we were all together, ghosts included, weathering the indiscriminate might of the formidable sea.

It was all over by the morning, and I looked up the ghost on my phone while we drank tea on the walkway. He seemed to be the lighthouse-keeper, called Raymond, and was often seen up there, repairing equipment or shining his torch at people. He died of a fever and a broken heart, poor Raymond. People had seen spooky footprints on the sand, had their kids get ill after visiting the beach, or had their dogs refuse to go near the lighthouse. A few hours later, when we brought Chico over to load him up, he slipped his mooring and walked fast away from the lighthouse. But it didn't seem conclusive to me. If we attributed Chico's every cussed mood to a ghostly presence, we'd have been jostling through the supernatural rabble every day.

I looked at the map and thought again about heading south. A bridleway ran straight over the hill beyond the dunes, and into the high and heathery Clwydian mountain range, designated an Area of Outstanding Natural Beauty. We could just do it, rather than blundering towards the unknown tangles of Chester and Wrexham.

'It's going to be ugly, I think, Flintshire...' I said to Rhys. 'We could—'

'Hey!' came a shout from the sand below. 'It's great! You have to do it!' A man with a round, friendly face and alarmingly good hearing was grinning up at us. 'I'm Mike! The Flintshire warden!'

He was the last of the three conservationists, and was cut from different cloth. He had nothing against Natterjack toads but seemed driven more by the need to get humans to enjoy the landscape. 'People in Flintshire don't even think of theirs as a coastal county,' he said when we'd invited him up to the lightroom and got him a cuppa. 'So a lot of the work is about regeneration, access and outreach.' He was also optimistic about the resilience of the natural environment, and told us about otters that had made a home for themselves in a pile of flytipped concrete rebar. He was just the man for his job.

He took my map and annotated it with great enthusiasm, showing the location of his millennium beacons, a big painted ship that used to be a nightclub, and the holy well of St Winefride that had dried up when the Halkyn lead mines were drained. His excitement for the area was infectious and I was chastened. Of course we had to keep on.

Mike also lent us a small bunch of keys that would open gates along the coast path. We took it in turns to hold them in wonder, like magic items from a fairytale. He even drew little Xs in places that would make decent wild campsites. We loved Flintshire already, on account of its guardian.

TWENTY-SEVEN

We left just as the waves began to tickle the base of the lighthouse. I emptied the pee bucket surreptitiously into the sea and wondered about those sick children whose mothers blamed the ghost. Rhys and I both wrestled with the tricky padlocks, the tide swirling around in determined eddies, everything suddenly feeling like a physical challenge against the clock.

The three of us walked down the main street of Talacre, eating pasties from the bakery. I tried to persuade Rhys to take it in turns to sneak into the holiday complex and use the showers in the tropical island swimming pool, but he wasn't brazen enough. We walked through the cloud of hot chlorine that burped into the street, and lost our only chance. Days before I had lain back in the tent with my arms folded behind my head and Rhys had said, 'Oh! That smell!' I'd quickly put them down again in shame, only for him to say, 'No, you're alright – it was me. I farted.' We stank.

Ten minutes later, fate intervened and the skies let rip with a series of ridiculous showers, each raindrop exploding like a water balloon. We were wet through in minutes, and took shelter in an MOT garage, between the inspection pit and the hoist, Chico standing perfectly still like he does when he wishes he was somewhere else.

We waited, enjoying the sweet summer rain smell of wet dust and grateful plants. Ragwort had a real hold around Talacre and field after field was full of the bright yellow, shoulder-high clusters of flowers on long stalks, the petals and leaves all fringed like a cowboy's leathers. Ragwort is poisonous for horses and donkeys, and people. It destroys the liver, but it's also bitter and was thankfully not of interest to Chico. The rain washed their dangerous little yellow faces clean, and they glowed beneath the navy blue clouds. For weeks all of the plants had been aggressively leggy and spent, flinging themselves onto the road, scorched white. We'd not had to worry about Chico eating cut grass – everything was hay. Huge dock leaves, once dark green, had turned bright red, draped limp on the tarmac. Chickweed rattled, pink and desiccated. But this rain revived everything and almost immediately ushered green back into the palette.

We dried off as we walked on, clammy and uneven, not feeling any cleaner for the dousing, our clothes getting tighter and then loose again.

'Ooh! It were *bouncing*!' said Ruth, leaning out of her pub and sympathising about the rain. She and her husband Ray invited us to camp in the Farmer's Arms' beer garden and we accepted straight away. The village of Ffynnongroyw was hardly any distance from the lighthouse, but we felt ready to stop. Ruth made us sandwiches, and Penri Jones, an 80-year-old local making light work of a bottle of red wine, serenaded me with the Welsh national anthem and then the love song 'Myfanwy', clutching his heart as he sang. I sang him one of the tunes I remembered from school eisteddfods, with only half the words and slipping into the alto part at the chorus, but he didn't seem to mind. After someone had taken Penri home in a taxi, we learned that he'd worked in the Point of Ayr colliery for 40 years, until it closed in 1996.

Ray tried to count the local people who spoke Welsh, but didn't get very far – there weren't many. 'Penri were right made up that you spoke Welsh to him, weren't he, Ray?' said Ruth, in her Liverpudlian accent.

We'd discovered whilst talking to the man who looked after the Talacre railway crossing that the local accent sounded very Liverpudlian to the untrained ear. We'd asked him when he'd left Liverpool, and he replied that he'd been born in Talacre.

Ruth fed us sausages in the morning, and we set off southeast along the Dee estuary, making use of Mike's magic keys. After days and days of nothing but sea wall, there was a lot to look at: a factory making enormous, shiny white pieces of wind turbine, a hypodermic needle on the pavement, the grounded and rusting Funship. The TSS Duke of Lancaster had been a bar, a casino and a flea market before becoming a giant canvas for street artists. The artworks include a giant geisha, a teddy bear crying toxic waste, and a pig in a policeman's hat. It was unlike anything else on the coastal path.

We had lunch on the grass outside a huge out-of-town haberdashery where we met an artist called Eric who painted birds. He'd known Rhyl's donkey man Ken, it turned out: 'He was always trying to get me to paint his favourite jack – a white and orange one.'

'That was Chico's dad!' we said, and we all looked at Chico, who felt shy and lurched away from us, dragging me sideways through his collapsible water bowl.

We spent the night camping under one of Mike's beacons, a stainless-steel fire basket designed like a Welsh dragon, which slashed some fearsome patriotic shapes into the setting sun. According to Mike, it had, on its first ever use, accidentally dripped molten fire onto the shoes of visiting dignitaries.

In the town of Flint a steady stream of people came to talk to us, generally friendly but slightly unhinged. Six children started up a quick-fire question round. At any one time three would be interrogating me, a couple would be poking Chico in the tail, and another would be hurling bicycles down the banks of Flint Castle's moat whilst roaring.

Child 1: 'Can I ride your donkey?
Me: 'No, he doesn't really do rides…'
Child 2: 'Can *I* ride your donkey?'
Me: 'No, he's never—'
Child 3: 'Can I ride on him?'

Me: 'No!'

Child 3: 'Can he tap dance?'

Child 1: 'Can he swim?'

Rhys had fallen asleep at a picnic table. A new crowd of children came over.

Child 7: 'My mum's boyfriend says your donkey is stupid.'

I wouldn't stand for this. 'Well, I think your mum's boyfriend is stupid!'

Child 7: 'Hm, he is. He's bald. And he doesn't know what one plus one is.'

Child 8: 'What's your donkey's surname? I think it should be "Forden".'

Child 9: 'Can I go underneath him?'

Child 8: 'Can I touch his hooves?'

The kids were getting more and more high-pitched with the excitement, and eventually I yelled at a little girl who had become obsessed with the idea of making Chico kick her friend.

'He'll only kick if he's really upset!' I said, wondering if I could get away with kicking her myself – *I* was pretty upset. 'Why would you want to upset him? That would be a MEAN thing to do!'

Chico lifted his tail and issued forth a mound of hot poo. The children lost their senses and leaped about like popping candy, screaming with the joy of it all. When they eventually all turned their attention to throwing the bicycles down the hill, the girl I'd shouted at asked if she could clear up his poo for me. She did her penance with two plastic bags and hardly any squealing, and I thanked her warmly. She even promised me she'd wash her hands.

'Ah, Flint Castle!' said a man who'd appeared by my side with his hands on his hips and introduced himself as the ex-deputy mayor. 'I'm very proud of Flint Castle,' he said. 'Well, it's the seat of Welsh government!' We were standing next to a sign that gave a potted history of its role in the final quashing of Welsh hopes for self-rule, but I didn't much feel like getting into it, especially not so close to the English border.

We ploughed onwards, our progress a little confused by the last-resort maps. Flint didn't sell OS maps, and we'd walked off the edge of my last one. I had the full set in Mum's spare room, but neither parent had visited for a long time – we were as far from Aberystwyth as we could be. The library let me photocopy their reference map.

'You're only allowed to copy one A4-sized section though, I'm afraid,' said the librarian. 'Ah, yes, of course,' I said, as my finger slipped onto the A3 button when her back was turned. In case it mitigates the felony at all, a black and white version of the map is, it turned out, almost completely unintelligible.

Rhys left us. I had 12 mystery bites on one knee and a bee sting that had swollen up really big, but apart from that I felt just about able to be cast adrift alone. Chico had almost stopped flinching at dark backpack-sized shapes, and I'd almost stopped flinching at Chico.

The Dee estuary became a long, dead-straight canal with a cycle lane on a dyke alongside. Before we'd even got to it, Chico wedged himself in a narrow bicycle gateway, too impatient to wait for me to take his panniers off, and backed up in alarm, refusing to try it again. The last of our Flintshire oddballs appeared at exactly the right moment – an elderly woman who had driven to this patch of scrub between the river and an industrial estate in order to sprinkle her bag of breadbin leftovers 'for the birds'. Chico's eyes lit up, and I let her offer him a small piece of pancake. He walked right through the gate, but I had some trouble stopping her from feeding him pieces of mouldy sausage roll as I lifted his panniers back on. The rats of Connah's Quay must have been fat, happy and carnivorous.

Chico and I crossed the Dee at Saltney, in relentless rain and emergency bin-bag waterproofs, and turned away from the water – our last connection with the sea. The border stretch stood ahead of us, starting ingloriously with a thicket of main roads, out-of-town shopping villages, Hawarden airport, and an aeroplane-wing factory.

But a mile later, as I arrived at my campsite – and shower! – the landscape looked just as I had imagined it in my hot, dry, concrete dreams. Fields of green crops shone in the recent rain, laced with poppies, and lawns were perfectly mown in cricket stripes. Poplars shimmered, dairy cows grazed, ye olde pubs under ancient oaks were open for business. The borderlands had begun already, and I was so ready for a change. As the sunset made golden linings around the clouds over the new landscape, I drank it all in, little knowing that things were about to get a whole lot harder.

This page, right: The pub at Porth Dinllaen. *Middle left:* Cae Mabon's roundhouse. *Middle right:* Chico, disinclined. *Below:* Back together after Anglesey.

Overleaf, above: The lighthouse. *Below:* Rhys and Chico relaxing in Rhyl. *Opposite:* Chico sure does love to roll in the Prestatyn sand.

TŶ COCH INN

PART THREE

THE BORDERLANDS

TWENTY-EIGHT

Chico and I stood at a junction, one of us paralysed by indecision, the other distracted by a dandelion. To the right was a simple mountain road heading around the west side of Ruabon mountain, into the prevailing winds, which smelled of impending downpour. The Met Office had issued a yellow-level rain warning, and there would be no shelter up there, not until the road finally wriggled down into a crevice called, worryingly, World's End.

The left-hand road stuck to the valley floor, navigating between dozens of little villages on the outskirts of Wrexham. Staying on the lee-side of the mountain seemed a wise choice, but all the roads went in the wrong direction, and there was no knowing which would be busy and dangerous. It would be a nuisance, tacking back and forth on full alert.

I had looked forward to navigating once freed from the coast. It made sense to me that 360 degrees of route-planning options would be easier than the 180 degrees of options I'd had until now, since the other 180 degrees had thus far been wet and salty. I could plot a straight course for Chepstow, untroubled by estuaries or headlands, and we could hammer along it – make up some valuable time. We'd pick the fastest option, no scenic routes. The Offa's Dyke Path usually took walkers two weeks and was 180 miles long, but as the crow flew, it was only 125 miles. We were nearly halfway around Wales!

Almost immediately, I realised that choice was not a good thing, especially for the chronically indecisive. I also realised it was not good to round up on a long walk. My jubilant 'almost halfway' became lacklustre and then downright mocking as two weeks later we still weren't halfway.

I'd planned to use the border as a rough guideline, but it was very faint on the map and when I teased it out with a pink highlighter pen, it transpired that it wriggled inconveniently all over the place. I wasn't even sure which maps I needed – the border meandered with no respect for the limitations of a piece of Ordnance Survey paper.

I had one offer of an overnight stay in the whole stretch, with my sister's friend Holly, which at least gave me something to aim for. We set out with a sinking feeling and found ourselves at the Ruabon junction.

I chose the mountain, of course. Just as the road wound into the full-frontal wind, the Offa's Dyke Path appeared from across the moor and joined us for a while, Prestatyn only 30 miles back along it. Chico wasn't keen on walking in the rain, and pretty soon chose standing in the rain as his preferred option. I tried the old rigmarole of pushing, pulling, touching him on the bum with the corral sticks – to no avail.

Standing still in the rain goes against every human instinct. A car came up on the single-track road and I turned Chico around and walked him back to a layby. Twenty minutes later – when we'd almost struggled on to the same point again – another car passed, and we had to go back to the same layby. A cyclist went by, calling, 'Good one! Lovely!' I wasn't feeling that way. When a third car arrived, I gestured, 'Squeeze past?' The driver, through his hyperactive windscreen-wiper strobe, signalled, 'Move him out the way a bit?' I gestured back, 'YOU BLOODY TRY!' and shoved Chico's rump as hard as I could, knocking him off his balance and gaining about six inches of road for the man, who drove tentatively by. This was rubbish.

Despite this occasional traffic and the single cars discreetly parked at each lookout point, enjoying the filthy view, it felt lonely up there. I began to wonder how we'd camp if Chico kept up his mutiny. I'd have to clear a patch of moorland of the thistles, rubbish and squashed frogs that littered the place. I had a lot of time to contemplate the mess – it was challenging my usual optimistic belief that all litter blew away from someone's picnic by mistake. Who made the effort to come up there only to throw their crap on the ground? Coffee cups, energy gels, something anaemic and deep-fried escaping from a polystyrene box. Sandwich packaging, plastic bags, a condom!

We eventually made it down, through World's End, where the deciduous leaves only served to assemble the raindrops into mega drops. I called a campsite – I needed some comfort. 'Do other campsites say yes?' asked the brusque and puzzled man on the phone. 'Yes,' I said, and he conceded. 'You'd better be here by six, though.'

The rain abated, but Chico had got into the habit of stopping, and even more so now that we had a deadline. I opened a bag of toffee popcorn for myself, and his head snapped up, the most lively he'd been all day. I fed him one little piece, and we were back in business.

I probably shouldn't have admitted it on Facebook. Within minutes Tamlin had appeared online, suggesting that carrots or horse nuts might have been a better option. I responded feebly that neither quite had the potency of toffee popcorn, that horse nuts decomposed like Weetabix in a wet pocket, and that I'd only given him one piece. Maybe two…

I was feeling the absence of Rhys's confidence, or maybe just missing the relative confidence of shared responsibility. Carol, my straight-talking donkey-walking guardian angel from the early days, had driven down from Lancaster to walk with us for a few hours the day before. I'd felt like a nervous learner on a driving test. I'd wondered what she thought as we weaved dangerously about by a road waiting for a break in traffic. I'd hoped she hadn't seen Chico's ears stand to attention when he heard the cellophane noise as she opened a packet of apricots. I'd tried not to let him graze whenever he felt like it – Carol didn't let him get at the verge at all when she led him.

She had declared Chico a 'fine pack animal', marvelled at his healthy hooves and admired his gait. I couldn't believe it – I'd got so accustomed to thinking of Chico as a terrible choice, a wayward juvenile in the process of being badly trained. 'You know he looks out for you when you go out of sight?' she said. 'Does he?' I was flattered but not convinced.

I was pleased that she'd given him her seal of approval, but when she left again, I was still in possession of a donkey who seemed to keep stopping, and she hadn't quite shifted my nagging sense that I was getting it all wrong.

'My horse really likes Coke,' volunteered a woman in the campsite, and I felt instantly much better. What sort of bad horsewoman discovers that vice? Three small pieces of toffee popcorn were hardly a sin at all…

We'd reached Llangollen Canal and strode out alongside it with delight – a guaranteed stretch of accessible path, flat and wide. Created, of course, for horses to pull narrowboats. The quiet dark water and sunlight percolating through the leaves, the occasional boat tied up, moorhens and ducks involved in turf disputes – it was lovely. A woman on a horse broke my reverie; her horse had spotted Chico and was terrified, prancing about. 'Take it away! Just take it away!' she shouted at me. 'Take it under the bridge! I'm worried about falling in the canal!'

Now I was too, and as soon as I got uneasy, so did Chico. He was walking on the far side of the towpath, as far from the water as possible. Most canals have the occasional underwater ramp, especially after a bridge, for rescuing boat-pulling horses should they fall in. I couldn't see any ramps on this stretch. What if Chico did fall in? I wondered if I'd be able to hold his head above water. How many passers-by would it take to pull him out? The idyllic scene was suddenly threatening.

I'd had a little dream of taking Chico along the Pontcysyllte aqueduct which carries the canal high over the river Dee. It's the longest and highest aqueduct in Britain, a beautiful architectural wonder in the form of a cast-iron trough held aloft by 19 stone pillars, built in 1805. The path alongside it was put there for horses, of course, and wouldn't we make an arresting sight, strolling through the air, 38m above the velvet-green valley?

No, we wouldn't. I lost my nerve, and Chico never had his in the first place. A loud narrowboat was the clincher, the sound of the engine amplified by the underside of a footbridge just before the aqueduct. Chico's hooves skittered on the stones, he bumped against the side of the passing boat and ran back along the towpath.

Rhys would have persevered, I expect, but I gave up. We dashed down some steep steps, Chico taking them three at a time to get away from the water. At the bottom of the valley was the far more sensible river bridge, and we sat on it, recovering.

Chico looked at me suspiciously. I thought we were getting on well, but it could have been that I was getting more accustomed to the daily adrenaline peaks. Human beings can get used to all sorts of things, and distractions were many. Luckily for Chico, the menacing loneliness of our bilateral relationship was about to be relieved by a string of unexpected companions.

First up was Steve, the third person ever to complete the Wales Coast Path/Offa's Dyke combo, and the self-designated secretary and online support of perimeteers. He'd caught several buses to walk with us, weathered my firewall of disorganisation, and arrived at our rendezvous point long before we did. Godfrey, a kind fellow who'd taken me in the night before, was worried about handing me over to a strange man. 'I'll know when I see him,' he said, and came along to vet Steve. When we saw Steve, neither of us could be sure – he was extremely laconic and missing some teeth.

'It'll be fine!' I whispered to Godfrey, releasing him from duty. 'Probably…'

It was hilly around there, and I was getting no sense of travelling across the landscape. Nor would I for weeks to come. Steve was a keen guide, but I wasn't really listening, intent as I was on the square of map at hand. We swapped anecdotes from the trail but were each just waiting to interject with a memory of our own. Steve told me his vital statistics: 53 days, two rest days, longest day 30 miles. I had none. No milometer, no path, scant idea of space and time. Just a donkey. I felt a little superior.

I arrived at my sister's friend's house. Holly was all heart, and had prepared for our arrival by laying scaffolding boards over the cattlegrid to her house. She was a fan of horses, and took Chico's rope, letting him walk all over the garden, enjoying him being in charge. I took off his packsaddle, made the corral, filled the water bowl, measured out his handfuls of food, scooped some poo from the lawn and offered to take him off her hands – walking slowly around the garden at his insistence looked pretty arduous to me. But Holly was enjoying it. I felt like a tired mum.

Holly's neighbour Leanne came over and gave Chico a long massage, her after-dinner fag in the corner of her mouth and a faraway look in her eyes, until he brought her round with a vigorous bite of gratitude, right on the breast. I sat at the outside table, watching them love my donkey but unable to participate. I must be a bad person. I was much more interested in my own dinner, and a shower, and checking the map. I did often feel guilty while I went off to seek the pleasures that made the effort all worthwhile – hot baths and cold beers and conversation. Reading and swimming, telling jokes and making food, lying in the sleeping bag, looking at the map – Chico had none of those things.

Along the north coast we had begun to be friendlier to each other. He had started it, I was sure – he began to be nice to me, and in return I felt warmer towards him. Giving him a good rub was the one thing he'd really enjoy at the end of a long day, a way I could show him I appreciated him. I *did* appreciate him, and yet my arms felt weighed down at the prospect – my heart closed.

'But your relationship is practical,' said Holly, kindly.

Later, as I looked through the bags for something or other, I came across a clipping from Chico's first farriering on the Lleyn. It was a crescent of hoof, strangely beautiful with its tiny white rays, undeniably organic, like the veins of a sea creature, or salt flats seen from space. I'd saved it – maybe I was a little sentimental after all. Now it was all shrivelled; I threw it into the shrubbery and carried on looking for some lost thing.

There's no such thing as time or space, said Holly, just the experiential understanding of the one-ness of everything. This was a relief, because it was already long after breakfast – pushing lunch, in fact – and Chico wasn't even saddled up yet. 'There's just vertical time – everything is now,' she said.

'It's a big thing to take in, I know,' she continued, 'but once the walls in your mind – the ones that say "I am Holly" are gone, there's so much more. If you are happy with what you have, that's great, but any time you want more, it's there.' She sat back and smiled beatifically. She and her partner Nick were planning to open a centre based on *A Course in Miracles*, a book of spiritual transformation written by an American psychologist taking dictation from an inner voice that she identified as Jesus. I was sceptical, although Holly looked so happy I tried not to be rude.

As I walked on, I mulled over the moment, which for me pleasantly contained an ice-cream that Chico was trying to lurch towards. It was a very long time since I'd lived so much in the moment, probably not since primary school, if then. My moment extended to making sure I had some sort of supplies for breakfast, lunch and dinner tomorrow, maps for the next week, a vague idea of the next few days' walk. Refilling my shampoo bottle, getting hold of food for Chico, charging up electronic things…

It was a full moment, only about three days long in its crystal clarity. The future unfolded path by path; my old Filofax had a three-month stretch of blank pages already; my ailing bank account was keeping a dossier, recording card payments in successive Spars, village by village around the country. Generally I didn't bother looking up the weather – we were walking regardless.

It was glorious, utterly self-centred, simple and immediate. It was a bit scarier without Rhys, but I was tough enough now to walk without a destination, and it was even more exhilarating alone.

But my moment was enormous, *cavernous*, and choked with a thicket of the past and the future when compared with Chico's moment. I couldn't say whether he had a concept of past and future but just wasn't pursued or driven by them because he'd already achieved perfect enlightenment. Or whether it was more that he was a donkey. He certainly had memory – if dogs had frightened him yesterday he was always more wary of any we passed today. But he didn't do forward planning. He welcomed the rain mac if it was raining already, but wouldn't let me put it on him in advance – the weather app might say it was going to rain at 2am, but as far as Chico was concerned, it wasn't raining on his moment. I regularly woke to the very first drop of rain on the tent, and went out to trail him around a dark field, waving his mac.

I was amazed by him, really. He walked without an idea of where we were heading, why we had come, when we would be stopping, whether we would ever be dry again, what would be for lunch. In fact, he knew very well what would be for lunch.

He'd spot something – thistles, vetch, plantain, ash branches – and that would be that: lunchtime. Maybe that was why he ate like he did, so single-mindedly – he could never be sure that there would be another meal.

A whole new level of the human brain must have been fired up when the first bag was invented, and along with it the concept of planning, saving, and deferred gratification – perhaps the whole idea of a tangible future.

We were very, very different animals, my travelling companion and me.

TWENTY-NINE

Chico and I had still hardly walked alone, and Chantelle and Chris were our next companions. They'd seen us on the road, stopped the car, and arranged to join us for a walk the next day. Chantelle was South African, tall and skinny, with long dreadlocks and Hindu deities on her T-shirt. Chris wore combat trousers, and his love for Chantelle on his sleeve.

We walked up the steep hill out of the Ceiriog valley, through narrow bridleways worn deep between ancient tree roots, so totally overgrown that they'd become murky, covered tunnels. We were clutched at by cat-toothed brambles, spanked in the shins by nettles, sweating from the inside, drizzled on from the outside, pursued by flies.

Chantelle had just arrived back from South Africa – her exile, she called it. The two of them revelled in being together again, calling each other husband and wife. Chantelle loved Wales – the mists! The rain! Then, 'Oh no – lambs! I missed the lambs, didn't I?' she realised suddenly. She'd lived in a caravan near Llangollen for a while, and during the heavy snow she had just sat inside it, the caravan surrounded by a puddle of meltwater. Then she met Chris and his car, and they could drive out and enjoy it. 'I love the snow!' said Chris.

He'd been brought up in Llangollen, 'a real border town', and they lived in nearby Glyn Ceiriog now. When we reached the top of the hill, he made an attempt to map out the area for me, distant hills in every direction, the soft light moving across them. We were in the Berwyn range, apparently. It was impossible to tell how far away anything was. Every hill changed colour, lit up like an empty dancefloor by momentary breaks in the cloud. Occasionally a quarry or distinctive ridge seemed to be a clue, but by the next breath it had all moved about. To make sense of it and get my bearings I needed a much larger scale map, but I was clinging to my 8km square, charting my floundering way through the choppy contour lines. I missed having the sea always on my left, where I could see a headland in the far distance and work my way towards it, reach it, and then watch it get folded away behind me. Identifying a particular hill was as futile as trying to name a wave.

Chris knew the land from running all over it; he wanted to run the full length of Offa's Dyke one day. Right now, though, he was fresh from the trauma of form-filling and bureaucracy. He and Chantelle had got married in South Africa, but they were having trouble satisfying visa requirements to keep her in Britain. He'd got a job instead of being self-employed and they were hopeful but exhausted.

We stopped in the grassy middle of a track and I made tea to go with Chantelle's banana cake. Chris rolled a joint and Chantelle found some field mushrooms to take home. I'd been complaining about a mosquito bite on my shin that, for some reason, had caused my whole calf to swell up, hot and tight, and Chantelle advised me to sting it with a nettle. I couldn't bring myself to, but got her to do it.

'My wife's a witch!' said Chris, and we all laughed as Chantelle's choice of nettle didn't seem to be a stinger. 'This nettle's broken!' she declared.

'Shouldn't you be chanting?' he said. Urtification, it's called, and it either reduces the inflammation, increases the bloodflow, or tricks the nerves by distracting them with the new pain. In any case it seemed to work, and having my sore leg stroked with a nettle by a gentle woman on the top of a mountain was very nice.

We were thankfully done with our picnic when a Land Rover pulled up on the farm track, and the farmer said, 'You're trespassing! The bridleway is one field to the south! This is my private track.' He was pretty hostile, and suddenly I saw us through his eyes – a bunch of crusties. Chris replied cheerfully, clearly well used to compensating for his appearance. He apologised for the mistake, pointed to where I was untethering Chico, and told him about our walk. The farmer had an Eisteddfod parking-permit sticker on his windscreen, so as he passed me I waved and called, 'Diolch yn fawr!' through the window. Thank you very much!

He stepped on the brake and snapped to attention. 'Siarad Cymraeg?'

Yes, I speak Welsh, sort of – rusty, I said. And we had a chat which began with me instinctively, shamefully, distancing myself from Chris and Chantelle: 'I just met these two on the road yesterday,' and then, angry with myself, 'They brought me banana cake; they live in Glyn Ceiriog. They've been showing me the beautiful landscape you all have up here!'

It was chilly up at 400m and, as I began to think about where I'd stay, we passed a riding stables. Chantelle and Chris hung back while I went to say hello, sitting discreetly at the side of the road so as not to influence my chances. What a strange and sad reality they'd made for themselves.

And yet, as I talked to the sudden crowd of curious teenagers and stablehands at Spring Hill Riding School, I was aware of my own effortful first impression, honed over the months – friendly and a bit silly, walking with a donkey, seeking assistance but not desperate, cheerful and unthreatening.

I took Chico a few miles further to the riding school's camping field but came back to pitch my tent by the stables in order to take them up on the offer of pizza. I found myself putting off leaving Chico, and sat with him until he wandered away from me. Then when I got up to leave, he came straight back over, so we sat a little longer. As I finally left, he looked at me from the corner, his white arrow-shaped face visible long after the rest of him had faded into the shadows of a tall fir tree. And he brayed. It was like... like a big chicken caught in a rusty bellows: wheeze-ugh-ugh-ugh! A mile further on and I heard him again, this time with a much better-constructed bray, a real hee-haw. I celebrated my short walk of freedom back to the stables by taking a route with three stiles and a kissing gate, but it didn't alleviate the funny, itchy feeling in my heart.

A dozen 13-year-old girls took my mind off it. They were at the stables for a teenagers' riding holiday which would end with a two-day trek and overnight camp. Steve the stable-owner catered for them with a barbeque and bonfire, burgers and marshmallows – it sounded brilliant. 'Most of them love it, but some totally freak out,' he said.

I'd not really met a teenage girl since I was one myself – what strange threshold dwellers they are. I'd been invited for dinner: platters of pizza triangles that kept coming, and industrial water carriers of pink and orange squash. The girls were all different heights but slender, with sweet, fresh faces, long blonde hair that was wriggly from elaborate French plaits, and adult teeth that they'd not all fully grown into yet. A few had brand-new breasts under one-piece pyjamas, some still looked like children in jodhpurs and pink wellies. They told me about their favourite horses, and sang songs, and before long wandered off to brush their teeth.

I slept on the front lawn, spread-eagled on top of the high, round hilltop. Above my eyelids was the tent and above the tent was the woolly cloud cover, but above that a meteor shower danced around the earth. Steve had told me that his camping field was on the Dee/Severn watershed – spit on one side and it would eventually wash out in North Wales; spit on the other and it would head the way we were going – to the Severn estuary.

My little sister Naomi turned up to walk for a few days, and we consolidated our stuff in the field. I'd been worried about her visiting and had found myself discouraging her in the preceding weeks. 'It's pretty rainy, but do come anyway! I'm sure it will be fine, but we can't count on shops or shelter, and we can't load Chico up any more, so you'll have to carry everything you bring, and it might be really cold, or hot, and I don't know where we'll camp. It's pretty hard work. But do come!' She's not known for travelling light (she often takes her favourite saucepans to other people's houses), doesn't much like roughing it, and generally turns up without waterproofs. Most of all, I'm just not very nice to her, which is hard work for both of us.

I've been her mean older sister for ever, and she is predisposed to deep analytical discussion about the nature of our souls, so it was a long time ago that I was forced to recognise that the things that frustrate me about her are the things I don't like about myself. Knowing this doesn't make me any better.

And this was a previously untrodden context, having Naomi invite herself into the strange world I had built for myself but where I was far from comfortable. I was inept, and I suppose I just didn't really want her to see me that way. I wasn't sure I had the energy to look after her – it was sink or swim around here, do or die!

She arrived having taken my warnings very seriously, every item of kit and food weighed and considered. She was completely ready, and chipper. She took hold of Chico's rope and led him without concern into a field of cows. A dozen scary cow moments of the past, and various well-rehearsed worst-case scenarios flashed through my mind, but neither she, nor Chico, nor the cows seemed concerned. She tied her waterproof trousers to his packsaddle and I imagined the trouser-based disasters that could ensue. It surprised me that she had come upon this travelling circus, seen it functioning, and assumed that was how it always was. She was unsullied by my fractious history with the beast. No wonder she was chipper.

She took the tent down wrong, and completely disassembled the corral. How confounding! No one could have seen my set-up as a tight ship, but it did appear that along the way I had got myself some routines, which she was breaking merrily. I tried to bite my tongue, but failed, and then apologised, several times a day.

Naomi was keen to lead Chico, but he was not what she expected and she was surprised. He sensed her inexperience and invented a new game – running down hills. It was very annoying and, as we were mostly on roads, dangerous. I saw myself in her – our pet-less childhood had given us no grounding in how to conduct a relationship with an animal. We were both eager to believe that we could do anything we put our minds to ('Girls can do anything!' said the feminist alphabet wall posters around our childhood bedroom. 'Amy is an architect, Fatima is a farmer…'). But we were both discouraged by Chico, and both took it personally. The difference was that Naomi was willing to think it through, and at the end of her few days with us she would submit her analysis.

In the meantime, we did have fun. We were heading through estate landscapes with the sweeping authority of costume dramas and heading for a village called Llanfyllin. We'd been told it had a hippy contingent that would take kindly to a visiting donkey. On the way, we snuck into the corner of a field to have our lunch. I'd usually find somewhere less obviously owned, but the borderlands didn't seem to have such crannies. I had a quick pee before we packed up and carried on, and at the next house a woman standing on the road said, 'Did you shut the gate?'

Oh dear. Yes – sorry.

'Do you need to use the toilet?'

Um… no, not any more… I guess that was a pointed question. But we must have looked contrite enough, and Carol invited us to stop for a cup of tea on the garden wall, served up by her young daughter Charlotte. They told us about the snows of late March – it was less than four months ago and the horror was still fresh. Snowdrifts were over four metres in places, and it got down to minus 10°C. Sheep were covered and lambed under the snow, breathing air through the drystone walls, their lambs freezing to death. Sheds fell down under the weight of the snow, burying sheep that had been brought inside.

'We were lambing wherever we could, all over the place,' said Carol. 'And it's the sheep farmers' harvest, of course. They feed the sheep from November, and there are just a few days when most of the lambing happens...' Her voice betrayed that it was more than the cold economics of the job. The whole area was traumatised by so much recent death, to animals in their care. The powerlessness. People kept mentioning it.

'I had days off school, and we went sledging! We had a cornice!' said Charlotte.

The Llanfyllin Workhouse is an old Victorian poorhouse, a bleak, imposing building where women, men, girls and boys used to be segregated and forbidden from seeing each other. The experience was designed to be such a miserable disgrace as to discourage all but the absolutely desperate. Later it operated as a much-loved care home, which kept running until the 1980s, housing mostly the elderly, but also some single mothers and occasional overnight hobos.

It was now a community arts centre, and when we arrived there was a circus festival setting up; everywhere there were brightly coloured people defying gravity. Bodies, bubbles, hula-hoops and toadstool umbrellas spun around in the air, and good-looking stilt walkers in bowler hats wandered by, finding high Victorian windowsills to perch on, dusting them with their satin bloomers. If only time really could have been vertical for a moment! Imagine the faces of the pauper children, many born in the workhouse to a life of shame and hunger, corn-grinding and stone-breaking, suddenly surrounded by that technicolour rumpus of fun. Even more interesting would be the shock of the circus folk, themselves so accustomed to pursuing enjoyment for its own sake, suddenly plunged into a tight-lipped world of sacrifice and virtue, and required to examine the twenty-first-century devotion to pleasure and personal happiness.

I had a chat with a woman called Felicidad (or Fe, or Fizz, or Fliss. 'I have many names,' she said, and seemed annoyed that I had asked such a mundane question). She crouched before us as only hippies do, wearing a knitted rainbow-striped skirt over her jeans.

'I used to work at a donkey place in the Pyrenees,' she said. She had to take the donkeys who needed a bit more experience out for extra walks – a nice job, she said, but not easy. She was amazed that families just turned up, put their children on the donkeys and set out along precipitous paths, assuming it would all be fine. She paused. 'Hm, I'd forgotten how much donkeys smell like monkeys…' she said thoughtfully, and we were both smelling Chico when Nao reappeared from buying the next map at the village shop and asked why I'd made so little progress in packing up.

Felicidad headed off to find me a wizard, but he wasn't quite ready for wizarding. I decided not to ask if he could mess with time and space for me.

Steve, a cartwheel maker with a workshop in the workhouse, was a New Age traveller. He told me about a time when he'd seen a picture of the common in Talybont – the village where I went to primary school, and that we'd walked through on our second day – on the wall of some fellow travellers' caravan. 'We don't know if it's a real place. It's so beautiful!' they'd said. 'It is real – it's Talybont common!' Steve had told them. They'd all gazed at the magical place.

To think that someone would have a Shangri-La picture of my local village made me laugh. Sure, I liked it there, but it was hardly the promised land. Was it? It was just the place I bought contraband sweets and waited for the school bus.

'So, you're just travelling about a bit with your donkey, are you? That's cool.' Steve wasn't surprised.

It was a simple question, but it blew my mind. Imagine if we *were* just travelling about a bit – how different that would feel from this mission I'd built. There'd be no weekly recalculating of the miles left to go, no nagging worry about that galling 'nearly halfway' that we'd still not reached. I wouldn't be pulled ever onwards by Aberystwyth, the very place I'd left, just because I'd set my mind on it, and told everyone, and made a Facebook page. Or if I *was* particularly drawn to Aberystwyth, I could turn west right then and be home in a fortnight.

I think I tried to carry on the conversation with Steve, admiring his cartwheels, but my mind went on reeling. If we were just wandering about, I'd have to like Chico's company. If I wasn't doing it for the challenge, I'd have to be doing it for the enjoyment. Or just because it was something to do? But it was so hard! Who would choose to do this without purpose? Without the satisfaction of a line on the map, without hourly reward snacks and regular kindly hosts? I wasn't in the moment at all – I was on a mission, and making a mountain out of it.

They must be really rock-hard people, those travellers – as tough as they come. And to be saddled with a social stigma at the same time... Steve smiled at me. He had a pink feather in his beard.

I felt like a tenacious, frostbitten mountaineer digging deep into my psychological reserves on the slopes of Everest, while Steve was a Nepalese teenager in wellies who'd come up after dinner to build a snowman and look at the sunset.

THIRTY

Chico, Naomi and I walked on, along some beautiful bridleways. One wound through a scene like an alpine oil painting, another cut across a wooded bank so steep that Naomi held her breath all the way up, watching how close Chico's hooves were to the abyss. I was glad that she was coming to understand that we were always a mere heartbeat away from disaster – at least it made me feel less alone.

We weren't far from Chico's previous home, Stonehill Donkeys, and we'd met three people – including the donkey masseuse Leanne – who had previously worked there. It was too far away for us to drop by, but as we walked I told Nao about the day I'd bought Chico, only 14 weeks before.

I'd been nervous, fanning myself with £375 in tens and twenties, and Dave had invited Dad and me in for a post-sale cup of tea. In his kitchen, all of us slightly high with the thrill of the transaction, he and Margaret had told us about the dangerous donkey who'd become notorious in Shropshire a few years before. The donkey turned up at livestock auctions, his temperamental nature undeclared, as various people bought him and then palmed him off again. Then it was Dave's turn: 'I said to Margaret, "I think I've bought that bad donkey that's been doing the rounds." We'd had him for a few weeks and had the grandchildren riding him in the yard and everything, but then one day I walked in and he went for me. He grabbed my shoulder in his teeth, lifted me clean off the ground, and shook me. He was wild!' Dave wasn't a small man. He'd called the Donkey Sanctuary and offered to have the donkey put down, but they took him instead.

'It was them who named him Gnasher. If you give a donkey to the sanctuary, they write with news every so often. For a few years I got letters telling me who he'd mauled that month – the postman, the farrier, the vet… I reckon he might have had a tumour that put pressure on his brain every so often.'

Dad and I had made all the right noises at Dave's story, but secretly I wondered whether he always rolled that tale out for people who'd owned a donkey for less than the time it took to drink one cup of tea. Then Margaret wrote me a receipt with the words 'Can be returned in same condition' at the bottom, and we went gingerly on our way.

'I feel strange, owning an animal. Like, what gives me the right to *own* another living creature?' I'd said to Dad as we drove away.

'He's your servant, Hannah. A tool for a job,' said Dad, but then pulled over frequently to feed Chico bits of carrot over the trailer door.

It rained in brief showers, the sort we could see coming at us across the valleys – patches of denser, shimmery wetness like shoals of fish. A breeze dried us off in between the dousings.

A man on a quadbike stopped to admire Chico. Arwel had a huge grin, red cheeks, and silver chest hair creeping out of the collar of his waxed jacket. His short silver hair and black eyebrows were wet through, but he didn't seem to notice. His beautiful black horse, Rosie, stamped and swaggered back and forth on the other side of the hedge as we chatted in the lane, and Chico responded, bravely.

He had a Welsh accent of the sort that was pretty rare around there. I switched us to Welsh, and we struggled along for a few minutes – Naomi even more uncomfortable than me and dropping Spanish words in every so often by mistake. Arwel did that familiar, shaming old thing of switching us back to English.

His family had been farming those parts for five generations, and these days he was rearing animals for halal meat. We were surprised by the unexpected worldliness. His best friend owned an abattoir in the Midlands, so they worked together. 'Modern Muslims generally prefer animals to be stunned before slaughter,' he said. We chatted for ages, Arwel unconcerned by the rain falling on our heads. He pointed out one of his fields on my map, six miles further on, and said we were welcome to let ourselves in when we got there.

Naomi is always keen to articulate feelings, even – or especially – uncomfortable ones; I squirm like a child when she does it. As we were saying goodbye to Arwel, she said, 'I'm sorry that my Welsh wasn't good enough to sustain a conversation, Arwel,' and to our surprise he replied, 'No, no, it's me! I haven't spoken Welsh since school – I find it very difficult! *I'm* sorry!'

When we got there, Arwel's field was perfect – apart from being mostly on a slope, in an area that the map called Freezeland, and under a productive raincloud. We tied the tent door to the corral sticks to make a tiny awning, under which Naomi deftly assembled a superb meal of dehydrated mashed potato, vegetables and mackerel. I'd never thought of Smash before, but it was a brilliant idea, and when she went home at the end of the next day, she left me the rest of her supply.

The next morning she stuffed her wet socks into a pocket of her backpack, trying to hide how glad she was to be going home. 'Cheesy! Wet! Socks! Get in there!' Spells of hot sunshine cheered us up though, as did another long bridleway. Naomi was doing well leading Chico, but then we stepped into a field with a huge herd of cows. They were black and ginger, running about in excitement before thankfully herding themselves into an adjoining field. I ran ahead and shut the gate after them, and then looked them right in their funny big eyes, their ears flapping, and their pointy grey tongues probing their rubbery nostrils, spilling strings of drool as they came up to the gate to investigate me. Nao tried to lead Chico to the far corner of the field – I was going to open the cows' gate again when Chico was out of harm's way. But he stopped, and wouldn't move another step. 'What's wrong with him now?' I shouted up at them. Nao figured it out. 'I think he's waiting for you! He doesn't want to leave you behind with all of those cows!'

It did seem to be true. As soon as I reached him he walked on again, and after we'd got him through the next gate I ran back down to release the cows, feeling all warm that he cared about my wellbeing.

We walked on through a farmyard, and the farmers, who called each other Mr Evans and Mrs Evans, filled a bucket with water for Chico. It had a hole in it, and Nao and I sang, 'There's a hole in my bucket, dear Liza, dear Liza,' for a few miles. A man in a shiny Jaguar leaned out and interrupted us.

'So, how long will it take you to get to Swansea then?' he said.

'I guess… a month, perhaps,' I said. It seemed a very long way away, and I was hazy about the southeast corner of Wales.

'I'll be there tomorrow, dear!' he said, and drove off.

Nao and I tied Chico to a tree in the corner of a field and had a thoughtful late lunch before we arrived at Welshpool, where her walk would come to an end. It had been good. She had been kind and capable and, apart from her cold feet at night, not whingey at all. And I had – I think – apologised for anything sharp I'd said and not meant, and, under her tutorage, scrutinised anything sharp I'd said and meant. But she'd still found it very tough. She ushered in her debrief.

'I had no idea it would be like this. It's been such a struggle. For my self-esteem, most of all – trying to do something and failing all the time.' She looked pretty stricken, as she thought back over it. 'Not being able to control him, or communicate with him… And when it was going wrong, I felt like *hurting* him sometimes – I got really angry! It was hard to control *myself*, let alone him! It scared me to feel like that… I felt quite bleak.'

She thought for a moment.

'That powerlessness… I guess it's all my own issues. If I was a different sort of person perhaps I'd have shrugged it off, wouldn't have taken it to heart. But maybe Chico wanted to teach me a lesson.'

I knew exactly what she meant, and what she'd felt, and we sat together awhile picking over our spread of emotions. Her bitterness was still raw but tempered with relief at leaving, and I had a kind of sweet release of having my darkest moments understood, plus a little self-satisfaction at being slightly more competent than her. We are all complicated animals.

I once heard an ocean-rowing athlete claim that his successes were simply down to not thinking too much. And when I was young I read some of Ffyona Campbell's books as she walked around the world, charging along at up to 50 miles a day, blistered and determined. Her first continent had been fuelled, she said, by anger towards her father; once she'd resolved that and found some peace, the second walk was much, much harder.

Being single-minded and combative helps crowd out the doubt, I suppose. But Naomi is all nuance. She firmly believes that honesty is her compass in life – being true to herself, and clear with other people. She meditates, she doesn't drink, she puts a lot of time into analysing her emotions.

I'm somewhere in between. I'm no unwavering ocean rower, but I do like to bolster my emotions with good company, by singing songs or listening to the radio. I sometimes pretend I'm cheerful, and that often does the job. And when all else fails, if those emotions are a bit too troublesome, I like to pacify them with a stiff drink.

Our next walking companion was already on her way, with lots of booze and a holiday spirit. As it turned out, her visit would be a welcome interval before this whole shonky parade ground to a halt.

THIRTY-ONE

Philine got off the train at Welshpool station, but found herself enjoyably waylaid as the only taxi in town had been taken. Two men on their way to a stag do had also been angling for the taxi, and took her on a spontaneous pub crawl of the town while they all waited for it to return. She rolled up at my tent, late, enthusiastic and excited to meet Chico.

She had several bottles of wine, a few beers, a carton of pink grapefruit juice, some brandy, posh snacks and no backpack. 'I thought we could put everything on Chico,' she said. 'Isn't that what he's for?' We had a midnight feast, sharing wine out of a cup and making light of the world as the very full river Severn surged by the campsite unseen.

It was a relief to have the cover of darkness in the busy campsite – the school holidays had begun and the place was full of children who had already got themselves deep into a multilateral feud, with Chico as the principal asset to be fought over, and me as some kind of reluctant adjudicator.

A group of scouts were under the impression that they were Chico's official keepers because I'd left them a note with my phone number earlier in the evening when I'd had to leave Chico to get supplies. Three girls from another field thought that they were, because they had requested permission to guard him and I had granted it, unaware of the impending turf war. They had also given me a bead with which to mend my wind-up radio; my debt of gratitude strengthened their claim.

A new delegation came from somewhere else entirely to report that they'd seen some other children slapping Chico's back while I was away handwashing my appalling socks. This was the catalyst, and as soon as they had retreated a little, the scout bunch stalked up to tell me that the corner lot – as yet neutral – were no good, and that one of their own scouts was 'very violent and stealing sweets'. The scout leaders were no help, wandering past with a huge, double-ended saw with vast teeth, and a coil of rope, to find some dead wood for the fire.

The bead girls ran over to tell me that one of the scouts had said that one of them was 'an S-L-U-T, just because I fed Chico a piece of tree, like you said I could!'

I wanted no part of it, but trying to sympathise with them all wasn't working very well. I reiterated each time that no one should feed Chico anything, unless they absolutely had to, in which case small bits of the willow were permissible. I had a vague memory that Tamlin had said willow was alright in small quantities. When I got back from filling my water, all of the factions were back in their corners, but the willow looked like it had been stripped by locusts, and there was a suspicious small pink cake on the floor near Chico's corral.

I was just done laying out my washing in the fast-retreating sun when a single small boy appeared on the battleground, wearing plastic sunglasses with star-shaped frames and a big football stuffed up his small T-shirt. His toes were pointed slightly inwards, and he spun his shoulders back and forth a little as he spoke, although whether it was nervousness or swagger, I couldn't tell.

'Can I ride your donkey?' he said.

He was very insistent, and specific in his request. He said he'd come a long way, and just wanted to borrow Chico to ride back to his tent.

'I want to ride a horse really,' he said. Then, with a nonchalant cowboy-like disregard for his physical safety that sat well on his skinny three-foot-high shoulders, he added, 'And if I fell off, I'd just climb on another horse and keep on going.'

I encouraged him to sally off and took my couscous to the far edge of the field to eat in the last bit of sun. I was slightly too close to the corner lot I had been warned about, and a grown-up envoy in a fleecy one-piece came to invite me over for a drink, making it clear that declining was not an option. They were from Widnes, six kids and seven adults although it felt like more of both. They had dozens of tents and toys, and I was given a chair and a shot of something cheap, sour and apple-flavoured. I admired the woman's onesie, wondering if I could get one for the autumn leg of the journey (we were still not halfway, and the spectre of walking in winter was beginning to bother me. The last shreds of the evening sun were still hot, but the shadows had a new chill). 'I don't even have to take it off to go to the bog!' she said, and demonstrated by deftly unzipping the flap across her bum, and wiggling her buttocks in their lacy thong.

A three-year-old called Isobel began rolling on the ground, screaming because her mother Ellie wouldn't give her a sip of Malibu and Coke. Ellie didn't look much older than the oldest of the scouts. 'Oh, give her a slug!' said a man who I assume was Isobel's dad, and Ellie finally gave in, saying, 'One sip then, Isobel! First you'll have to give me your dummy…'

I stood up to go, but some sort of Jägerbomb was handed over, the bitter liquor in a plastic shot glass, suspended in the energy drink. I drank it, enjoying the thorough anti-wholesomeness of energy drinks before bed.

Everyone was chain-smoking fags, except for the woman who was sitting on an inflatable chair. She was smoking an e-cigarette instead – a wise move, I thought. They asked about the walk, and were incredulous.

'How can you manage 1000 miles when I go crazy after a few miles in the car…'

'Well, that's sort of the point,' I began. 'It's much better than driving—'

'… with these two saying, "Are we nearly there yet?" after ten minutes!'

'Yes,' I said, 'I have so little to worry about in that way. Walking is so slow and thoughtful and calm…' I sensed I'd lost them. 'And I haven't been in a traffic jam for three months! Or had an email! Or a parking ticket!' They looked a little more convinced.

A small boy wandered past with a balloon, and the 'give her a slug' man bit it, making it burst. Then he hung a handbag of not-yet-inflated balloons over the boy's shoulder, and said gleefully, 'Now you look like a poof!' The boy wandered stoically on, blowing up balloons and trying to bite them.

I made my escape, full of brightly coloured chemical alcohol, and went back to wait for Philine in my tent. The water was rising in the river as the day's rain ran off the mountains – I'd chosen a tree on the opposite riverbank to mark its progress against, as a warning in case we had to vacate suddenly. The train to Aberystwyth from Shrewsbury and Birmingham – my usual route across Wales – passed every two hours and blew its horn. We could always just head that way, 50 miles back home. Even that sounded a little daunting, and yet Chico and I were about to overshoot, and attempt to take in the rest of the borderlands, industrial South Wales, the estuaries of Carmarthenshire, and the great, long, twisting coastline of Pembrokeshire. It was inconceivable, and at this rate it was going to be very cold by the end. It was cold now, on a clear August evening – I was layered up in almost all of my clothes.

Chico was weighed down. Rhys had done us a food drop, leaving two weeks' worth of donkey food and a bag of treats from Dad's Christine's garden, including a bright yellow courgette the size of a small marrow. Chico's saddlebags were 11kg each, which made it a coordination challenge to lift them onto him without the packsaddle being dragged down to one side. But once laden he didn't seem concerned.

I was so thrifty that it didn't cross my mind to throw away some of the minibar we now carried. Thrifty and thirsty… We stopped after a few hours and had wine and quiche for lunch by a field trough. Chico merely wet his lips. It was a beautiful day, made more so by the wine. A dramatic cloudscape brought occasional drizzle and washes of sunshine that lit up the fields of crops; a watery rainbow glimmered across the land. A bright green field of rippling, feathery crops had a dead oak in the centre, like a shipwreck at sea, bare branches poking jaggedly in all directions. Tall flouncy pink flowers took up whole banks – I'd learn later that they were rosebay willowherb. And then the blackberries began, like little love letters from autumn, bittersweet in both ways.

The market town of Montgomery was having a fun day – we could hear the music across the fields. We avoided it, not yet recovered from Welshpool and the campsite. Instead we opted for the little village of Church Stoke, and a few bottles of cider in a pub.

Over a few days we gained height, the crops giving way to livestock, and no option but to climb high and drop low in between. We were in the Clun Forest, and it was hard work. The alcohol wasn't really helping. Fields were perfectly ploughed, like they were spread with chocolate, and in the distance cornfields glowed as if they were lanterns. Everything else was green, farmland in every direction. Someone told us about the 'Radnorshire gate' – field gates held closed with twists of barbed wire. We slipped through a few, making illicit shortcuts. It was a quiet landscape, more cows than people, but everything meticulously cultivated.

I declared that we were crossing the tropic of Aberystwyth. Were we halfway now? Pembrokeshire was a pretty big landmass with a particularly large estuary, but then the north had included the Lleyn Peninsula and Anglesey… I couldn't be sure. We'd not reached the halfway point of the Offa's

Dyke Path yet. Anyway, why did it matter? We had a beer and toasted the halfway mark in case, feeling briefly jubilant in the sunshine. Then we strolled down into the Clun Valley, where we found a campsite that let us stay despite oddly being closed so the owners could have a summer holiday. The grass was a perfect lush carpet, unmown for weeks and six inches tall, and Chico had the run of the field – stalking around and chewing furiously like he'd never seen grass before. Philine turned cartwheels. Chico began rolling and enjoying our enthusiastic praise, and Philine provided his internal monologue: 'I don't know if you saw that just now, but I rolled right over, *both* ways? Good skills, eh? HOOF FIVE!' She high-fived the air in his direction.

Philine certainly didn't suffer from Naomi's accursed introspection. She'd come to quite like Chico, but she never let him affect her mood. The fun things had been fun, and the hills had been a bit much, but hey, she was leaving in the morning, so who cared?

THIRTY-TWO

Clun Valley did not want to give us up. Perhaps if it hadn't been called Clun – such a congealing, dull thump of a name – I wouldn't have minded being stuck there. It was certainly pretty. But as soon as Philine's taxi accelerated out of view, I felt lonely.

Chico had chosen to be near us all morning, but the instant Philine had gone, he turned bad. He wouldn't come for his food, so I eventually took it to him, but in his greedy field of perfect grass it must have been a bit like offering a dry cracker to a five-year-old in a candyfloss factory. He definitely didn't seem to think much of me. I picked up the packsaddle and he walked purposefully to the other side of the field. I was a bit worried – this was unusual.

Even if Chico settled down into a browsy, lacklustre mood, he was always – absolutely without fail – very quick for the first ten minutes. Too quick, really. We learned right at the beginning to keep the corral up or the gate closed until every single other thing had been done: bags packed and loaded onto him, water bottles filled, boots on, maps checked, hosts hugged, and… release the beast! We'd race along with him, knowing better than to try and curb him, until his speedy thrill of freedom subsided into the slight disappointment of another day of the same, made bearable by hedgerow distractions.

On this bad Clun Valley day I managed eventually to bully him forward in the field just enough that he could see the gate that I then went and opened, noisily and with theatrical gestures. It worked – he was curious enough to move his hooves through it and onto the road. His thrill of freedom was very brief, though. We got to the far side of the valley, 200m away, and Chico stopped.

He was given to stopping – this I knew. It shouldn't have been a surprise. And yet he hadn't stopped since that day on the wet Ruabon mountain. All the time with Naomi and then with Philine, he'd walked. Even back on Ruabon I'd sensed it was rain-related – a weather-specific refusal. Before then there'd been unpalatable bridges and rivers and gaps in the fence, but they were all physical obstacles and going back was always an option, however much trouble that would cause. Not since the end of the Lleyn Peninsula had he stopped with such absolute but unattributable certainty.

The effect, whenever it happened, was very perturbing. It was as if an electromagnet had been switched on beneath him. He was immobile, and I couldn't go further from him than the length of the two-metre lead rope. I was anchored. I was like a goblin with one foot nailed to the ground, hopping around, screeching and beseeching.

With every last dreg of will I managed to get him as far as the turn-off to the bridleway that ran through a farmyard, where a farmer was stacking up giant bales with a tractor. I opened the gate and we began heading up the hill, never more than five steps at once. It took arduous hours. Was he ill? Had we overloaded him so much that he was exhausted or sore? He'd been up much bigger hills over the last few days, but then this one was forming a particularly off-putting barrier – 200m high and stretching as far as we could see to east and west. And only just after breakfast. And when breakfast had been such a supremely delicious field, and there was so much of it left…

We got halfway up the hill, each step hard won. His body language was insolent and uncommunicative, but every now and then his great, velvet chin quivered, just like a child about to cry. I hardened my anthropomorphic heart.

Then he looked up the hill, looked at me, wrenched the rope from my hand and ran all the way back down to the bottom, his saddlebags bumping and rattling, sometimes treading on the rope, jerking his chin to the ground, graceless and desperate. I lumbered after him, my own backpack working against me.

The farmyard gate stopped his progress before the road, thankfully. I took his rope and let us through and then, for lack of anything else to do, tried the two roads that went over that side of the valley, to no avail.

I could see the previous night's campsite and Chico probably could too. The owner drove past, wound down the window and said to my hot, stricken face, 'Oh dear. You're welcome back at ours!' I thanked her, and knew there was no way we were going back – I'd rather sleep where we stood than suffer the indignity of putting the tent back up in the same place.

And that's pretty much what happened. We were back at the farmyard, and had established that he would not go up the bridleway, or in either direction along the road. We had tried everything and we were stuck.

I asked the bale-moving farmer, Ben, if we could camp right there, in the corner of the farmyard where bits of tractor went to die. My donkey and I hated each other and, short of asking to borrow a gun, I couldn't think of anything else to do. I was spent. Thankfully he said yes.

There was no joy in making camp when the last one was less than half a mile away, tired though I was. I corralled Chico carelessly into the corner, where he promptly rolled in a cowpat – some sort of resentful dirty protest, I expect. Then I left our stuff in a pile, fed up with it all and the whole stupid *everything*, and hitched a lift on Ben's tractor into Clun.

It was hard to stay miserable on a tractor ride, and even more so when he insisted on taking me right onto the main street, met another tractor coming the other way – both negotiating their enormous trailers onto the pavements of the Norman streets – and brought Clun to a standstill. I slid down and found that the pub served homemade black-pudding scotch eggs and local jerky, as well as their own ale. By the time I got a lift back with a nice man from the pub, I was almost cheerful.

That horrible donkey was still there, lurking in the dark. I put up my tent on the slope and spent the night bracing myself against rolling downhill and listening to tawny owls hooting in the chilly, misty moonlight.

I woke up feeling achy and nervous. Would he go? Should I bother packing up camp? I did, and rigged Chico up, trying to be nice to him. I'm sure he could tell that my every muscle was tense. I left the bags behind, opened the bridleway gate, and – nothing. Nothing had changed. We were in exactly the same bleak position. I tied him to the gate and walked away from him, without a plan, pathetic sobs of total impotence forcing their way out of me. He brayed at my retreating back, a miserable wrenching noise that was so like the one I was making that it just made me cry harder.

Should I call around to see if I could find a field where Chico could rest? Should I get a vet? If only there was breakdown cover for donkeys. I still didn't have any phone reception; maybe I could borrow a landline. I looked in the window of the farmhouse, feeling a deep envy for all of the things of a non-nomadic life – the jar of kitchen implements, the beautiful hanging baskets, the everyday disorder of living.

And then Tess appeared. Farmer, mother of Ben, wearing a T-shirt from some heavy-metal band. She didn't mention my tear-streaked face but asked if she should try walking with us for a little while. I held out no hope whatsoever but was so desperate for any idea that might come even briefly between me and failure that I said yes please – if she didn't have any more important farmery things to do.

She fetched a staff and her little dog Jake, and untied Chico's rope. I opened the dreaded gate, and… Chico walked through it and right up the hill, fast and strong. He hesitated a moment at the previous day's highest point, and then forged forward. Tess, Jake and I had to skip along to keep up.

I hardly dared draw attention to his progress, but kept my eyes forward, my breath held. I couldn't believe that any single step would follow the last, but it did – they just kept coming. In no time we were at the top, and with a gate closed behind us – he couldn't run down again. Level completed! Our bags were all sitting pessimistically in the farmyard, but Tess offered to drive them up to us. She was a cheery angel, claiming she was glad to have been distracted from doing the farm's VAT return.

We were on top of a big plateau now, called Llanfair Hill. There would be no more up that day, just a long flat, followed by a downhill to the town of Knighton. He did it, although I walked very nervously.

In all directions there were beautiful views across the Shropshire Hills, fields like a patchwork quilt in greens and golds, embroidered with stripes of harvesting and ploughing, brocades of old trees and dusty tracks, and fence posts so old and gnarled that the grain stood proud like candlewick.

We passed a crowd of fat lambs, like the stuffing bursting from the quilt, all fuzzy and hemmed into corrugated iron squares while two young men weighed them and sorted them into rough dates of demise. I glared at the wriggling creatures: 'Back off! Don't put my donkey off his unreliable stride! I'll do you in right here!'

The nice man in the pub in Clun had given me several numbers for emergency refuge, in case my donkey broke down again; smallholders I never met because we did make it to the campsite in Knighton. The last stretch had a few small uphills along the road, which I managed by holding Chico close so he couldn't graze at all, and then snapping hazel branches from the hedge and holding them in front of his nose. When he grew bored of hazel and began to stall, just as the road wound uphill one last time, Steve – the unofficial secretary of the coast path – and his fiancée Liz appeared ahead of us. I kissed them, and handed Chico to Liz.

Sure enough, he walked fine with other people around. I suppose I'd hardly led him at all – there'd been Carol, Steve, Chantelle, Chris, Naomi and Philine to do that, and before that Rhys, Mum and Dad. Did he think we'd left Philine behind by mistake yesterday? Or was it just that he liked being number three, a junior, following the momentum of a group of people? That was sensible, in a way – two can be risky. What if one of us got eaten? And when things grind to a halt and communication breaks down, two is much, much lonelier than one.

THIRTY-THREE

Steve and Liz were just passing; I had to bite my tongue not to beg them to stay. The worst and weirdest of it all was that no one who'd walked with us could see anything but a happy strolling donkey. I felt like I might be unhinged, or in some sinister fairytale.

I put my tent up in the campsite – a simple field-and-loo affair for walkers, with the Heart-of-Wales train line running along one side. We were right on the Offa's Dyke Path and, as walkers came by to meet Chico, I realised how sociable it could have been if we'd only been able to walk on the proper path.

The next morning we were joined on the road by a woman called June who had arrived prepared with boots and walking poles. There was something really reassuring about her. She had silver hair in a bun, kind eyes and a careful way of moving. She'd heard we were in need of walking companions and would set out with Chico and me. I was deeply relieved. Just beyond Knighton were big hills in every direction, and I didn't think we'd make it alone.

As we set out, June told me that she'd had a knee replacement the year before and this was a big deal for her – her first proper walk. She might only make it to the other side of town, she thought. I was grateful for anything. In Knighton she answered people's questions and looked after Chico, tied in the town square, while I bought camping gas and brandy and got the man in the hardware shop to help me fix my radio with a nut and bolt. The radio and the brandy were very important right now – the erratically immobile donkey survival kit. I got back to find a woman from the local paper waiting to take a picture of Chico, June and me.

'There's a lot of metal and plastic,' June said of her knee as we walked on. 'When I kneel it feels like it belongs to someone else. They don't tell you beforehand that you might not be able to kneel. Some people just force it, for religious reasons... For me it's so that I can get down to kiss my dogs.' She gave a little smile. 'They're dachshunds.'

'They couldn't be any lower!' I laughed.

We climbed the steep hill, sweating and chatting and not mentioning her knee or Chico's uncomplaining progress. The views back over yesterday's Llanfair Hill were beautiful – a dark, forbidding landmass, and behind it the scene of Dreaded Clunday.

At the top of Reeves Hill we were walking right on the border, England's Herefordshire to our left, Wales's Powys to our right, Shropshire now behind us. The moody land rolled away in all directions, but up there the fields alongside the ridge road glowed, rays of sun rippling through the tufted barley. Rosebay willowherb lined the road, taller than we were. 'They call it red willa around here,' said June. 'Or fireweed – it does well after a fire.' We were among Marches people, she said, their borderland identity taking precedence over being particularly English or Welsh. I'd heard the accent in Knighton – a hybrid between a lazy, rolling, hay-chewing Bristolian sort of intonation and a singsong Welsh one.

'Ah, purple vetch!' She pointed at a tangle of deep purple flowers and long, dark green leaves on the verge. 'Beautiful! And I don't see it often – the yellow vetch is more common here.' Chico leaned in and, before we could react, ate it.

It was time for June to turn back – she'd come four miles and had all that downhill to do. She was very pleased with her knee, and I was so glad that we were at the top of a hill again, with only flat and down to do alone today. As we geared up to say goodbye, she said, 'I've been trying to think of a song involving a donkey, but I can't think of any, so I'll leave you with an Irish song of farewell.'

Oh, here we go, I thought. Being sung to – that's just the sort of embarrassing, earnest thing Naomi would do. I immediately chastised myself. What a ridiculous thought – open your heart, Hannah! 'Oh, lovely!' I beamed. 'And I'll sing you one back,' I said. 'It's a round, but of course I can only sing one part… I've been singing it to Chico a lot – it's a Goethe quote,' I rattled on. She smiled, then composed herself in a grave and intense sort of way.

And she sang. It was beautiful. It was pure art, an amazing gift, and an expert craft. I didn't want it to end. June marked the time with an internal rhythm that she was anchored by, concentrating, unhurried and unselfconscious. Her voice untethered, soared into the heavy air, to the serious, dark blue clouds and the bright streaks, the low notes combing through the golden barley. She sang the story as if she'd felt every delight and sorrow – a handsome damsel wearing no make-up or jewels, but a Galway shawl, inviting a man back to sing songs with her before he departs, leaving her forever, but remembering always the Galway shawl. It was as if her soul was made out of music and she occasionally opened her mouth and let some out.

I did sing my song to her – like a child giving a finger-painting to a great artist. But like a child covered in paint, there was joy in the doing of it; the outcome, I hoped, wasn't important. It was a song about magic and boldness after all, and June had ushered some magic back into the walk where there had been none for a while.

We shared some flapjack while Chico polished off all of the rest of the pretty vetch, and June wrote down her name for me to look up: June Tabor. 'Singing is what I actually do!' she said.

She turned around and headed back, singing as she went.

As soon as she was out of sight I phoned Dad. Christine was very excited. 'June Tabor? She really is the queen of British folk music! She's largely responsible for having saved and reinvigorated folk music for the nation. I've seen her live whenever I could – she brings such a deep emotion to the room, transports listeners to other worlds and lives. Wow, Hannah!'

Well, to think I'd been discussing animal poo with the queen of folk (Chico's had been rather loose since the rich Clun Valley field, but June's dog was having the opposite trouble). Oh god – and I made her listen to me sing! And her so famous and all! I sang her song for several days, although the range was far too ambitious for me, and the Irish twiddly bits I just warbled. I only stopped when someone pulled over at a junction days later and said, 'I heard you this morning, sort-of-singing past my garden!'

We floated down from the mountaintop to stay in the paddock of June's friend Teddy, a trout farmer, who in turn called ahead and arranged for me to stop for tea with another friend of his and June's – the lead singer of Oysterband, John Jones. Teddy told me that they had walked together to Aberystwyth a few times. 'It's only 45 miles from here, takes us two days. And my daughter sometimes rides her horse to Borth.' The pull west was worse than ever.

Still, the prospect of meeting another famous person kept me heading south, through Presteigne, where no one gave Chico a second glance, and out along the main road for miles. John Jones put Chico in his stable, his horses galloping about the field in excitement. We took tea in the garden with fellow band member Alan Prosser, the chocolate sliding off the biscuits in the heat. I was not living in the moment at all – I sat and sweated as I told John that I was worrying about being cold when the winter came, struggling through short, dark days. He sympathised, raving about the landscape to come if only I could follow the Offa's Dyke Path unhindered. 'Walking's about being free, isn't it?' he said. 'I don't want to break up a partnership, but I'd hate to think you were missing all of this by going around on roads. This is the best bit of Offa's Dyke –

the Wye Valley, the Black Mountains. Hay Bluff! It's seriously steep, and maybe it would do you some good, to experience that.' The thought of our recent six-mile days pained him. 'I'm a fiendishly fast walker,' he said. 'I would want to get on.' He was planning a walk from his house to northern Spain, playing music along the way.

'I'm just suggesting it, as a walker. You're writing your own rules, after all.' Maybe he was right. I'd done it for Anglesey – maybe Chico just needed another break, and I needed the striding energy and the hit of freedom. This limping along was the worst – if Chico wouldn't go, maybe it would be better if he stopped completely.

We managed a few hundred yards before he stalled again. It was an arduous afternoon spent getting to Kington's campsite of obnoxious drunks, who somehow managed to be disinterested and incredulous at once. I slept badly, lying wide awake at 4am, doused in sweat and worrying about the miles left to do, Chico escaping his corral, and his dodgy stomach that I could hear churning squelchily outside. I'd worked out a rough estimate of the miles done (520) and the miles left to do (533). We were pretty much halfway at long last, but far from feeling jubilant, I felt weary and low. I'd thought that things would start easier than they had, and failing that, I'd hoped they'd *get* easier, but this felt like one long slog. And everything I'd managed already, I had to do again. Only in colder, darker weather. This was a ridiculous idea. What the fuck was it for?

THIRTY-FOUR

By the morning things were worse. Now I had a dodgy belly too, and both of us were itching. I'd been bitten by everything going, but these bites were different, in less exposed areas – knicker crevices and the like – and had appeared in the night. I began to get suspicious. I guessed that my own stomach issues might have had something to do with the fact that, since accidentally throwing my penknife away in Flint, I'd been using my farrier's knife for picnics as well as for picking out Chico's hooves. I stopped that.

We struggled up Hergest Ridge in the drizzle, achingly slowly, taking two hours to walk less than a mile. We passed dozens of shaggy wild horses, loose on the open hilltop, that thankfully wouldn't lower themselves to getting het up by some passing strangers. Several fields of cows had been the same, much too well-bred to make a fuss. The people too – it had been a long time since anyone shouted 'Donkey!' from a car window. People seemed to pretend not to see us at all, rather than risk being uncouth. We'd met some really kind people, but it felt like that might have been the sum total of them.

We were accompanied into Hay-on-Wye by Arry, the first person to complete the Wales Coast Path/Offa's Dyke Path circuit. She'd run it in 40 consecutive marathons, arriving back for the day they officially opened the route, in May 2012. Annoying. She was determined to meet Chico and had driven all the way up from Cardiff.

Arry turned out to be really sweet, and ridiculously self-effacing. 'Sure, I ran it, but I didn't do it with a donkey!' she said. We tried to discuss favourite bits, but Arry said she'd hardly seen anything – running was too fast. 'No favourite teashops! No favourite pubs! My best part of the day was sitting in a bath of iced water… I'm going to have to walk it one day.' Arry was, unsurprisingly, a fizzing bomb of energy. She'd brought her smiley boyfriend, carrots for Chico and fudge for me, and her sister Petra stopped by too – she lived nearby and was a trainee vicar. Petra showed what would happen to a fizzy energy bomb if that energy wasn't sloughed off by daily long-distance running. She pulled up by the side of the road and leaped out in her dogcollar and equestrian boots; when I mentioned the itching, she delved into Chico's hair, appearing a moment later with a louse on the end of her finger.

Lice! I declared it time to rest – the Hay Restival. While Chico hung out in a field next to an enormous and very dignified shire/cob cross horse called Mable, and a knee-high shoelace-biting pony called Kiwi, I found a merino wool jumper in a charity shop, re-waterproofed my jacket, and ate some green vegetables. I also had chips in a pub while the publican told me that his mother used to ride a cow. He nodded off on the bar, woke up later, apologised for snoring, and told me all over again about his cow-riding mother. Outside was a poster for a missing tortoise, and I had an amaretti-and-Marsala-flavoured ice-cream. Hay-on-Wye, eh? The great, wide, dark green Wye wound around the town, only inches deep but as full of promise as the Amazon. Canoes launched beneath the bridge and wobbled about in circles as their paddlers learned to balance.

A vet called Barney returned my out-of-hours SOS call and said he'd hidden a tub of louse powder in the undergrowth opposite the vet's practice in town, and could I stick a tenner through the letterbox. In the morning, in a vest, rubber gloves and a face mask, I set to killing hundreds of sucking lice, rubbing the white powder of death into Chico's hair. It was they that had been biting me too, but they wouldn't live on me, so I was thankfully spared the powdering.

After a few days we set off again, but any renewed optimism was swiftly quashed. The rest hadn't done the trick, nor had the massacre of the lousy hitchhikers. I needed a more decisive solution.

During our achingly slow progress up Hergest Ridge I'd conducted a quick poll of anyone who'd answer the phone to see whether, by the unwritten edicts of the walk, I could get away with leaving Chico somewhere and carrying on without him, as John Jones had suggested. Or could I stop for winter when it got too horrible? Or cut off Pembrokeshire? The poll was inconclusive. Rhys said I couldn't leave Chico behind but I could have a week or two off with him. My book-writing friend Lois said I shouldn't let the truth get in the way of a good story. Sarah-the-barrister said I couldn't stop for winter as I'd only confirm everyone's suspicions that UK-based adventures are a bit soft. And Mum thought I could do whatever I wanted, as long as I was happy.

Eventually it occurred to me that Chico might simply be bored. The adrenaline of the first 500 miles had either subsided or just become ordinary. That killer backpack hadn't put in another appearance, although he remained vigilant. He was accustomed to making a home in a new place every night. He liked an adventure, of course, but there had to be some *purpose*. This border landscape was beautiful, sure, but it was a bit… samey. Up a hill and down a hill, then up a hill and down a hill – there was no sense of progress. 'Are you just bored?' I asked. Chico looked blankly back at me. Were these thoughts in his skull, or mine?

I was becoming obsessed with contour lines. I could see walkers on the Offa's Dyke Path at the top of the ridge – it was also the border, running along at 700m. We were at 400m in the valley, and I wasn't in the slightest bit tempted to add any unnecessary hills to the journey, even though I could hear John Jones's lament at my loss – so near, yet so disinclined to incline.

These were the Black Mountains, long ridges running south from their northern escarpments. At the bottom of my map were the towns at the heads of the Valleys – Ebbw Vale, Tredegar and Blaenau. They felt very southern, foreign to me – another part of Wales I knew nothing about, except for a sooty sense of closed coalmines, deprivation and unemployment. Perhaps we were getting somewhere new, albeit as slowly as the glaciers that had formed those ridges.

It was ten days since Dreadful Clunday. It felt like a month.

Then came one of the weirdest overnights of the journey.

Lyny had pulled over as we struggled through Longtown and offered me her seven-bedroom house, with a field outside for Chico. I had said yes, yes, yes, please! She'd called her feller Billy to tell him about me, and on the phone had said, 'It's okay – she's not a hippy!'

'Ah ha! I might be!' I thought, but kept quiet.

Lyny and Billy had moved a few miles away, and this was their old house, in the final stages of being straightened up ready to rent. There wasn't a single piece of furniture left in it, and almost nothing else, except for a gun and a very loud ticking clock. When Billy had washed his paint brushes and left me to it, I walked from room to room, trying to decide which to sleep in. Although the house was enormous, the ticking could be heard from everywhere. On the patio sat their two dogs, Splodge and Deaf Sally. It was three years since they'd moved house, but the dogs refused to go with them. Billy had thrown his hands in the air: 'I've made them a perfect kennel over there, but they're not happy. I locked them in once, so they'd get the idea, but they ate through the plasterboard and ran back here. I'm not quite sure what we'll do when this place is rented.'

Lyny was an estate agent and she sang in the local pub; her business card said 'Lyny' on it. Her dad had called her Lyn, thinking there was no way she could shorten it into something he didn't like, so she lengthened it instead.

Billy could trace his family back to 1680 in the hidden valley on the far side of the ridge. He rented a quarry nearby and had supplied the roof tiles for the twelfth-century Dore Abbey, hand-quarrying the 440-million-year-old Herefordshire sandstone, which, he said, had little fishes in it.

There were surely no ghosts in this house – it was less than 30 years old. I lay in my sleeping bag on my mat on an otherwise uninterrupted expanse of cream-coloured carpet and made myself think that thought a few more times. I got up and opened the door, and then got up and closed it again. As well as the clock, there was a freezer somewhere – the humming was getting louder and louder. There was a bluebottle in there too, my comrade, stuck indoors and rattling against the double-glazing. It was ages before it occurred to me to get up and open the windows – the cold air was like an embrace. Outside, next to the sleeping dogs, was a trampoline, and I considered dragging my bedding out and sleeping underneath it. I wasn't used to indoors – it felt a bit like wearing a motorbike helmet in bed.

THIRTY-FIVE

It was an unremarkable piece of road on which to set the scene for the great turnaround moment of the walk. Right outside Lyny and Billy's house was a small round hill, a mere pimple in the mountainous landscape. The road didn't even go right to the top, it just skirted it. But it did mean that the very first step of the day was an uphill one, and it was one that Chico refused point-blank to undertake. We had come to the final impasse.

In Billy and Lyny's drive the two dogs watched us going nowhere, and on a bank above the road their neighbour hung out her washing. I stood in front of Chico, holding his slack rope, and we looked at each other. Ten minutes of pulling and pleading had passed, and we stood in silence.

It was the road to Ewyas Harold and cars passed every now and then, back and forth, mostly taking it slowly past the stationary donkey while I waved and made an apologetic, grateful face. Chico'd had a long night in a big field, plenty of grass and rest. There was *nothing* wrong with him, I was sure.

I'd had enough.

I hung the lead rope over the arm of his packsaddle, turned, and walked away from him up the hill, leaving Chico and the laundry neighbour looking at each other. I wasn't angry, I was just through with this maddening, demoralising, exhausting stalemate. I had no plan, but for a few seconds it just felt really good to walk at my own first-steps-of-a-new-day pace, the pistons and levers of my body responding to the incline, increasing the traction, my breakfast converting into energy. I peeped over my shoulder, ready to run after him if he'd turned back towards Longtown, but he hadn't, and he wasn't standing still either.

He was walking after me, his eyes trained on my back, his ears pointing forwards and his head bobbing up and down. His front hooves gripped the road and his strong muscles powered him up the hill. I'd not seen this sort of purposeful forward momentum for a long time.

Laundry neighbour was doing battle with a tablecloth, oblivious to the monumental event taking place before her eyes. A squeal of excitement rose in my throat but I stifled it and walked on, keeping an eye on Chico behind me. A car appeared and I ran back down to him and held his rope, mostly for appearances, but then hooked it up again and carried on walking ahead. Chico grazed a little, but when I'd got further than he was happy with, he picked up his hooves and hurried after me.

The next time he hung back I stepped sideways into a layby and heard his clip-clops speed up, an edge of nervous urgency to them. He rounded the corner, caught my eye, and slowed to a walk again in relief.

It was the first time in ages that we had made such communicative eye contact. Suddenly we were comrades! The coercion was over! I felt like a parent whose baby smiles right into their eyes for the first time. Validation! This donkey knew me, he wanted to be walking with me. We strode across the landscape, walking on air.

We were about to join the river Wye in its last due-south dash for the Severn estuary. I couldn't wait to get there – there were bridleways along its wooded banks, and its wide wandering waters would lead us out of these endless green hills and down to the sea, like a tour guide with a little flag. The land was changing again and everywhere around us were tumps – little hills, which look exactly as they sound.

We walked without the rope whenever we could, Chico always behind me.

'There's luvli!' called a voice from a passing car – the first South Walian accent I'd heard.

'Sight for sore eyes!' shouted a second. It looked like the buttoned-up and empty stretches of border were over at last.

'You must have a good relationship with your donkey,' came the third comment, the driver impressed that we were walking along separately but together. I smiled. What a difference a day made.

Chico would stop to sniff poo, stare down sheep, eat a little of everything in the hedgerows. I would forge ahead and get out of breath, and then stop for a short break while he caught up. Even when I took his rope again, he walked comfortably alongside me now.

It seemed we were both equally refreshed by the new terms of our independent relationship.

This page, above: Crosscountry in the Shropshire hills. *Below left:* Chico wanted to go back for more blackberries. *Below right:* Arwel, the friendliest farmer.

Overleaf, above left: Top priority at the Hay Restival. *Above right:* Beautiful old roads. *Below:* Dawn breaking on the Severn estuary floodplain. *Opposite:* The deserted but manicured borderlands.

PART FOUR

THE SOUTH COAST

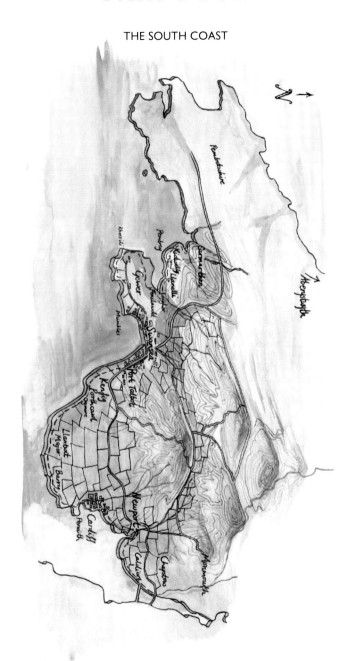

THIRTY-SIX

Winter had ceased to worry me. It seemed that the future was only so paralysingly scary when I wasn't the agent of my own destiny. Standing by the verge and waiting for snow was more than I could bear, but striding forward into the changing seasons was fine. With a donkey that walked, anything could be overcome.

Autumn was here though, and with it the first scrumping opportunities. We found a plum tree in Skenfrith and filled our bellies, shaking the branches and catching the falling treasure. Chico ground up the jammy flesh along with the stones as I sang, 'It's raining plums, hallelujah!' and loaded up my backpack with enough for several more days.

In Monmouth, even being rejected by two surprisingly curt campsite owners couldn't spoil our mood (one of them strode towards us at her threshold, holding her palm up like a traffic policeman. 'No!' she declared, before I'd said anything). We slept in a park right between the two campsites. I felt pleased with myself and we had one of the calmest nights of all, Chico lying alongside the tent in the rough, tall grass, shielded from the road by a bank. Some small creature surfaced under my tent and burrowed around beneath me, and even that didn't trouble my serenity. I awoke to a beautiful, pearly, autumnal dawn softly settling on the spires and outlines of the pretty old buildings stacked up the hillside.

We packed up, crossed the medieval bridge and hit the river that would take us back to the sea, along fantastic adventure bridleways that wound steeply up and down, high above the Wye. It couldn't have been more different to the weeks before – we were off on a caper together.

Rhys arrived, ready to join us for another stretch. I'd been desperate for his company over the dark weeks, but now Chico and I were a team, and had been through such a lot to get here, somewhere deep down I wondered if we needed anyone else.

Beneath the new exuberance, though, I was very tired. The arrival of backup made me realise how exhausted the donkey battling had left me, and as the chilly evening drew in, I began shivering. We stayed in St Briavels, on the east side of the Wye in the Forest of Dean. It had been common land once and the houses were scattered and invisible, linked by secret footpaths and tracks and all swallowed by thickets of blackberries and ancient trees, like a fairytale. Our fairy hosts, Anna and Tim, plied us with homemade oak-leaf wine and wild boar sausages.

I slept until 10.30am – an all-walk record – but woke up feeling like I hadn't slept at all. Anna and Tim boiled eggs and made coffee, and I sat and ate, and ate, and ate, trying to find some energy.

Anna's friend Warren put us up that evening, meeting us on the road as the enormous sky turned into tiger stripes of wild neon pink and orange – like celebratory streamers for our arrival at the coast. He'd mowed us a clearing on the floodplains below the end of his garden. Beyond us, across a hundred yards of reeds all painted beige with the mud of the Severn estuary, was the water, and beyond that were the sand flats of Slimeroad Sands.

On the far side, England was already dark. A mile down the estuary stood the majestic Severn Bridge, its two enormous sentinels with their petticoats of wire ushering the flow of warm yellow headlights back and forth across the channel as the river and sea and mud and sand mingled and eddied in the dark beneath it.

Chico seemed to be itching his backside. Rhys looked up the worming procedure and reported that it was best to wait until after the first frost. I didn't really know why that should be, and by the next day Chico had stopped itching in any case, so the idea of worming him fell by the wayside. But the damage was already done – frost had been mentioned.

A few days later, Mum joined us and admired the sloes that hung heavily above the blackberries we were stuffing into our mouths, on the paths behind an industrial estate.

'Sloes are best gathered after the first frost,' she said.

'Shush about the first frost, will you!'

We walked past a pub with 'Book now for Christmas!' signs. Regardless of the midday heat, winter seemed to be on the agenda. It was September: new term, new season, new compass bearing. West!

We had a rest at Jez's house. Jez, his wife Jo and their daughter Jeanie lived in Rogiet. After the airs and graces of the borders, I got caught out asking the way to Roj-ee-ay, with three syllables, a soft 'j', and in a French accent. The alcopop youths of Caldicot town centre screwed up their faces and said, 'What? What? Oh! Rogg-it! She means Rogg-it!'

I collapsed a bit at their house, in Hotel de Wheels, their campervan that was parked under the treehouse, between the hammock and the raspberries. They let us stay three nights, the longest I'd been in one place since we'd begun.

Jez was in the process of walking around the whole of Britain, 6440 miles by road and path. He was a university lecturer in art and was documenting his project with films of the journey overlaid with conversations from along the way, as well as with a GPS line along online maps. We sat around in their dappled garden, drinking tea and having sleepy, earnest conversations about walking as art. Jez saw it as a kind of drawing in space. It was performance – the art was in the walking, but Jez wanted his work to be useful and valuable as a resource too. It was – we scrolled through his videos to check for stiles.

Chico was relaxed in the semi-detached garden, pruning the raspberry canes and watching our comings and goings. At the back of the house was a huge conservatory with the dining table, play area and sofas, and the doors stood open all day. It didn't take long for Chico to invite himself in, following Lilo, the big white cat. He tried out the feel of the confined area, listened to the sound of his hooves on the tiles, checked out what the humans were up to, and then headed out again.

The next day was a school day – Chico, the same age as Class One, was about to attend his first school assembly. We were as taken by surprise by schooltime as I had been every day of my own school life, getting up too late and running about Jez and Jo's house jamming bread in the toaster, wet clothes in the dryer, phones on to charge, all at once. Jez, off for his first day back at uni, was just the same, declaring, 'I'll get the 9.20 train!' and a few minutes later, 'I'll get the 10 to 10!'

So I arrived at Caldicot's Welsh-language primary school addled, under-caffeinated, and very out of practice, having encountered barely a single Welsh-speaker since Bangor, or an appointment since March. It had been almost a quarter of a century since I was at primary school, but the little things came steaming back across the decades – art on walls, tiny toilets, squeaks on hall floors, disinfectant, carpet tiles, the smell of school dinner, morning hymn-singing – and rendered me an uncomfortable child again.

Ysgol y Ffin, the Border School, is one of only two Welsh-language primary schools in the whole of Monmouthshire, a county that has a long history of being shuttled between being Welsh and English. Its very even-handed Latin motto is '*Usque Fidelis*', meaning 'Faithful to Both'. There's not a lot of Welsh spoken down there, where the closest city is Bristol, and Herefordshire and Gloucestershire are very nearby, but the Welsh school is growing. Neither Jez nor Jo spoke Welsh, and were really proud that Jeanie now did. Jeanie shrugged and got on with it, as kids do.

Chico did a walkthrough in front of the whole school, to the gratifying sound of gentle sighs of love and wonder. The hundred-plus kids, cross-legged on the floor, asked good questions in shy whispers: 'Why? Where do you sleep? Were you lonely when you walked around Anglesey without the donkey? Are you going to walk past my house?'

While telling a boy that we'd already passed his house, I attempted to suggest that he see if he could spot any little piles of tell-tale Chico chocs left behind. A sea of blank faces, including the teachers', gazed at me, and I began floundering, realising too late that I couldn't remember the child-friendly word for poo. Eventually I hit on 'cachu', which I fervently hoped wasn't quite as bad as saying 'shit' in school assembly. I checked later on, and it was. I should have said 'baw', meaning dirt.

And then it was patting time outside, class by class, with each child feeding him a couple of horse nuts and Chico doing brilliantly among the throng of little people in quite a wide variety of school uniforms. The kids, made braver by each other, fed him well – flat handed, but not so convex that the nuts rolled off before Chico's whiskery, dexterous lips could tickle them up. One really small girl enjoyed the whiskery feeling so much that she fed him her whole hand, sending it in, palm down, as if posting a letter. In the slow motion of horror I watched Chico clamp down on it; fair enough – kids had been posting food into him for ten minutes. Her face registered the mistake and, I suspect, the understanding that it was her own fault, because she didn't make a sound and no one except her, Chico and me noticed it happen.

It must have been a bit scary – he'd bitten me a few weeks before when I was being sloppy about the flat-hand thing, grated a little skin off and left me with a slightly swollen finger joint. While he held my finger in his teeth it was like being in a vice – very firm, and with much, much more power and pain possible should he feel like it. Thankfully he released her, and the little girl thrust her fingers into her own mouth to comfort herself before getting over it and disappearing into the playground.

We headed back to Jez and Jo's with a pile of carrots scrubbed to half their original size by an enthusiastic dinner lady, and a plastic bag of Chico chocs to go. I put the carrots in the supper and the chocs in the compost.

I'd begun wondering if Jez, Jo and Jeanie might let us stay in their garden for ever – we could offer to contribute to the mortgage. But the next morning I recognised the familiar onward pull of the journey. Chico seemed to be feeling it too: he'd gnawed some chunks of wood out of the garden gate while he watched people passing in the street.

We walked over the M4 right next to the tollbooths, and watched the cars fan out into lanes, pay, and accelerate on their way, £6.40 lighter. Only the ones heading for Wales were charged; like a giant non-return valve, getting out of Wales was free.

Watching all the frantic gear changes, the ceaseless moving, I felt suddenly frightened of ever stopping, and simultaneously scared of the size of the journey so far. It was too big! I'd begun to forget the names of the kind people along the way. I was scared to experience anything else: I was full and surely anything new would push out the old. My memories seemed to be calcifying into a few anecdotes. I couldn't remember the subtleties, the fragrances. I'd had some epiphanies of the road, I was sure, but what were they? I was just a hungry, grumpy lump in constant orbit. I was writing a diary most days, but I began to supplement those notes by scrawling disconnected memories on bits of paper, the edge of the map or the back of my hand, just in case my mind really was overflowing.

Reens dominated the next few days – drainage ditches that crosshatch the Caldicot Levels all over. We walked along them, passing Cock Street Reen and Old Convenient Reen and Prat Reen, and thankfully missing Pwll Uffern Reen, which means

Hell Pool in Welsh. The Severn estuary was hidden beyond a sea wall to our left, and we headed over to have a look.

It was beautiful – shiny and calm, the pearly sea and the pearly sky only parted by the thin lilac stripe of Somerset, dotted about with industrial structures. On our side of the estuary the grass was a lurid bright green, with fishermen in ones and twos. While I was trying to stop Chico from eating the litter that lay everywhere, a man appeared from behind an outflow pipe and started chatting to Mum. His short-sleeved checked shirt was open, revealing a firm round belly. Below it was a pair of blue shorts, thin with age and very short indeed. They didn't do much to mask the shape of his body as it was, but to make matters worse he had a distinct protuberance within, making a tent of the fabric that stuck out as far as his stomach. He seemed oblivious. I ran over to give Mum some backup.

'I'm a spiritual healer, see?' he was saying. 'I come here to get my chakras sorted.' He didn't elaborate on how exactly he achieved that. 'I was just behind the pipe there, moving the sea grass from this side of the pipe and replanting it on that side. Helping nature out; paying it forward, see?' He stood a little too close.

Without requiring any encouragement he began to tell us about comet ISON. 'It's coming in our direction from over there, by Gemini, and it's going to be spun towards us by that guy,' he gestured at the sun. 'It will be 15 times brighter than the moon, even by day. All of the people in power know about it, but they're not letting on. Obama has instructed that all schools have three days' rations on hand for the children. And did you hear about the Russian hovercraft that just came up on to a crowded beach?'

'Hannah!' yelled Rhys, running up to where Chico had begun to swallow something bright yellow. To Chico's annoyance, I managed to drag it out of his mouth – a Russian cigarette packet, and behind it a babywipe.

While I was distracted, the man lurched closer, grasping my hands in his very soft, warm ones. 'I really admire what you're doing,' he said. 'I take my hat off to you.'

We thanked him and ran away.

We camped at the Newport Wetland Centre after successfully getting Chico through a wheelchair-accessible kissing gate. We were jubilant.

'Hey!' said a man with a garden full of ducks and geese that backed onto the wetland, and we froze, guiltily. 'Are you camping?' We hoped to, I said, tentatively. The sun was going down again, as usual. 'D'you want some eggs for your tea?' Tom handed the eggs over the fence, and a heron flew by across the ginger-coloured sunset.

'A heron!' I said.

'Ah. Frankie,' said Tom.

'Oh, you know him?'

'All herons are called Frankie,' said Tom, without explanation.

I've called all herons Frankie ever since.

Chico spent the night eating damsons off the bush, the crunching of the stones like firecrackers in the complete silence of the small hours. In the morning we packed up and headed back to the kissing gate, realising as we approached it that we'd be in big trouble if we were stuck inside the nature reserve. There was no guarantee that Chico would consent to being backed through the gate again – his mood was less plucky that morning. We charged forward, hoping not to allow him a pause in which he might register our drop in confidence. We turned him around, bum to the gate, and Rhys lifted Chico's chin up onto his shoulder and began to push. 'Back, back, back!'

'Hey!' came a voice from very nearby, on our side of the fence. It was a man in a Newport Wetland Centre truck that we'd not even noticed in our hurry. Uh-oh… Rhys, Chico and I all stopped dead and looked at the man, Chico only able to swivel his eyeballs like a patient in a dentist's chair. We'd been busted.

'Hey, the main gate is open, look! I just opened it, go out that way!'

Oh. Now we looked silly. Our single-minded focus on the problem at hand had blinded us to the solution that was standing wide open, two feet away. That seemed significant. We let ourselves out, waving at the man in the truck, who didn't seem to think anything of our night's trespass.

A few more hours of reen walking and we came across the Newport Transporter Bridge – a sort of suspended ferry across the river Usk that cost 50p to cross, and free for donkeys. A high boom and track ran between A-shaped towers on either side of the river, and suspended from it by long cables was a platform at bank level. The platform had the look of a Victorian train station about it, with highly glossed woodwork and handrails in several shades of blue. It had been built in 1906, when Newport was a busy port with lots of maritime traffic heading further up the Usk. We'd just passed the old steelworks on the east side, which used to be staffed by workers who mostly lived on the west side of the river. Before the transporter bridge was built they'd had a four-mile trip upstream and down again to get to work. I liked that this huge and somehow brusquely elegant piece of engineering had been brought about to convenience the workers.

Chico was unnerved by the peculiar sensation of being suspended; he stamped nervously on the wooden boards, and then released a big poo – thankfully one that still held together in distinct briquettes. The staff swept them cheerfully off the side and onto the mudbanks far below. 'It's really great having a donkey on board!' they said. 'Even the poo – that's great! We've got a picture somewhere of a horse and cart on the bridge once…'

Visitors were allowed to climb up the towers and walk along the boom, 54m up in the air. I tied Chico at the bottom and left him with Mum while Rhys and I ran up the hundreds of steps and looked at the view – fluffy white clouds evenly spaced around the deep, royal blue sky, and the oddments of industry that from up there looked like scattered toys: rows of blue flatbed trucks, reels of orange piping, warehouses and cranes, wooden wharves, triangles of scrubland and shining docks. We called and waved at Mum, but Chico couldn't figure out looking up and didn't know where our voices came from; by the time we got down he'd had another poo, this one fully liquid, and was trying his hardest to pull down the fences. We soothed him and got a move on.

Newport has a reputation for being a bit crap and rough, but it seemed to me to have made an art out of not taking itself seriously, becoming the capital of creative self-deprecation. It's the home of comedy rappers Goldie Lookin Chain (whose songs include stadium anthem 'Your mother's got a penis', and 'Guns don't kill people, rappers do'), and also the professional masochists Dirty Sanchez, who hurt themselves for slapstick telly. Both gangs are funny, rude and unapologetic.

We skirted around its perimeters, along a main road and into a Lidl for cheap chocolate bars – I was getting into the habit of scoffing sugar for short energy spikes. We worked our way through a few parks and back onto more irrigated reen land. It was hard to navigate in a suburb with only the Ordnance Survey map, but we had Cardiff to come tomorrow – this was nothing. I spuriously blamed Rhys for our erratic zigzagging, who in turn got all dictatorial: 'Tent up within an hour! No more of this setting up in the dark!' Was that my fault, it being my adventure? Maybe it was, I hadn't realised…

I wasn't sure what Mum and Rhys were there for – even six arms was never quite enough, and Chico kept wandering open-mouthed into piles of cut grass, or blindly into oncoming traffic. I was ceaselessly grumpy with all three of them. Chico brayed when Rhys went out of sight sometimes, and I thought, 'Why are you braying for *him*? Did all that bonding with *me* count for nothing?' No one understood what we'd been through, including Chico himself, it seemed.

We only came across a few people in Newport, all of whom were obliging if not totally trustworthy with directions – a skinny man in a rasta tracksuit with a tattoo of a pair of boxing gloves behind his ear; a woman with no teeth wearing a dressing gown; and a man in a suit, already drunk at 4pm on a Friday, and taking a long time to get to the point, considering we were cross and heavily laden (my new chocolate collection was a significant extra weight).

We hit on a field that all four of us found acceptable, farmland but not recently farmed, through a broken gate and over an earth bridge across a reen. The ground was flat as far as the eye could see, baked hard and still bristly with the stalks of its most recent crop. There was just enough green stuff for Chico to eat, and the sky was enormous and sliced up by wires running between pylons, silhouetted against another extravagant sunset. We named our field Kansas, and had brandy in our tea to facilitate settling in.

As we crept into our tents, Rhys said, 'Do you want my toothpaste?'

'No thanks – it tastes like sweets.'

'Well, it's minty, like almost all toothpastes,' said Rhys.

'Mine's salty,' I said.

'Like your character,' he replied. Ah, it was all okay – we were friends.

A train passed through Kansas, somewhere under the pylons, and Rhys tuned the radio in to something classical and began to fall asleep.

'The ground is hard,' he said, shifting sleepily to get comfy.

'It's knobbly,' I agreed.

'Like your personality,' said Rhys, and drifted away.

THIRTY-SEVEN

We spent three nights in Cardiff, capital city of Wales. The first was with Joe, my old best friend from school, his wife Sandie and baby Ifan. They lived in a terraced house with a tiny garden that could only be accessed through the building. We'd been plotting how to manage this for weeks, and they'd evidently taken the mission seriously. To make a clear corridor through the house, they'd used Ifan's plastic tablecloths to cover the beige carpets and had moved a sideboard into the middle of the living room. On the counter in the kitchen were two buckets full of hard green apples – they'd stripped their little tree.

I'd intended to arrive early so that if Chico refused we'd still have time to find alternative lodgings, but of course I'd failed and it was late in the evening – there was no backup plan. Thankfully Chico didn't seem concerned. He followed me straight into the house, down the hallway, through the living room and kitchen, and out of a back door into the garden – very impressive.

Of course, by now he was beginning to think he was half human, and had been practising in Jez and Jo's conservatory and the primary school. Once we got him in the garden, he turned round and tried pretty firmly to come back inside with us. We got a Japanese takeaway (*Japanese!* How cosmopolitan!) and ate it cross-legged on the carpet, with Chico's long face pressed against the window, misting it up with little puffs of breath.

Mum headed off on the train back to her car, genuinely pleased to have joined us for a part of Wales she'd never have sought out for a walking holiday. Rhys, Chico and I spent the next day walking slowly across Cardiff to be in position for an interview with Radio Wales the following morning. Cardiff is very green in the middle, and we were looking forward to some urban wild camping, although a tramp on a bench must have guessed our intentions because he advised us not to pitch the tent in the castle grounds or the cops would move us on. As we looked for a less manicured corner, Gloria, the manager of the council-owned Cardiff Riding School, called us over and invited us to put Chico in their grassy car park, saying we could sleep on the floor of their portacabin classroom. We were delighted. The night was chilly and we put on the radiator and made use of their electric kettle. Chico tried to follow us in, understandably confused about when he was and wasn't allowed to come inside. The chipboard floor wouldn't have withstood his weight, although he might have been interested in the posters of horse anatomy and dressage skills.

We were ready for the *Jason Mohammad Show*: hair finger-combed, best anecdotes rehearsed, worst clumps of mud brushed out of Chico's mane. The friendly audio engineer, Mark, was waiting in the radio van, ready to send the interview on a 4000-mile journey from the car park via a satellite and on to the studio, even though the studio was less than 10 yards away, one floor up. The staff jostled to look out of the window at the donkey. Chico found a blotchy old banana from a BBC employee's abandoned packed lunch and polished it off. Jason appeared, and almost immediately it began to rain, the fat raindrops making transparent circles on his crisp shirt. His production assistant leaped to attention, holding an umbrella over his famous head.

'This is a career highlight!' he laughed on air. 'I sit in a studio on network television on BBC1, doing the football results on a Saturday, and by the Monday I'm feeding a donkey outside BBC Wales. Is this what my career has come to?' Then he sounded gratifyingly nervous. 'I'm not very good with animals! What do I do? Come on, Chico, my man, eat this carrot and I can go back in the dry...'

I thought feeding Chico was vastly superior to feeding football results to the nation, and tried to convey telepathically to Chico that there wouldn't be any serious repercussions if he accidentally gave this man a little chomp. But he didn't. Sheesh, what's the point of having a donkey on your team?

We walked all the way through the city along the river Taff, on a path speckled with undeniably autumnal leaves. We met many nice young men, and they all asked to 'smooth' my donkey – the Cardiff word for stroke. A crowd outside a pub looked at us, wide-eyed with the effort of coming up with something funny to say, and then boom! one of them got it: 'Sion! Your taxi's arrived!' Next came Eddie and Luca, shy punks with excellent mohicans and far too much black leather for the hot afternoon. Rachid was a young Moroccan who claimed his Welsh wife missed his donkey from back home; they were planning to bring it through the long-winded quarantine system to live with them in Cardiff. A few fierce-eyed men on consecutive street corners were sweet and earnest about Chico. 'Crack dealers,' said Rhys, knowledgably.

Cardiff's bay area was very clean and shiny and we walked right around the waterfront and across the barrage. It used to be the docklands, with mudflats and a huge tidal range that held off the development, and a heady, long-standing mix of ethnicities, gambling dens, a red-light district, sailors and dockworkers all jammed in together. Now there were chain bars and restaurants, a leisure complex and an arts centre, sculptures and yachts, all around the huge freshwater lake created by the barrage that blocked the mouths of the Taff and the Ely rivers. We chatted to people, asking what they thought, and as they blinked amongst the mirrored surfaces, chrome handrails and sparkling water, most seemed a bit uncertain. I guess it just needed to accrue some of the dirt and character of time.

People were certainly making use of the new public space – a gang of teenage girls were doing tricks on penny skateboards, and lots of people were out strolling in the sunshine. A man with an almost unintelligibly thick Pakistani accent asked if he and his wife could have their picture taken with Chico. They'd been married that morning and she was wearing the first hijab I'd seen in 600 miles. 'Where are you from?' I asked. 'I'm from Cardiff,' he said, 'but my wife's from Newport.'

We stayed in Penarth with a friend of Mum's, corralling a space in the middle of a lawn edged with yew. I texted Carol for advice: 'Carol, you know how everything kills donkeys? Am I right in thinking that yew really will kill him?'

'Yes,' replied Carol, straight away. 'Yew wl kl hm, keep hm away fm it, don't let hm pk up any bits that hav bn blown on2 the grnd.' She took to texting full words, by which I realised just how serious this was: 'Honestly, it's just the worst thing.'

Chico found the window of our room, turned his bum to it and kept guard.

THIRTY-EIGHT

In Cosmeston Park the next night, we got catty with each other as we struggled to choose a camping place from the various indiscreet options. Rhys cooked us meatballs by the lake and secretly I felt grateful to be cared for but just complained about the greasy washing-up. In the morning, it took ages to get everything back into bags – always my least favourite bit of the day. I talked to passing dog walkers to avoid having to do it. All of these things I had done alone for that month in the borders, but somehow I was now struggling to do even my half. As he packed everything into the wrong pockets, Rhys suggested that I think about changing my habits – get up earlier, pack up faster, maybe leave breakfast until the mid-morning break. I was deeply aggrieved. Postpone breakfast? I was running on empty as it was. And we'd have to take stuff out of the bags again, bowls and spoons and muesli! Spooning out dried milk on a windy headland? Stupid idea!

Things became frosty and, as we got to the sea at Sully Point, erupted into an out-and-out row. I was 'juvenile', Rhys was 'intolerant', Chico ate chunks out of the wooden tables outside the Captain's Wife cafe. 'Team Hannah just has Hannah in it!' said Rhys, outraged.

Three old women leaned against the outside wall, all of them wearing lilac jackets. 'Very dangerous tides, Sully Island,' one interjected, unbidden, nodding at the island that was 400m out to sea.

'What? I…' I frowned at her. Rhys had turned away from me.

'Many people have been drowned. It's a death trap,' said another, nodding at the enormous sign above our heads that said: 'Warning! Warning! Dangerous tides! Many people have been drowned attempting to visit or return from Sully Island. The causeway is a death trap. Please take great care.'

I hadn't even known that it was possible to walk to Sully Island – the tide was in, and the island was very, very unwalkable to, 400m of sea away. And in any case, we were mid-argument about making poor progress. Waiting until low tide to walk to a death trap with a donkey was not what I wanted to do, at all.

'Well, we just want to walk along the coast,' I said.

'Don't go to Sully Island – death! People die!' said the third woman.

'I CAN SEE THAT!' I said. 'I DON'T WANT TO!' They were like the council of monkeys, only all of them were the monkey with his hands over his ears.

'Is that donkey a girl or a boy?' said one of them, undeterred by my outburst.

I looked at Chico. His extremely long black penis had put in a very obvious appearance, strangely timed considering the tension in the air. I looked back at the lilac monkeys, but they didn't seem to be joking. 'Um, a boy?' I said.

We escaped, walking along the coast to Barry. Between a trading estate and the sea our path ran over beautiful rosy cliffs, layered and chipped away along the horizontal seams, making flights of steps up and down. Chico tried to drink the salty puddles that were trapped and evaporating in crevices of the red rock. 'Stop him! Stop him! Salt water will make him go crazy!' shouted Rhys. Chico was very certain he wanted it though, and surely had some instinctive understanding of what his body needed – except for Russian cigarette packets, admittedly... I pulled him half-heartedly away from the many puddles.

We got lost around the docks, and finally reopened tentative lines of communication while eating lunch at the Atlantic Cafe, a portacabin caff in the industrial estate that was staffed by women in classic diner-waitress uniforms. We cleared the ground around Chico of litter, cut grass and broken glass – a laborious process that left pretty much nothing behind except gravel.

Across the causeway, Barry Island was like a small Welsh version of New York's Coney Island – a long, misty beach, a log flume built on a corner plot, and insistent, tinny amusement-arcade music spilling onto the deserted plaza. It began to rain hard and we sheltered under the awning of a closed kiosk. Everything was very clean and fresh from summer, well painted and litter-free. But it was September now, and the place was deserted on a Wednesday afternoon; a man replacing bulbs on the strings of lights above the promenade leaned out of his truck and said apologetically, 'It was nice this morning! You should have been here then!'

We camped in Porthkerry Country Park, after a further altercation. We were wet and although the day had stayed close and warm, our cold shoulders were wearing each other out. There weren't many wild-camping opportunities on the map, even fewer on the ground, and finding a spot whilst damp and round-shouldered with self-pity was especially hard. Wild camping took confidence, a self-assured sense of proprietorship over the whole world, a sanguine attitude towards the shortcomings of the chosen patch, and a thick skin in case of local opposition.

Rhys saw a 'No Camping' sign at the entrance of the country park. 'Well, that's that. We can't camp here then. We can't disobey a direct instruction.'

Where had this sudden dutiful line-toeing come from? Hadn't we camped on a protected, cordoned-off dune in Conwy? And the nature area in Rhyl? And the Newport Wetland Centre, for heaven's sake! And general non-specific council-owned land all over the place? I was sure that if we'd looked, they would probably all have had 'No Camping' signs of some sort. Rhys was definitely just coming up with new rules to make my life difficult!

In the UK, wild camping without consent isn't a criminal offence, but it is trespass – the landowner could choose to sue the camper. It doesn't make any difference whether it's council- or privately owned land, whether it's land you can sometimes go onto, or land you can never go onto. Well, it did in my head, but that was just down to the fact that I'd rather be caught out by a council employee than an angry landowner.

If a landowner gives consent, it's not trespass, of course. We loitered fruitlessly around the warden's house for a while, knocking on windows and making a dog bark inside.

The absence of a 'No Camping' sign doesn't make any difference either, but the presence of one does rather underline the lack of consent. I did understand why it made Rhys uncomfortable. But, as usual, it was getting late and the ceaseless turning of the globe forced an end to our moral wranglings. We set up the tent in a corner between the pebble beach, a cliff with a 'Beware: Falling Rocks!' sign, and a bit of scrub with a 'Beware: Adders!' sign. There wasn't a soul in the park, and we were a long way from the nearest houses.

Rhys curtly refused dinner, and went to sleep.

I lay in the tent, in the dark, wondering. There weren't any opening times or gates on the park. What exactly constituted camping? The sign had a picture of a tent with a red line across it – what if we didn't put up a tent? And what if we just lay on the ground but didn't sleep? Or we could walk in the night and sleep on a picnic blanket in the day – would that be alright?

Suddenly, in the not-far-enough-away-for-comfort distance, there was some wild laughter. It was a horrible sound. I looked at my phone – it was 1am, and my battery was almost dead. Rhys's already was; there'd be no phoning for help. The laughter was manic, cold, and devoid of humanity. It was laughter that came from insane boredom, a schism with rationality, quite likely drugs. It was the desperate laughter of someone hunting madly for distraction. I was absolutely certain that if the laughers found us and Chico, they would hurt us.

Rhys didn't wake up, but I held on to him, and eventually silence unfurled, and long after that, sleep.

The next evening, once Chico had made a break for it after having only one hoof checked and had then run all over a golf course, and after we'd packed up and set off and got through the villages of Rhoose and Font-y-Gary, and East Aberthaw and West Aberthaw, and Gileston and Boverton, and found our way to Llantwit Major where we'd pitched the tent and charged the phones, I called Sarah-the-barrister to ask her about wild camping.

'It's about limited implied consent,' she said. 'If I were to invite you to my house for dinner, you couldn't assume I was also giving you permission to slide down the banister.'

Right. So I guessed that meant no wild camping, really. Except very quietly.

In Llantwit Major we camped in a closed campsite, with the permission of the owners who brought us a paper bag of biltong made in their on-site sausage-making factory. Once Chico was happily settled, I took Rhys to the pub and bought him a big dinner and all the pints he could drink. There was a time and a place for chairs and tables, knives and forks, and not doing the washing-up with fingernails and spit, and this was it. A full belly in lieu of a proper apology.

Ever onward, very slowly, through the rain. We were stuck on the back roads – the footpaths clung to the coastline, but we didn't know if there were stiles, and the map showed no farm tracks to escape via if need be. And with all the rain we were happy to stick to a faster route. This was the Vale of Glamorgan, a segment of rich agricultural land between Cardiff, which had seemed to appear very fast after the big west-turn, and Swansea, which persisted in being stubbornly far away. I realised I'd only ever travelled this corner on the M4, which cuts a straight line further north, and takes little more than half an hour in a car.

Despite the rain, it was full of moments of beauty. The distant fuzz of the Mendips was still visible across the Severn estuary, with a foreground of soft green paths between stubbly fields, and crops which smelled unmistakeably turnippy. A big green trailer was parked in a field by the road, displaying a sign that said 'PLOUGHING – SUN 8 SEPT'. Asking around later, we were told it was for the European Ploughing Championship the week before, undertaken exclusively with vintage T20 Fergusons.

The land was quiet, but the people we met were warm. A woman ran out with a bag of windfalls and a box of biscuits. An estate agent, dolled up as if she was due at a wedding, skipped across the road in six-inch heels to declare that she'd called the *Barry Gem*, and then acted the star reporter. Two more women shouted, 'He's lush!' at Chico from across the road. A little further on a man gave us his copy of the *South Wales Echo* with Chico and me posing by Penarth pier like unsmiling rock stars; someone else told us we'd made the cover of the *Penarth Times*. Jason Mohammad's umbrella-holding production assistant, Angela, called to say that a man called Gareth, landlord of a pub called the Prince of Wales in Kenfig, 25 miles further on, had invited us to stay the night and have dinner when we got there.

'I'm not sure I could handle the fame!' said Paddy, a Wales Coast Path guidebook writer who was heading in the other direction. He walked his steady 15 miles a day quickly and quietly and wrote up his guidebooks diligently as he went, compiling his inventory of cafes and guesthouses within a mile of the path. He was soon to finish in Chepstow but had decided to carry on up Offa's Dyke 'for the hell of it', for the third time. To dampen down the panic of stopping, he'd long ago learned to have the next walk lined up. This time it would be one on Corsica, then Lanzarote and Fuerteventura in the next few months, and then the South West Coast Path next year, for the second time. I wondered what would happen if he did stop.

Paddy went on anticlockwise and we went on clockwise, but as he stepped off the kerb he turned and said, 'Don't forget to go to the Prince of Wales in Kenfig!' Oh, okay, we said. What was it about that place?

Though the people in South Wales were warm, so far the pubs had been markedly less so. Several wouldn't let us charge our phones, and one also got very cross about us trying to dry our boots, even though they had a huge log fire that gave a false impression of a warm welcome, and the rain was thick in the air outside.

'*I think you've had enough!*' said the log-fire landlady, returning my phone and its ungainly cable tail to me in an indignant rage. The young barwoman who'd given me permission caught my eye apologetically. I used up some precious battery, while we were hurriedly finishing our expensive meal, to find out what it cost in electricity to charge an iPhone. Less than 0.01p, it turned out. Rhys stopped me from going over to offer the sour woman one penny – 100 times the payment we owed her.

'I'm trying to run a business!' said another angry barman, whilst refusing to fill up a water bottle, even though we'd just bought two pricey coffees.

'A *hospitality* business!' I retorted, as Rhys dragged me out of the door. Honestly! Needing other people was getting to be tiring.

Perhaps the publicans around there were just contrary folk, trying their hardest not to be typecast by the 'friendly South Walian' epithet. Or maybe they started out being friendly and it wore them down. Maybe they were genuinely worried that if they let us charge a single phone, all of the traffic on the M4 would divert to take advantage of the good times, parking all over the road while people ran in to thrust phones into sockets already bristling with small appliances, piling their shoes before the fire until no one could get in the door and the air was choked with the smell of steaming insoles, like a backstreet fish-poaching factory, and draining the local reservoirs as they filled up jerry cans from the sinks in the bathroom and loaded them into the boot. One needed to be vigilant when meting out friendliness, or things could get out of hand.

'Go to sleep, Han,' said Rhys.

THIRTY-NINE

While I was grumbling and arguing, Chico was being quietly brilliant, and he was about to surprise us. Alongside our camping spot was just the sort of river that he would never agree to cross – 30 feet wide, over a foot deep, and running fast with the rain. In all of the fording progress since the terrible six-incher of day three, we'd not encountered anything like this, and to make matters even less hopeful, the evening before he had refused to tackle the inoffensive rivulets that this same river had made over the beach, further downstream. We'd walked a few miles upriver and were expecting to have to go a few miles more that morning, to get to a road bridge.

We'd been allowed to stay in the riverside paddock of the stables in Ogmore, along with five friends who had driven over to visit us. All morning, Chico had witnessed a constant stream of horses being herded back to the stable, past our field. They'd each had to cross the ford on their own, and managed it without fuss – they clearly did it all the time. One of the last was a tiny, unflappable Shetland, the water level higher than its stocky legs, and halfway up its round belly. It ploughed through, tossing its mane, the raindrops bouncing off the river and into its eyes. Chico was watching.

I didn't expect success, but walked across a few stepping stones, holding the end of Chico's rope. He looked worried but took a few encouraging steps in before stopping. I quickly pulled off my boots and waded in with him, and with great bravery we walked together across the ford, the water pulling at our ankles while the slimy pebbles slithered around underfoot. Chico was mightily proud of himself at the other side, and too excited to stand still while I hopped about pulling my socks back onto my wet feet as the rain fell even harder around us.

We gave Chico a lot of praise, and then headed into the Merthyr Mawr dunes. The Prince of Wales in Kenfig was on the horizon, and people kept mentioning it as a mandatory experience of local kindness and good eating. But we were going to have to work for it – a day of highs and lows stood before us. First of all, it rained all day. The drops were big and cold, tossed about in the air by squally, obstreperous winds to make all combinations of splats and spray, drizzle, needle dashes and drumming marbles, like a compendium of raindrops.

We were bent double so the tops of our heads went first into the wind and rain, our faces hidden inside our steamy coats; and Chico, following along behind on his rope, looked the part too, ears blown flat behind him, legs held out wide for stability, the rain mac slapping his wet flanks.

But it was beautiful! We felt wild, shouting to each other, our voices whipped away and sent across the dune grass that was dashed back and forth like a seascape. The sand was the colour and texture of demerara sugar, in bare paths through the lush, low green growth. Sometimes the tracks ran in trenches so deep that Chico's eyes were at the level of the grass, his bags wedging him in, and he'd force himself through with the extra energy he reserved for moments of fear at getting trapped.

These were the second-highest dunes in Europe – some up to 200ft high, and hard going. We learned later that scenes from *Lawrence of Arabia* had been filmed there, and we paid unintentional homage by battling forward, our footsteps dull and graceless in the sand, breaking through the dark wet layer and scattering the soft light sand from underneath. The air was full of it, sandblasting our wet faces.

As we reached the last bank of dunes, there was the sea, a churning, crashing mass of living, shining shades of grey, topped with bright white froth, seething into the wet butterscotch sand. We'd escaped the Severn estuary at last, and this was the wide, wild sea; the open throat of the Atlantic, howling right into our awe-filled faces.

We made it onto the path at the end, spurred on by the firm ground underfoot and by the smell of chips that came from the first steamed-up car and weed from the second.

We skirted Porthcawl, and a man in a tacky red sports car stopped to shout, 'The rain in Spain falls mainly on Wales!' with a gameshow host's accent and face, and bad teeth. On Marlpit Lane we came across a fallen tree, blocking the whole road. A couple driving towards us had warned us about it, claiming it was unmovable but, filled with the strength of the day's wildness, I dragged a clear path, and Chico launched himself through it before I was ready, getting branches hooked up on his packsaddle.

The wind battered the high branches, and Rhys and I took different routes along the road, showing what felt like significantly different attitudes to risk. Rhys walked on the side furthest from the trees, figuring that he'd rather have the smaller branches fall on him if another tree came down. I walked on the tree-side, on the gamble that this made me less likely to be hit by the trunk and more likely not to be hit at all, though if I was hit, it would be certain death. Chico walked his own sweet way, to his own logic, indecipherable to us.

Eventually we arrived at the Prince of Wales, which was full of a welcome-committee of locals, drunk on the several extra pints they'd had to put away while awaiting our delayed arrival. Our friends from the night before were there too; they'd decided against joining us for the walk but had still been fed huge Sunday roasts by Gareth and Julie. 'Bring him in!' shouted everyone as they peered out of the front door.

I wasn't at all sure about it, but I am a sucker for spirited exhortations, so Chico, Rhys and I walked into the pub and up to the bar, where a roomful of people cheered and someone fed

Chico a yorkshire pudding. Through my steamed-up glasses I peered at him closely for signs of panic that could precede a fear-poo, but Chico just checked the place out, his eyes bright and his ears swivelling, and then followed me back out.

Gareth's friend Len led us to his stable, where we left Chico looking sideways at his three red horses like a kid on his first day at big school. We went back to the pub, where more roast dinners were brought forth.

Gareth was a born landlord. 'A friend reminded me recently that I used to look at this pub when I was a boy and announce, "I want that,"' he said. 'I'm an entertainer and a custodian,' he continued, and proved it by telling us a little of Kenfig's tumultuous history.

Its location on the Bristol Channel made it both desirable and vulnerable. The Normans built a wooden castle and walled town there in the twelfth century, which was burned down by the Welsh, rebuilt in stone, and then attacked again. This cycle was repeated up to a dozen times over the following 250 years, including by superstars like Llywelyn the Last (last true prince of Wales) and possibly Owain Glyndŵr (the other last true prince of Wales, a few centuries later), and on one occasion the town was destroyed by a lightning strike. Then came some sacking by a confederacy of barons, and the Black Death. Meanwhile, great storms in the 1300s destabilised the coastal dunes; sand began to encroach on the land, filling in the river, covering the buildings and turning the marshland into a lake called Kenfig Pool – the second biggest lake in South Wales.

The old village of Kenfig was abandoned at the end of the fifteenth century, and the nearby Prince of Wales alehouse began doubling as the guildhall for the new village. Its upstairs room had served as a meeting hall ever since – at times hosting a Sunday school, a courthouse and a mortuary – and it still functioned as Kenfig's town hall. We were to sleep up there, in the town hall, and Gareth proudly showed us around.

The single, long room was furnished with banqueting tables, flags hanging from the sloping ceiling, and paintings of various barons and burgesses high on the walls. 'I often come up here,' Gareth said, 'and just look around and think of all that has happened over the many hundreds of years. I once lay on the top table and fell asleep – a deep, deep sleep.' He grinned.

'When it was a courthouse the judge would sit at that end of the room, and the sun would stream from behind him through the windows in the gable end, blinding the defendants. Intimidating them.'

Unsurprisingly there were plenty of myths and stories about the place. In the town hall, a Sunday school organ was said to play music to itself, footsteps walked across the boards, and discussions were heard in the empty room. 'There's often a little boy standing just there, too,' said Gareth, pointing at my dingy sponge bag on the floor. His straight face was impossible to read.

He was so proud to be the guardian of this rich history, and also the local hub – the pub had won an award for its community spirit and been visited by Charles, current Prince of Wales, who presumably felt the presence of Llywelyn and Owain jostling at the city walls as he drank half a pint for the cameras.

We stood in a rare moment of silence.

'It's so quiet here, considering it's only half a mile from the M4,' I said.

'Yes,' said Gareth. 'I make them close the motorway at 6pm. Sometimes 7pm, if it's busy, you know.'

FORTY

We were on the knuckle of the next corner, and up ahead were the lights and chimneys and flames of Port Talbot and the Margam steelworks, like a vast factory of some serious hardworking gods, forging and hammering. And beyond was the wide Swansea Bay, with the Mumbles and the Gower Peninsula on the far side – a distant headland of promise that I'd been wishing for through the great green borders all that time.

Gareth had found us a host for the next night – a bed-and-breakfast owner called Gail who was equally effusive and hospitable and lived eight miles further on. Rhys and I dithered, getting stuff done, but by the time I went to get Chico – after having been fed lunch at a wake in the pub for someone's 93-year-old auntie who'd-had-a-good-innings – it was late afternoon.

Chico wouldn't leave Len's stable; he was flirting with one of the red horses. I'd been worrying that he was getting too dependent on us – the morning before he'd been braying to me even though he could see me washing the pans in the ford. But now he was offhand, and it took a long while of cajoling to get him away from them. I gave him time to say his goodbyes. We walked through Gareth's field, and Chico decided he'd rather stay, running around in circles, waiting for me to get close and then pelting away. Scoundrel! He was clearly having fun, but I wasn't. I had to contemplate the possibility of asking to stay in the town hall another night, which just seemed too much. We'd been the recipients of everything Gareth and Julie could lavish on us, and our role was to know when to leave. Chico, however, had no such concerns, and we, as always, were bound to him. By the time I caught him it was 5pm. We slunk sheepishly away.

Every adventure – every life, I suppose – is built around a personally assembled set of rules. What counts and what doesn't. I liked it that our route around Wales was self-assembled, determined by our energy levels, the weather, and offers of accommodation. We were spinning our path behind us, not tied to a circuit. Rhys caught a train or hitched a lift back to the old Volvo every time we ran out of food for Chico – that was the only thing we hadn't worked out how to be independent in. Other than that, with the kindness of strangers several times a week, and regular village shops, we could walk forever. For me, that was realness. I'm not the type to draw a chalk mark on a pavement, get a lift from the support vehicle to a hotel where I can sit in a bath of ice and drink protein shakes, and get a lift back to my chalk mark in the morning. For starters I've never done anything that warranted an ice bath or a protein shake, but more importantly it's the chalk mark that I don't get. I'd rather plot a course that walked into the hotel and out again the next morning – I suppose I just prefer that my route really is the route I've taken, my body moving through space, rather than think of it as something separate that I am visiting. That idea of the route – The Route – suggests that someone else made it up, sanctioned it, declared it a thing-to-do-before-you-die, or a top-ten-best-so-and-so. From there it would be a small step to pedometers and calorie-counting apps, and all of a sudden what should have been a person walking through a landscape would become a bunch of graphs and personal bests. Then I'd have to find some other way to make the experience significant and superlative – do it all faster than anyone else, or backwards, or naked, or carrying a fridge…

I suddenly realised I should write Mr Grimley of the Wales Coast Path a thank-you letter – all of those stiles and kissing gates had caused me to be walking around Wales in a way that was utterly connected to the landscape and people. Rarely could I trudge along looking for the next path marker, and the experience was all the better and more involved for it.

And then I had a chalk-mark moment. There was bound to come a time when, in demanding hospitality so constantly, we found ourselves being offered something that we didn't want but couldn't refuse. The day we left Kenfig was that day.

The sun would set at 7.30, and we'd vacated the Prince of Wales too late to get to Gail's house before dark. We were going to be annoyingly late, as so often before. Every day of the journey so far, the one non-negotiable part of the whole escapade had been the moving of a donkey from one place to another. And suddenly Gail was offering us her brother Gareth, his wife Lisa, and their horsebox.

'It's fine,' she said. 'He can take you right back to the same place on the main road in the morning, so it's not cheating. It's a steep hill to ours, and it'll be dark by then.'

And that was that. It felt like cheating, but to cheat there must be an external arbiter of right and wrong. I was cheating myself a bit, but that seemed far preferable right then to making a fuss. The steep hill and the dark didn't worry me in the slightest, but making Gail wait for us did, just for something as invisible as an internal arbiter. And, more than anything, that arbiter seemed to care about taking this journey as it came. If we were suddenly given wheels, so be it.

Chico didn't want to get in. Gareth and Lisa looked after retired racehorses, and the very posh horsebox had a padded divider so that Chico couldn't turn around. We coaxed him in bum-first, and he didn't like it, squirming about in panic. I thought we should just get on with it. It was about two miles, and Gareth drove impeccably around roundabouts and over speed bumps and up the steep hill, but by the time we let Chico out he was terrified. The floor was covered in fear-poo, and he was drenched in sweat – it dripped off his neck. I felt terribly remorseful and pretty carsick myself: it had been a traumatic two miles for both of us slow creatures.

Lisa brought a towel and a bucket of food, and we dried him off and fed him. He pulled himself together faster than it took for my queasiness to subside.

'Racehorse food, that is,' said Lisa. 'That should sort him out.'

Gail took us in and showed us around, and then gave us – whether knowingly or not – the most superb and unexpected gift: a totally unsociable evening. 'I'm off now. Here's the wi-fi, there's the telly, tea and coffee over there, fruit, yoghurt, bara brith, bathroom, shower, washer-dryer… Sleep well and see you for breakfast.'

Rhys and I lay on our twin beds, listened to the solitude with our eyelids sagging, and fell asleep by nine.

FORTY-ONE

There was no question of going near the horsebox the next morning, and we walked down the steep hill with renewed gladness to be on foot despite the rain. The map looked very built-up for quite a long way ahead – the intricate cells of housing in Port Talbot, Neath and Swansea linked by the pink arteries of the A-roads and their neat roundabout valves, and the thick tendons of the motorway and its perfectly engineered curves and sliproads. Between them on the map sat the criss-crossed white patches of steelworks, the map far more clean and blank than the reality. I remembered a geography field trip that involved vast cauldrons of molten metal.

Within the first hour Chico came to a standstill, next to an unremarkable hedge on the pavement by a roundabout. I tried to encourage him a few steps back to stand under a tree, but to no avail, so we took his bags off and sat on the ground next to him and ate welshcakes, waiting for the rain to stop. After a little while we realised that it wasn't raining on us – Chico had chosen well, clever animal. A little further on, we walked under the motorway, and even the cathedral-sized space was nowhere near as dry as Chico's bush.

We parked Chico outside a supermarket while I went in for morale-boosting sugary things, and when I came out, Rhys was trying to tell a man in a yellow hoody about the 1000 miles. 'You're walking to *Swansea*!' He was astonished. 'Well, yes – Swansea's the least of our problems,' we said. An old woman came up to mutter at us, turning 'cruel' into two syllables: 'Croo-el. Croo-el.' I tried to explain that Chico was much better off there with us, having an adventure. With the rain mac over them, the bags did look enormous, his face was soaked and his soggy ears were at half-mast. 'He's having a great time!' I persevered. 'Better here than going crazy with boredom in a field, spending hours working out how to open the gate…' She looked me in the eye and shook her head. 'Croo-el,' she repeated, and shuffled off. Her umbrella was printed with pictures of a fluffy kitten and a fluffy puppy, nose to nose in a nauseating kiss. 'She's bound to be the sort of woman who has some massive cat back at home that she's feeding to death,' I hissed.

Further on, through rows of houses, we were beginning to steel ourselves for Briton Ferry, where we'd have to walk along the cycle path by a busy dual carriageway, first on a long bridge high above the railway line and the river Neath and then under the motorway. We were a little nervous, and to make matters worse, just as we approached we met a man who gave Chico three carrots in quick succession. 'Enough carrots!' I said, trying not to sound ungrateful. Moments later a woman ran up and asked if she could feed him a mint. 'Just one, then,' I said, but as we chatted she carried on stroking his nose, slipping more to him surreptitiously, hidden under her hand. Chico was complicit, manoeuvring them out of her fingers with his rubber lips. When I looked down, half the packet was gone.

Great – now the donkey was wired, high on sugar and just in time for Briton Ferry. He picked his hooves and his chin up high and goosestepped energetically towards the unbroken stream of fast traffic.

It was strangely beautiful up there, amongst the heavy clouds and pylons and the motorway that wound about on tall, round pillars. Below us was a Gypsy site and warehouses, and a marina and sand flats in the river, a church and lots of cranes, and a dinky transporter lorry passing on the M4. The air was pale and gleaming and the wet grass was bright, and here and there were little surprises – two excitable horses in polka-dot rain sheets, and a bush of huge red rosehips. The

Mumbles glowed in the distance, and occasional sunbeams escaped through the clouds, one of them hitting us eventually.

We wouldn't make it much further, so we decided to head for Pant-y-Sais park and see if we could camp somewhere there. A man leaning on his car in the car park intercepted us before the entrance. 'It doesn't go anywhere. Are you looking for the canal? It's over there.' He pointed. 'And the cycle track is over there!' He was very eager for us to leave, but we weren't ready to let go of our hopes. We walked on along the path to the park, and sure enough, it didn't go anywhere. It was a boardwalk over a wetland, and it had been burnt down. 'Arsonists!' shouted the man after us.

I tied Chico to a picnic bench while Rhys scouted the area, returning to report that another car had been indicating to turn in but had carried on driving when he saw Rhys. 'There's something not quite right here. And it is a wetland. But there's a tiny place here we could camp...' I followed him under some low branches to a small, damp place covered in ivy and brambles. As we emerged, discouraged, a car drew in – another man on his own. None of them seemed to have dogs... And in any case, there was no park...

We grabbed the donkey and called a stables we'd passed a little way back. No questions, no nonsense, the stables owner met us on the road and directed us into an overgrown paddock. 'The car park back there... is it popular with... er, do people...?' we floundered. 'Yes, it's Wales's number one dogging location,' she said, and left us to our own devices.

FORTY-TWO

'If you can't trust your drybags, what can you trust?' I said, taking advantage of the sunny morning in the paddock to peel wet tissues and bits of paper out of the dingy panniers. The forgotten remainder of the bag of biltong from Llantwit had not fared well, and one backpack pocket was full of bits of peppery wet meat and shreds of brown paper bag. One of my new shoelaces, only a week old, had rotted through and snapped. In an impulsive sun-worshipping moment, Rhys and I both began stretching in a kind of made-up yoga. Rain was fine, as long as it was always sunny the next day.

We walked into Swansea along the Tennant Canal, glassy and quiet and framed with millions of cornflowers and tall, elegant reeds. An old railway siding was beautiful too, in a desolate sort of way – bare, gravelly ground bisected by rusting rails like a musical stave, with big purple buddleias dotted about like the music. On the far side a brick building had been daubed with the plain black words: 'WHEN THEY COME DON'T FIGHT'.

We passed Swansea on the long, curved beach – a perfect sandy bay that suggested Swansea might be the best town in all the world. 'Graveyard of all ambition, they say!' said a woman who overtook us, she and her husband each carrying an end of a huge driftwood log. Chico rolled the moment we got to the sand, no doubt happy to be off the tarmac.

'You don't see that every day!' said pretty much every person we encountered, pointing at Chico.

The Gower Peninsula is shaped like a big rectangle, 12 miles long and six miles wide, and it would take us five days to walk around it – five long days of varied and increasingly glorious views.

Fran lived at the shoulder of the Gower, in Dunvant, up the hill beyond Swansea. She, her sister Ann and some neighbours all walked to meet us and escort us in, more neighbours waving from their windows.

Poppy the donkey and Pippy the Welsh Mountain Pony watched Chico's arrival with great interest, and Fran showed us our lodgings: a mint-green beach hut in the garden, with a pitched roof and white scalloped eaves, a double bed inside and a veranda outside, surrounded by wildflowers, but several miles from the beach. It looked heavenly. It was the prototype for her new business venture, called Laughing Donkey Beach Huts.

Fran and Ann ran the local Cats' Protection League, and the house was full of cats – rarely did I see the same one twice. Some of them were Fran's and some were waiting to be re-homed, but many others seemed to be in too bad a state for that and were dragging themselves around her house, living out their last days in the warmth of her love and attention. 'That one's got a throat tumour; that one's got eczema,' she said, introducing them. A ginger cat with respiratory problems sounded like a little gremlin, and Tig, a 19-year-old tabby that was Fran's own, lay asleep almost the whole time, his face pressed to the tiled floor. Occasionally he stood up on stiff legs, wobbled for a while, then lay down again. Shut in another room a huge pregnant cat called Clover prepared to repopulate the house.

We washed Chico in Fran's garden to get the old louse egg cases off him, and although he didn't much like it, he'd stopped holding things against me. It seemed that he was beginning to believe I was on his side. I rinsed him with the hose and then jugs of warm water, and we towelled him dry. His hair was all fluffy once he'd dried off in the morning sun.

We set off late across the common, into over-enthusiastic traffic heading home from work, far too fast for the narrow road. We cursed loudly as a car overtook us, accelerating towards a motorbike on the other side. There were no fences, just the stripe of tarmac across the brow of the common, and great Highland cows with huge sharp horns stood about, glowing their shaggy ginger colour in the warm evening light.

We three were all cheerful, leaping over bogs and glad to be striding out. Suddenly we were back in holiday-Wales and out of the cities. For the first time I had a sense of the end of the walk, still a very long way away, and on the other side of the unknown inlets and headlands of Pembrokeshire, and yet somehow no longer so many different cultures away.

As we made progress around the Gower's south coast the next day, we were able to walk on cliffs at last. The sheep-nibbled grass and craggy headlands looked like real Welsh coast to me, the rocks pitching down to the perfect creamy sand of Oxwich Bay below.

Rhys was trying not to admit that he had a hangover. 'You take him – he's mean to me. He bites me and kicks me,' he said, handing Chico's rope over. His hangover was down to a woman called Carolyn who'd put us up the night before, in her old family home on the cliffs above the bay. It was a huge hotchpotch of a house, once stately but now very retro and a bit tired. The main building was an early-seventeenth-century monastery and the extension had been built 100 years later, with long gardens running down to where an eerie sea mist crept over the clifftops.

The kitchen had been redecorated after a fire in the 1970s and everything was covered with fabulously garish patterns. Carolyn had little interest in all of the old treasures – I expect she was desperate for a long break in a clean, uncluttered magnolia sanctuary. 'Did you see that the curtains match the wallpaper?' she said. 'It's vinyl wallpaper, so to make the curtains you just peeled the paper off the back and hemmed them!'

Every drawer was full of Hellmann's Mayonnaise lids and there were more roasting dishes than could be used in a year of dinners. Off a corridor were several rooms piled high with tools – all ancient – and the carpet was stuck to the concrete floor with duct tape. On every surface there was evidence of bulk buying – packets of dog food, cartons of cigarettes, crates of wine bottles.

'I expect you'd like a glass of wine?' came Carolyn's welcome. She poured them to the top, and introduced us to her mother. Janet was 84 and had advanced dementia. She mumbled to us, and lost her thread halfway through her sentences, but her features were proud and her shoulders square. She had neat, rosebud lips and long grey hair, and wore a fisherman's Guernsey.

'Other way up, Janet,' whispered Rhys kindly when he saw her tapping the underside of an unopened pot of fromage frais with her teaspoon.

When Carolyn had put her to bed and sat back down at the table, with the bed alarm next to her in case Janet tried to get up, and the phone at her other side to guide in yet another new agency nurse who was lost in the lanes outside, she told us about the solution the family had settled on.

'Daddy left us well provided for,' she said. He'd died a while back, and there was enough family money that Carolyn and her two sisters had all decided to give up their jobs and take it in turns to live with their mother. They each had two weeks on and four weeks back at their own homes.

'I'm afraid you'll have to take us as you find us!' she said, topping up the glasses as her ancient, toothless dog Daisy licked my toes under the table. Every so often Carolyn would leap up to smoke in the doorway; she was counting the few remaining days until a sister came to relieve her.

Carolyn was clearly proud that her mother was able to live out her days in her own home, cared for by her daughters, but still there was a great sadness over the house. The freedom of the family money seemed like a mixed blessing, in a way. Carolyn didn't have her own work any more, and seemed a bit adrift between worlds without something of her own to hold on to. She couldn't really do courses or sports; her home life was spent waiting to come back again, to witness what she'd loved of her mother disappear day by day, and to watch herself become frustrated and trapped.

Beyond Oxwich the thick fog continued all day, inside and outside our heads, and we camped at Port Eynon. The campsite was still busy for a late-September weekend, and whispers of 'look, a donkey...!' shushed towards us through the mist. Rhys used my map case and a piece of notepaper to make a sign saying, 'PLEASE DON'T FEED THE DONKEY!' I drew a smiley donkey face, and we hung it on Chico's back.

At Rhossili we looked out over Worm's Head, the unmistakeable long and knobbly headland at the westernmost tip of the Gower. The sun had come out and hundreds of people milled around on the cliff, taking the sea air before heading off for pub lunches. We were welcomed by the Coastwatch volunteers who crewed the lookout station and had been notified of our arrival by eyes and ears back along the coast. They were all extremely smart in their shirts and ties, and ribbed navy V-neck sweaters with gold epaulettes. While we looked through their binoculars at huge seals lolling on the headland, Chico munched a hole out of the smooth turf at our feet, making a big effort to wrinkle up his lips and his nose to get his front teeth far enough out to take a proper scoop. The earth beneath was red.

Arry – the long-distance runner I'd met in Hay-on-Wye – and her boyfriend Andy ran up, midway through a gruelling Saturday circuit around Rhossili. Forty back-to-back marathons, she'd done – ice baths, protein shakes, the lot – and while we sat on the grass together I asked her about it. She told me it was the sponsorship and the importance of her chosen charity, the Velindre Cancer Centre, that had made her carry on. She had lost both parents, in quick succession.

Right from the beginning of the walk I'd been asked, many times, if I was doing it for charity. Enthusiastic givers tended to come in waves – the Lleyn Peninsula had been a benevolent place, as had Herefordshire, and now the Gower. People would come over, or leap out of their cars, waving notes and just assuming we were doing it all for charity; their generosity was astonishing.

It would have been strange and ungrateful to decline their donations, and so after I'd felt puzzled for the first few weeks, it was the walk itself that had come up with the solution. I'd decided to share any money that was thrust into my hands between Iain and Lindsay's equine therapy project near Porthmadog, Felin Uchaf's architectural volunteering centre, and Moelyci's community-owned hill farm. Those three small, unusual and inspiring causes had turned up within a few weeks of each other, back on the Lleyn, and were part of the journey.

But I never rattled a tin, annoyed though people often were with my passive attitude to collecting money. It felt important that we weren't 'doing it for charity'. Once a woman had run over to see if we were and I said, as I always did, 'Well, yes, but…' She ran back to her friends shouting, 'I *told* you! I *told* you! She *is* doing it for charity!', as if it would be incomprehensible otherwise. Another day a woman came right out and asked me bluntly whether I'd lost a family member to cancer.

I don't have anything against all of the impressive feats undertaken for charity. They attract attention and make hard cash; they can be cathartic; they can show solidarity with people who have struggled with illness, or gratitude to those who have dedicated themselves to helping. God knows, there are a million worthy causes.

And it can certainly galvanise people to do really incredible things. Like Arry. But it was important to me that I was walking because I liked walking. I liked Wales, I loved meeting people and on the whole the rewards of the adventure were immediate, not deferred. It wasn't a transaction, or a hardship I was enduring for a greater good, or something that I could only do if it was going to achieve something else. It was a big adventure, because it was there, for its own sake and its own magic, and I was puzzled that this was so puzzling to people, that many people needed a frame through which to understand such an undertaking.

One person said, 'Oh, well, if you're not doing it for charity it must be for a world record?' I suspect I might hold the unofficial record for slowest long-distance walker for some time. Another person on the Gower asked Rhys if he was on a gap year, which it seemed to me (considering he was 39 and his beard and moustache were by now pretty wild), was just another way of trying to frame it.

And yet I was scribbling what Arry had said on a piece of paper, and Rhys was filming the play of light across the miles of sand. I was taking photos and drawing my route in highlighter on the map; we were documenting madly, storing it all up for something else, some other time. Future purpose. I thought again of Holly and her spiritual vertical moment, Chico and his earth-chomping one, and Steve the New Age traveller cartwheel maker from the borderlands, and the endless wandering of nomads. I was about to try to formulate some thoughts in Arry's direction, but she and Andy had leaped up and were jiggling about, ready for the next 10 miles.

I realised it was true. This was a big adventure, for its own magic, and it was working. It wasn't always fun, and we were tired. I was sneezing like a pop-gun (was it Fran's cats? Carolyn's cigarette smoke? Janet's vintage house dust? Hayfever, or a cold?), and all of our kit was in various states of disrepair. It wasn't always fun – many times every day it wasn't fun at all – but it was still the finest summer ever.

It had taken 700 miles to realise it, but this was absolutely brilliant. Thank you, world! Thank you, people! Thank you

Rhys, and Chico! I thought of Carolyn's four fallow weeks and, with the irritating enthusiasm of someone high on sudden simple happiness, I wanted to go back, grab her by the hand and take her walking.

FORTY-THREE

The next day – the day of the three moors – was one of the most beautiful of the whole journey. We'd slept well in a little caravan belonging to Chris, the young landlord of the King's Head pub in Llangennith. He had also launched a brewery and was effervescent with entrepreneurial energy. He designed us a route over the moors – sticking to the high ground rather than the busy roads nearer the Gower's north coast. Chris's mum, Anna, brought out framed pictures of people cockling with donkeys and ponies at the next village along. The following day we'd find out just how significant this was to the people of the Gower.

From the top of the first moor, Llanmadoc Hill, we were stunned by the view, like a map laid out before us. We were on the north, inland edge of the peninsula now, heading briefly back east along the Loughor estuary, with Llanelli and Burry Port on the far bank – our route in a few days' time. The three-mile-long Llangennith beach and the lighthouse were back to the west, the way we'd come. There were green hummocks and white houses down below us, and beyond them were swirls in the currents of the Loughor and wriggly streams running through the mudflats. Such colours! Such distance! The bracken on the moors was all shades of red, gold and green. On the second hill, Ryer's Moor, we met a pasty man with a plastic bag and a drip on the end of his nose. 'I'm lookin' for magis,' he said, 'magis' rhyming with bhajis.

'Ah, magic mushrooms? Will you dry them?'

'No, I'll have 'em this afternoon!' he said, and wandered on. It was a Monday. Days of the week meaning nothing to Rhys and me either, we looked for some too, but found all sorts of different-coloured mushrooms and left them where they grew.

Next was Cefn Bryn, the 'backbone of the Gower', where we got lost in the bog looking for Arthur's Stone. It was worth looking for – a Neolithic burial tomb from 2500 BC. A giant capstone sits on a number of smaller ones, and was even bigger before a vast chunk fell off in 1693, possibly because the patron saint of Wales, St David, chopped it off with his sword in annoyance at the importance of the stone to druids. Or it might have been lightning.

From the ridge we could see down to Oxwich Bay on the south side too – it was in shadow and we realised the sun was setting. We hurried the rest of the way, our three shadows and eight legs stretched out long before us on the road. We crossed the fourth, bonus moor – Welsh Moor – by the light of our headtorches and slept in the garden of Chris's business partner, who was away in Dubai. Chico was scared in the stable, so I brought him out and corralled him with us on the grass, pleased to be able to comfort him.

We walked down to Penclawdd where we'd arranged to meet Hannah, a news reporter for ITV Wales. She turned up, a one-woman band, doing the filming and interviewing all herself. 'Is this an 'And finally...' piece?' I asked. 'Yes,' she said. 'If you walk along there, I'll just come off the blackberries here, to show that it's autumn now.'

She interviewed Rhys as well as me, and when she asked him what he thought about the trip, he said, 'I thought she was crazy! I mean, she doesn't even like *dogs*!' As soon as Hannah drove off, he looked at me. 'Why did I say that? I only said what I thought she'd be expecting. I didn't think it was crazy – I thought it was brilliant!'

Penclawdd has a cockling history that goes back to the Romans; the low-tide cockle beds of the estuary yield famously tasty cockles. It always used to be the women of the village who did the cockling: tough and well-respected, out in all weathers, they made a living right through the industrial revolution and Penclawdd's various mining and industrial booms and busts. They'd take their cockles to Swansea market, the boiled and shelled ones in pails balanced on their heads, and the live cockles in huge baskets on their arms. Even now licences are strictly limited and only hand-raking is allowed.

Some plasterers in their thirties leaned out of their white van and told Rhys that they remembered ponies and donkeys being used for work out on the estuary, and on my side of the road a man pulled up and said, 'Do you know you're in donkey country now? My grandmother had a pony to pull the trap, and the donkeys had great big bags of cockles on their backs. Sometimes she'd ride on top, with her rake and her riddle.'

It was a man called Wyn, leaning on his spade, who explained why the donkeys were so fondly remembered. He said he recalled his friend saying sadly, 30 years ago, 'That's the end of it for the estuary. They've authorised vehicles.' Wyn was clearly still angry about it and looked pretty fierce, as if he might punch Rhys. I tried to ask him a question but he said, 'Shut up and listen, will you?', continuing, 'Now there's vehicles out there dropping oil and diesel, and people tip rubble. You can see a tractor out there now. I think it's terrible.' Then he was done with us. 'If you hadn't talked, I'd have finished this hole and have it full of concrete by now!' We left him to it.

Bryan, a John Lennon impersonator who ran the food van in the industrial estate, said in his Liverpool accent, 'They call men "donks" around here. I'd be offended if someone called me a donk, but then I'm not from round here. They don't mind. You want a cortado leche leche on the house? That's what we used to have in Tenerife.'

We walked on with our milky coffees, and bought laverbread from the seafood warehouse. The woman there, Heather, finished hosing the floor and brought out a live lobster and a crab to show us, their powerful bodies writhing angrily in her hands. Outside stood a mannequin in a slightly ragged Welsh-lady costume, holding a price list. 'The men are out,' said Heather, 'so I've done all the mussels myself!'

Fran, the cat-woman from our first night on the Gower, passed us on the road and took all our bags the last ten minutes to her parents' house. Our day's mileage was low, but we'd been standing around all day chatting, and my knees had started making some strange clunks. Was it my new shoes? Or the damp autumn air?

We sat on Margaret and David's sofa, with Fran and her sister Ann too, and ate cherry cake while we watched the news, laughing at Rhys saying contemptuously, 'She doesn't even like *dogs!*' It was like being with old friends.

Margaret sent us off with bags full of apples and tomatoes from the garden, and we stopped for a picnic in a park before we crossed the Loughor Bridge and the county boundary into Carmarthenshire. The tomatoes were the most delicious I'd ever tasted, so sweet that they could have been served as a dessert. 'I make them a comfrey brew – that's the secret,' Margaret had said.

While we munched, we talked about the new job Rhys was about to take up, lecturing on a film course in Yeovil a few days a week; his name had been put forward by Jez back in Caldicot. Rhys was thinking he should find some lodgings in South Wales, in order to be close to Chico and me and not too far from Yeovil. As we mulled over the practicalities, a man and woman cycled by. 'Hang on!' said the woman, looking at me. 'I know this baby!'

Ann turned out to be an old friend of my parents' from the 1980s. She'd owned the restaurant next door to their wholefood shop in Aberystwyth and remembered me in my baby bouncer, blocking the doorway so every customer had to give me a bounce on the way in. I'd not seen her since then, but she'd heard about the donkey.

Within the space of a 10-minute chat, she'd offered Rhys her spare room in the Mumbles. Fortune smiles on people who sit in parks and declare their needs to fate.

FORTY-FOUR

Rhys stayed a few more days. I was happy with him leaving, but preferred if it was always tomorrow and not today. He walked the length of the new Millennium Coastal Path with us, a 13-mile stretch of neat, wide path running from Llanelli to Pembrey, through parkland that had been recovered from 2000 acres of industrial wasteland. It was a feat – well thought-out, curling through landscaped hills and beaches, past sculptures, harbourside cafes, and a rugby pitch.

We camped in a hidden hollow so completely surrounded by gorse bushes that we didn't need to put up the corral at all; we just pitched the tent across the entrance. There was nowhere to get water so we economised, eating dry food and sharing one cup of tea, and in the morning I had a tiny wash with tissues and raindrops off the grass.

We were cheerful. I disco-danced to a local radio station on top of a train tunnel that went right through one of the landscaped hills, and a cafe gave us two big bags full of picnic – crisps, sandwiches, apples and chocolate – and a bin bag of such exceptional quality that I couldn't bring myself to use it for clearing up Chico's poo so tucked it away for waterproofing instead. I was really enjoying the few and precious treasures of the road.

A young woman called Morgan had spotted us on Loughor Bridge and invited us to stay in the mobile home that she and her mother, Caroline, had in the corner of their paddock, near Burry Port. They bought us fish and chips and then went home to Llanelli, but left us with their paddock cat who purred to us. There was no electricity, so Rhys busied himself making lanterns out of torches and water bottles, and in the morning leaped up, saying, 'I know what he wants! A hug! Whether he looks like he does or not!' and ran out to see Chico, who'd been peering in through the glass door. He came back to report that he'd tried out putting the cat on the donkey.

The next morning Rhys packed and went. As Chico and I set off around the coast from Kidwelly to Ferryside, he kept stopping, looking for Rhys. We were both a little jumpy, and I remembered an odd moment on the path the day before when Chico had reared up at me three times, his front hooves right up in the air. It hadn't seemed all that aggressive, but was scary because he'd never done it before, and it was a reaction to me stopping him from rolling in a pile of old bonfire charcoal. Funny animal.

We got our first view of the Carmarthenshire coastline to come – the pretty village of Llansteffan across the Towy estuary, beyond which, on the other side of the river Taf, was Laugharne. And beyond *that* was some distant coast – could it be Tenby and the beginning of Pembrokeshire? We were back on an ancient pilgrimage route, this one running through South Wales to the cathedral at St David's. But for once we were worse off than the pilgrims – they'd have had boatmen vying to take them across the river Towy from Ferryside to Llansteffan, and across the river Taf from Black Scar to Laugharne. We, however, would have to go the long way round, walking a protracted four-day M-shape around the twin estuaries. I felt daunted; there was an edge of foreboding. But then came a flood of memories from the borderlands when we were last alone together, and Caernarfon before that. I began to try talking to Chico again – it felt like I was seeing him for the first time in a month.

Rhys texted from the Mumbles, missing us, and asking, 'What's that meal I make with veg and crème fraiche?'

Caroline, owner of the Burry Port paddock, had told me the address of her ex, Alan, who lived in Ferryside and was happy for us to stay in his garden. I found his terraced house, and a light was on, but there was no answer, so I had two cups of tea at the Cabin cafe. A little blonde boy announced, 'I couldn't walk around Wales, I have asthma. I couldn't, could I, Mum?'

His mother agreed, but I protested – it seemed a terrible shame to write himself off before he was even 10.

'Does your donkey like Kendal Mint Cake?' said a man with a wide smile, and fed Chico a crumb between my 'yes' and my 'but…'

There was still no one at Number 3, and Chico was getting restless. Was he in pain? Tired? Ill? Belly, harness, lice, worms? Or was I just getting sole-parent doubts? I walked him along the road a little, and he did seem to be opting for the softer verge. Was he footsore? We stood under a tree and I picked up a hoof to check. Sure enough, there were several deep red smears on the black hoof. Blood! Good grief! My heart thumped, and then I noticed that it wasn't quite the right colour. In fact… hm, yes, there were some sort of dark red berries all over the tarmac, and more on the tree above my head. I dropped the hoof and kept walking, and remembered all over again that I wasn't really cut out for animal ownership. Just because things had been going well for a while, didn't mean I could let myself relax.

I walked back and tied Chico to a tall garden gate on the other side of the road from Number 3. Still no Alan, so I texted Caroline to get his number, and then…

CLANG!

I looked round to see Chico racing towards me, the wrought-iron gate now flat on the ground and attached to his lead rope. Not this again! I leaped out of the way as he dragged it past me, and then began racing after him along Ferryside's high street.

Despite the weight of the gate, he was getting away from me. As I ran, my eyes scanned the road for cats and old people – that gate could do some terrible damage. A car pulled up alongside me and the Kendal Mint Cake man leaned over and pushed open the passenger door. 'Get in!'

We caught up and drove alongside the donkey as he ran, sometimes slowing a little, then picking up the pace when the gate banged or sparked.

'Should I try to drive onto it, do you think? To stop him?'

'No, I don't think so…'

It ricocheted off the kerb, slowing Chico a little, and the road curved around and began to go uphill, which slowed him some more. Kendal got past him and pulled in, and while Chico dithered for a second, I leaped out, grabbed his headcollar and put my forehead to his for a few moments before leaning back to untie the rope from the gate, which smelled of bashed metal. He wasn't too sweaty and didn't seem scared at all, but as I walked him back down the road I realised how much I was shaking.

A van pulled up and a couple leaned out. 'Is this the donkey that was wandering about?'

'Er, well… he was galloping full pelt, pursued by a gate?' I replied.

'We got a phone call,' they said. 'Looks like it's all under control!' They drove off and I wished I'd asked for help with the gate.

A text appeared with Alan's number and I called him as we walked back. Chico had run about a mile.

'Hello, I'm the one with the donkey. I think Caroline might have…? Yes? We can go somewhere else if it's a bit odd, having a donkey stay in your garden! No? Great – thank you! What should we do then?'

'Well, I suggest you go up onto my terrace – there are great views of Llansteffan Castle across the water,' said Alan.

It turned out he was in Newcastle and was expecting us to make ourselves at home. His lamp was on for security. I felt strange settling into his front garden, but glad to have the chance to recover alone. Kendal came by and we drove back to collect the gate, which was so heavy it took all our strength to manhandle it a few feet into his car.

That donkey was strong. As I lay in my tent, sleepless, turning over unnecessary worries that were trying to take root in the fertile ground of my recently traumatised mind, I made myself think about how truly amazing it was that this powerful animal was with me. Since that game-changing day on the hill by Longtown about a month ago, I'd quickly got used to him being mostly willing to walk along with me. It was good to remember that he was so strong he could do whatever he wanted, which meant that, whenever he did what *I* wanted, he was making the decision to be amenable. He was choosing to be on my side. I fell asleep at last, smiling, camping on top of some holes he'd already made in Alan's lawn.

I leaned the gate up against its rusted, broken hinges and posted a note through the gate-owner's door. We walked on, tentatively. I was back to the sort of straight-line, no-distractions, quick march of the early days, when a man leaned out of his car to say, 'What do you call a three-legged donkey that plays the piano?' He couldn't see that I was in a nervous state, and I figured he'd go away faster if I just went along with it, so I guessed, and answered in the manner of a person trying to finish a chore: 'Honky tonky wonky donkey?' He looked a bit put out and drove on.

Chico was fine, of course, and after an hour or so I was too. I let him off the rope on the smaller roads. We walked through old estates, passing a majestic red-brick stately hall that had crumbled down to the lintels of the upper windows and was now crowned by a roof of sunshine and brambles. I could see lush green fields to the left, but we'd have to cross the Towy river to get to them. And to do that we needed to head north to Carmarthen, then turn south again; a day later we'd be a mere half a mile away.

FORTY-FIVE

I lived in Carmarthen once, as an 18-year-old art student in my first year after leaving home. We were only just older than children, excited about choosing our own food – Earl Grey tea and screw-top bottles of cheap Spanish beer. We slept in hammocks in the woods, made things all day long, and thought we were the first people ever to see the beautiful world so clearly. We bought records in charity shops and stayed up all night, falling in love with each other and smoking cheap Indian cigarettes. We climbed the drainpipes in the middle of town and took a thermos of hot custard with us to drink on the rooftops. I took my bed into the potting shed of the rented terraced house and lived with the tomato plants and flowers, surrounded by cheerful Paul Klee posters that were slowly being eaten off the walls by the snails. Earl Grey teabags still smell like romance and promise to me now.

All that was long ago, so I decided we'd push on through the town and out the other side – cutting it fine, but better than making camp on the east side and losing good walking hours. Carmarthen is a market town surrounded by a whirligig of roundabouts and dual carriageways and I was keen to get it over with.

As we passed through, several unrelated people began chatting to us in a car park. One man started singing, a woman in a flowery dress stopped eating her McDonalds to join in, and an Italian art student looked puzzled.

'Donkey, donkey, don't you stop,
Just let your feet go clippity clop,
Your tail goes swish and the wheels go round,
Giddy up, we're homeward bound!'

Chico wasn't into clippity clopping – the car park was edged with some distracting clover. I eventually coaxed him away, and left the good townsfolk talking to the student.

Getting out of town was a fight. As we stalked along the hard shoulder of the dual carriageway, I swore about land that existed only for cars, as if somewhere along the way people had grown wheels and become a new sort of animal – fast and dangerous, with a very small brain deep inside the big metal armour. We charged up an embankment and onto a single road, but it was still fast and full of blind corners. After an hour the dusk was drawing in too; this all felt perilous. I eyed up a putting green that seemed to be deserted, but wasn't brave enough to camp on it.

The only house had a scary Alsatian standing guard. We began to hurry by, but then I noticed an old man leaning on the gate and smoking a pipe. His head was bald on top and softened by fluffy white hair on the sides, and he wore a fleece waistcoat and bright blue Crocs. I didn't usually like to ask for help unbidden, but on this occasion it seemed wiser than risking any more of the main road – which, according to the map, was also about to plunge into a deep, dark wood. 'You don't, by any chance, have a little patch of grass we could camp on, do you?'

Derek gestured at the field behind me. 'You could use the car park,' he said. 'I'll call Kay.'

Later on, Derek's wife Maralyn – known as 'Ma' – told me that it was always 'call Kay!' in their house. Kay, their daughter, came out and offered me their caravan, which was parked at a rakish angle (as so many people's caravans seem to be) in the field. She brought out some hay for Chico, as a treat, and introduced me to her two donkeys – Millie and Daisy.

'I didn't want them,' she told me, as we pursued them around their field. 'I had a shire horse, my beautiful, gentle big girl, but she died last year. It was terrible, and I didn't ever want to care that much for an animal again. So for Christmas I got a chaise longue – I was so happy. And then my damn family made me come outside, and there was a donkey. They'd got me a donkey.'

When we went inside and the kettle was on, Ma told the tale again, adding that Kay had stood looking at the donkey with tears running down her face. 'That's it then, I'll have to get another one,' she'd conceded.

Ma was sitting in the living room of the warm, well-worn house, in an armchair with her legs elevated. She was wearing a nightgown, and next to her was an oxygen machine with a tube that snaked into one nostril. An air conditioner chugged in the middle of the room.

I had a shower (First! Shower! Since! Gower!) and on my way back and forth both Kay and Derek told me, separately, that Ma had lung disease and was only just out of the critical care unit. The prognosis was bad, just three months more perhaps, but not to mention it because they hadn't told her. We all drank tea and chatted, the room full of people and laughter. Kay left to go to her job, an overnight shift at a care home in Carmarthen. Her brother Leigh arrived to do their own night shift, sleeping on the sofa next to Ma, who slept in her chair nowadays. In the kitchen, where Kay and Derek wrestled with the truth, the top of the stable door was open, and the cold air from the clear, dark night outside came in, relief from the heat of the range that roasted away, keeping Ma just right. Derek stuffed his pipe and talked, while in the yard Tango, the Alsatian/black Labrador cross sniffed around, a complete softy. An old, fluffy lapdog was called Bitey – I didn't ask why.

In the morning Derek picked up his flow of conversation, while I made myself rounds of toast. His stories wound around, loosely connected or not at all, through the ages and the local geography. There were no facts to pin things to; it was like watching an impressionist painting emerge.

'This place cost £5000 when we bought it. Before, my family had a 100-acre farm. I remember taking the milk churns down on a zinc sledge – that would have been 1947. They were horse-and-cart days, they were. A whirly came up, happened last year too – took the roof half off the caravan, did you see the rocks holding it down? I was about five or six and the whirlwind came through the woods – turned the oaks to matchsticks. We were making tumps of the hay, and the whirly took one clean away. I remember thinking, it will be down in a minute, but it never came down again.'

Many of the stories included deaths, from a little dog that had eaten slug pellets under his dahlias, to the Pendine murderer hung in Swansea in 1953. A local boy had been killed on the way to his own wedding on his motorbike.

Eventually I roused myself from the cloud of vague poetic memories conjured in the sleepy heat of the stove. Derek showed me a painting of his own – a beautiful dappled path, soft layers of paint, just like his stories. I went to say goodbye to Ma, who, as I turned to go, said, 'I went to heaven, I think.' I stopped and sat down. 'I know it sounds crazy. This isn't me, in here! I'm an outdoors person, I am. We went out on Saturday, the first time in months. I put flowers on my parents' graves. On the way back I stopped Kay and said, that's the gold! The sunset! That's the gold I saw in heaven!'

My heart ached. 'I had a scare, I don't know if they told you? I was in the critical ward, but I'm getting better now.'

I asked Ma to give my love to Kay when she got home, and she said, 'Kay is a wonderful person. It's been hard. I wish she would talk about that shire horse...'

Eventually, at two in the afternoon, I managed to leave their house – a place where nearly every one of the dozens of stories seemed to end in death or loss. But for all of the slow heartbreak, the house overflowed with softness – love and life and warmth.

I hugged Ma and kept my voice breezy. 'Stay away from the gold, Ma!' At the gate Derek and I hugged each other over and over, and as Chico and I set off down the road his eyes filled with tears.

As we walked, on the approach to Dylan Thomas's village of Laugharne, I began to memorise his poem 'Do not go gentle into that good night'.

I recited out loud his repeated line 'Rage, rage against the dying of the light', and felt the ache of love and the welling up of their grief. It had seemed so different to Carolyn's house on the Gower. Was the difference down to the taint of madness? Or incontinence? Or the sadness of the loss already endured, the grief for Janet's forgotten self, the being stuck in a stasis where love was congealed and healing couldn't begin?

Love doesn't save you from grief – it makes you vulnerable, it hands over your heart, casts it out of your control. As Chico and I walked together through the Carmarthenshire farmland, I could really feel that something good had settled between us. He wasn't obedient and docile like a beach donkey – he'd wilfully wander away to look at something and then come crashing through the undergrowth with branches sticking out of his packsaddle – but he would respond to my voice and eventually follow me, walking through gates I held open for him, and falling in behind me as we covered the miles. He seemed to understand me, and the journey, and the joy of exploring.

I looked back at him, the strong, young animal walking behind me, nodding his head with every vigorous step. Vital, full of the sap of life; I pushed away the thought that he would ever be old. I'd pass him on first, pass on the responsibility and safeguard my heart.

This page, left: Morning chores. *Above:* Weighed down with gifts on the friendly south coast. *Below:* Comparing manes in Cardiff.

Overleaf, above left: Chico eyes up our borrowed caravan. *Above right:* Derek bids us farewell after an emotional stop near Carmarthen. *Below:* Chico navigates on Oxwich Bay. *Opposite above:* Rhys and Chico have a little moment over lunch. *Below:* The South Wales Echo comes up with the walk's best pun.

ADVENT-EEYORE

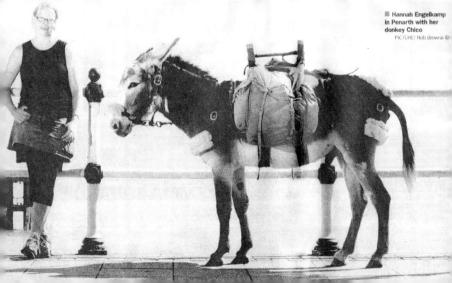

Hannah Engelkamp
in Penarth with her
donkey Chico
PICTURE: Rob Browne ©

PART FIVE

PEMBROKESHIRE AND THE HOME STRAIGHTS

FORTY-SIX

Despite there being such a long, long way still to go, in passing Carmarthen I'd suddenly felt homeward bound. It seemed to come from something other than actual proximity. Hope, perhaps? Or that, in still failing to live in the moment, I was finding myself spending walking hours thinking about the exciting things of the future, like doing evening classes in Welsh, watching films, wearing different clothes, learning about wintertime animal husbandry and the price of hay. My thoughts turned to earrings, computers, London, routine. Hazel, the owner of Chico's field in Aberystwyth, left a message asking if Chico would be staying in her field again on our return; if so, she'd get on the case mending the shed for him. That was a step too real and I stalled for time. Daydreaming was one thing, but I didn't yet believe we'd actually make it.

Perhaps it also had something to do with walking through Carmarthen and hearing Welsh spoken in the streets again, and in a Mid-Wales accent. But then almost immediately we had left the language behind again. We were now south of the Landsker Line, in 'Little England beyond Wales', the name given to the southwest corner of Wales between Carmarthen and the top of St Brides Bay, including south Pembrokeshire, some of south Carmarthenshire, and half of the Gower. I'd assumed the epithet came with the influx of English people – retired artists and bed-and-breakfast owners and the like. But it's much older than that: the region was first recorded as 'Anglia Transwalliana' in the sixteenth century, and the distinction probably goes back even further. The Landsker Line is remarkably obvious, a clear delineation of language and culture, with Welsh language and culture predominant to the northeast side, and English culture and language to the southwest, despite the distance from the border. It's not known why the region came to be so English, although the area was settled and raided by waves of Vikings, Saxons, Flemish and others, before being placed under military control by the Normans, who built castles all over the place. As with the Lleyn Peninsula, I suppose that this corner hadn't been a remote outpost, but a land of harbours in the busy highway of the sea, predisposed to becoming home to mongrels. I wouldn't speak Welsh again for over two weeks, until we crossed north of the Landsker Line, near St David's.

My habits were also changing. I was choosing indoors when I got the chance. The night after leaving Ma, Derek and Kay's warm house, I hung out in a campsite utility block, which had a little more atmosphere than the village pub (in defence of the pub, it was quite a nice utility block). The mobile reception was so good that I watched frivolous American comedy shows on my phone, my feet up on the washing machine. Chico's hair had begun thickening up for winter, and he seemed almost grateful – at least unusually cooperative – when I put his rain mac on him on drizzly nights.

But it had been a mild September, and I was very glad for that. I'd still not worn all my clothes in my sleeping bag, used my tiny hot water bottle, or been rained on while both setting up and striking the same camp. I had sent my bikini home, but still had the suncream on board, and had used it twice the week before. The first frost hadn't been mentioned again.

When I lived in Carmarthen, my sort-of boyfriend Jo lived in a woodland beyond St Clears, where I helped him build a huge roundhouse in a clearing. He was now in New Zealand, but I had tracked down his dad, who'd said I was welcome to stay in the woods, and that I would meet a woman called Sarah up there, and her baby, Sylvan.

It was dusk as we arrived, and 20 minutes darker under the trees. Chico was nervous, but I remembered the old track and felt my confidence encourage him along. There was the roundhouse: a huge turf roof with a hole in the middle for the smoke from the fire, an earth floor, and outer walls made of piled-up logs to burn, so that the space changed over time as they were used and replaced. There was an old leather sofa and a candle in a jar. On the first day of building, 16 years earlier, the tall upright trunks were sunk into holes in the ground and when dusk fell they glowed with foxfire, the bioluminescent fungi that sometimes lives on rotting bark. Nineteen blue-green pillars in the darkness – it was no wonder we thought we might be magic. There was no end of boldness and genius back then.

I corralled Chico by the roundhouse and walked over to see if I could find Sarah. I heard a stick crack in the silent darkness behind me and turned to see that Chico had walked straight through my corral to follow me, his mirror eyes gleaming in the light of my headtorch.

Sarah came to the roundhouse, a mother and artist about my age. Sylvan was sleeping in her lorry and I lit a fire and made cups of tea. We sat and talked about the woodland – the oaks that she thought of as male, spindly and competitive. The trees were more feminine in the valley, by the stream. She'd seen a panther down there, she thought – shining eyes bobbing along, too tall for a cat. There were a lot of sightings in Wales, and bits of sheep found in the branches of trees around there. The police generally took it seriously. 'You'll be alright, though,' she said. 'You've got a fire.'

I lay on the leather sofa, watching my fire burn down and trying not to listen for panthers. Chico patrolled the area, coming into the roundhouse to roll on the earth floor in the first soft light of dawn. I thought he knew I was there, but when I shifted in my sleeping bag he jumped and tore out into the clearing.

It rained hard the next day and we walked down to Laugharne to see the famous boathouse – site of modern-day coach-party pilgrimages by American fans of the poet Dylan Thomas. Wet through, we were put up by Adrian, whom we'd met outside a petrol station the day before. He'd invited us to stay in a holiday home he kept an eye on for the owners, and insisted on lighting me a fire that set the chimney alight and filled the whole house with smoke. I took him to a pub to buy him a beer in thanks, and to see what the other people there thought of him. He drank his beer very fast, with both hands on the bar, leaning forward like a runner under starter's orders. There was a scorpion tattoo on one arm and a swallow on the other, both homemade and fuzzy with age. Adrian bought himself a second pint and then a third, 'celebrating,' he said, because he'd picked up the dole that day and didn't have to suffer the awful, patronising experience again for another fortnight. I got nervous. 'You don't have to worry about me!' he said, but I did a bit, and slept uneasily. He was a good soul, and gave me a waterproof hat, but alcohol and frustration made him unpredictable.

The next day I was joined by a couple of old friends, Gareth and Tom. Gareth had lived in Pendine as a little boy and wanted to come back to make a few new experiences of the place that sat uncomfortably in his memory. He and his mother and sister had fled the village, escaping his father, who'd been a drunk, though well liked locally. Accompanying a donkey over the troubled ground might do the trick, he thought. 'I took my first steps on the beach at Pendine,' he said, 'and I want to put my feet on the sand again.'

As we walked, a man with soft grey curls and a leather jacket leaned out of his car and said, 'Is that donkey your pet?'

'Well, what's the definition of a pet?' I asked him.

'An animal you care for, love, and will look after for ever!' he said, with feeling. I laughed and said I wasn't sure then –

certainly the first and maybe the second, but I couldn't say about forever. He got a bit cross with me.

Next we met a farmer called Rob, herding his cows through an underpass that linked his fields under the road. 'I built it too narrow,' he said. 'They don't like going under in single file. *Come on, girls!*' He encouraged them, but there was very little movement going on.

Rob admired Chico, and showed me some land of his on my map. Out on the headland was his family camping corner, complete with fire pit – it sounded perfect. We walked down to Pendine to get supplies for a feast, and just before we set off up the hill to find Rob's spot, Gareth noticed he'd stepped in a dog poo. He ran down onto the beach to wash his shoes, and returned, laughing wryly at the crude significance – all this time he'd been looking forward to setting foot on the sands of his childhood again, and now it had come about through washing away the shit. We linked arms and set our sights on the top of the hill – greater things, new memories layered over old.

It was exactly as we'd hoped – the camping spot of our dreams. Secluded at the end of a long, muddy farm track, we were high on the cliff, 90m above Pendine. To the east we could see out along the Pendine sands, across the twin estuaries of Carmarthenshire, and to the landmass of Pembrey forest and the Gower. And at the end, wriggling into the shining sea, was Worm's Head, twelve days back.

Gareth and Tom constructed a Jenga tower of kindling and Rhys arrived from the Mumbles. We sat around, a warm hearth surrounded by a group of friends, circled by a ring of old and gnarled elders, and beyond them a soaring semicircle of Welsh coastline, unceasingly washed in the darkness. Chico had the run of the whole field beyond our corner and he explored its far peripheries as the sun went down. Then, in a moment between jokes and stories, I saw that he'd come into the circle of elders and lain down, just beyond the light of the flames but close enough to feel their warmth, and the warmth of his people.

FORTY-SEVEN

Rhys, Gareth and Tom walked with us for the next day as we crossed into Pembrokeshire. We were heading to Tenby, where we'd been offered a courtyard for Chico and beds for the rest of us. There would be no grass, so as we passed a stables we asked if they could spare some hay, and stuffed Chico's saddlebags full. The beautiful beaches of Pembrokeshire with their lovely names lined up before us like a display of welcome – Marros, Telpyn and Amroth, then Wiseman's Bridge, Saundersfoot and Monkstone – and with the sturdy bravery of a team, we tried out the coast path itself. It was steep and exciting, with steps up and down and tight overgrown tunnels, and Chico loved it – testing and expelling his fears one by one and being cheered on by his crew. Every gate opened fully for us, except for one kissing gate, which Tommo lifted clean off its hinges. There was nothing we couldn't manage!

We walked into Tenby as night fell, and Chico seemed happy with his courtyard – Marcus and Abi lived in the old greengrocer's store, and their courtyard had been the parking place for the grocer's horse and cart. Now Chico stepped through the little door in the big blue gate, off the cobbled streets of Tenby, and made the place his own. Their twin three-year-old daughters sat on Chico's back for photos and Chico didn't seem to mind at all.

In the morning everyone walked us along Tenby's South Beach. 'Motherhood will be a breeze for you after this!' said Abi. She'd seen Chico being tricky and obstinate when we were taking too long to get going. I grinned. His pulling and weaving had caused me so much anxiety over the months, and now I knew it was an expression of impatience; he'd be fine as soon as I turned my own shoulders in the direction of travel. Abi's twins were gorgeous little blonde whirlwinds of energy, exhausting and insistent, so I took her compliment with pride.

Behind us the tall, ice-cream-coloured houses of Tenby were piled up on the rock and reflected in the shining wet sand, heavy-bellied gunmetal rainclouds scowling above them. The seven of them – Rhys, Gareth, Tom, Abi and Marcus and the twins – bid us goodbye and walked back to the town, and Chico turned to follow them a little way. I called and he came back to me, perhaps understanding at last that other people came and went. As we climbed the next headland and lost sight of them, I felt a great flutter of the excitement of the road, enhanced when the coastal path took us through a field of cows, all sleeping in the dunes, and then one of frisky horses.

We camped outside the youth hostel at Manorbier, in a thick, cold sea mist. Indoors was company, warm lounges, wi-fi and bookshelves of novels and DVDs, hot showers, a tuck shop and the smell of cooked dinner: a practical, comfortable temporary haven for the restless. But I knew that Chico was likely to bash through his corral if I left him, and the campsite wasn't enclosed, so I stayed with him. I cooked up some laverbread and watched Chico make a kind of hissing noise at the sheep on the other side of some trees. As friends had become parents I'd seen them cease to be worried about missing out on things, or seem happy to go home early, and I thought I might be beginning to understand. My current life – my purpose – was out there, and I was genuinely happy to be hanging out with Chico. It still felt like sacrifice of sorts, but worthy sacrifice that brought its own rewards. I wandered into the trees to see if he was winning against the sheep, and he knocked me over into some nettles and bit me.

Ah, my dear donkey.

The coast path kept treating us well, so we kept risking it. Manorbier would be the last shop for a while, so I stopped to stock up on bread and brandy, tying Chico to the lamppost outside where he delighted all the customers. I explained that the brandy was in case of cows, and the woman behind me in the queue asked how. 'Well, the cows scare us, and then the brandy settles my nerves later on!'

We'd been chased by cattle a few days before and I was taking more care, but there were no cows that day, just a herd of horses kept on the Ministry of Defence land, behind a tall chain-linked fence. Chico swaggered past with the air of a rock star before excited fans. Did he understand that the fence kept him safe, or was he just reading my confidence?

The mist cleared and Chico looked superb walking along the tops of the sheer cliffs against a backdrop of opaque, mint-coloured sea edged with the white lace of distant breakers and framed by red rock and dark green foliage, still lush and rich.

Our daily advance across the map was minimal – the peaks and gullies of the coast slowed our progress right down. The Pembrokeshire Coast Path is 186 miles long and in total has 36,000 feet of ascent and descent – 'the same as Everest!' said a hot-looking woman as she laboured past us. At the cafe at Stackpole Quay I had a cream tea and enjoyed watching Chico distract a grey-haired class of landscape artists, their teacher's briefing about reflections and translucence slowly petering out. I was shown up a little when Chico ran off, disappearing into the car park so that all of the many people in the cafe, car park and souvenir shop became engaged in a game of spot the donkey.

After a treacherous cliff section, we walked down a flight of tight steps to Barafundle Bay, where Chico snuffled about in the warm, soft sand, picking up seaweed and eating driftwood, and watching a huge, dead seal very closely. It took some effort to get him to leave the beach, leaping up a bank, and then labouring up the steep wooded side of the bay. And at the top there was the first stile in many days.

I couldn't bear to go all the way back to Stackpole, plus there'd be the shame of passing all the donkey spotters, so I led us inland from the beach, through trees and out onto farmland that was fenced off by a single electric wire at hip-height. As I fiddled despondently with the padlock on the gate, Chico ploughed under the wire – it hadn't crossed my mind that he wouldn't consider it impenetrable, as I did. It hooked on the wooden cross of his saddle, and as always when his progress was halted in a way he didn't understand, Chico's instinct was to keep going, ramping up the power. He pushed and pushed into the field, the line sawing into the saddle like a cheese wire. I tried to get close, ducking and holding my hands in front of my face in case the wire snapped and recoiled at me, and trying to yell calmly at the donkey, who was consumed by the vigorous task of moving forwards. Thankfully, the saddle slid over sideways, dumping the bags. Chico popped under the wire and stood in the field looking puzzled for a moment before eating a little grass.

I grabbed him and reassembled his set-up, and saw that the next wire on that side could be unhooked – thanks to Chico's unorthodox technique of brute force, we could go on. I held him close, feeling cross and alarmed; the rest of the farm was all single-wire fences too, and I didn't want a repeat performance.

I finally began to relax and let Chico off the lead again on the beautiful seven-arched bridge into the Bosherston lily ponds, hooking his rope back onto his packsaddle as I always did, leaving slack enough for him to graze. He immediately lifted a back hoof to scratch an ear, and hooked it through the rope, tying himself up for a moment of donkey yoga and leaping about on three hooves with his head to the ground.

Everything felt a little treacherous that afternoon, and we hurried on to find a campsite, not stopping to appreciate the boardwalks of the beautiful lily ponds, and sinking wearyingly into the deep sand of Broad Haven. Poor Chico didn't share my relief at having reached the campsite – while I was setting up his corral, he broke his tether in order to come over to where I was, and then got hissed at by the owners' alpacas in the neighbouring field. I'm pretty sure he was questioning my judgement as leader, and the soft boom and clatter of artillery in the distance, the way we were heading, didn't help.

We had got to Castlemartin Range, where the Ministry of Defence owns a huge chunk of the far southwest corner of south Pembrokeshire, and the sea beyond. In the morning we walked around their fences, along the road, enjoying moving fast after the serpentine coast path of the past few days. A khaki MOD Land Rover passed going one way, and a National Trust minibus passed going the other – the two big landowners down that way. Someone called, 'Hello, Chico!' out of the window.

We walked onto the ridge, the landscape lit up by the bright sun, and beautifully at odds with the dark, foreboding clouds above. It was a strange mixture of accessible and inaccessible out there – tall fences, red flags, warning signs and diversions, and then plentiful footpaths and a public lookout point with several cars parked to watch the explosions. The wind whipped around, flicking my hair and hood and the camera and map – I was getting annoyed, fidgeting and juggling things all day.

As we passed, a helicopter that had been circling for a while with an ominous buzz began to fire ahead of us, four bursts with each circuit. Ta-ra-ra-ra-ra! Ta-ra-ra-ra-ra! Ta-ra-ra-ra-ra! Ta-ra-ra-ra-ra! At first I waved into the sky, feeling observed, but as it went on and on it became increasingly oppressive and intimidating, until we'd walked underneath their circuit and the firing was right above us. Chico and I both jumped at the beginning of each round, our muscles tight with the onslaught.

We hurried on, but each time the helicopter came back around and we didn't seem to have got away from it. To the north we could see rain coming towards us too, a slanting patch of opaque grey sky. A rainbow appeared right above the distant nest of chimneys and pipes at the oil refinery. The sky was busy.

The rain arrived and fell sharp and cold, the wind flapping everything around. I tried to get Chico's coat onto him, but it flew about, and the helicopter kept firing, and Chico wouldn't keep still. The rain was soaking into my clothes and I yelled at Chico with mad ferocity, 'STAND! STAND! STAND STILL!' as loud as I could into the wind. I felt instant remorse, but he stopped moving and stood completely still as I secured his mac and put my own waterproofs on over my wet leggings and skirt. The moment we were both dressed, the rain moved on, of course. I offered Chico a piece of carrot to apologise for shouting, expecting him to refuse it, but he grabbed it and munched it down. He could be naughty like a toddler, and even a little sulky, but he didn't know about manipulation. He wouldn't turn down some carrot to make me feel bad.

We walked down to Freshwater West, a long, west-facing beach hemmed in by dunes that piled up on either side of the road. The grey-green waves rolled and smashed on the ginger-coloured sand, and broken sunbeams chased the skittish clouds around. The helicopter still circled, but we were in another world already, and looking out west felt like sudden progress. A few people were surfing out there; a few cars were parked in the car park. Chico paraded in front of the adjoining field of menacing little bullocks and got in the way of the cars – I still felt a bit fraught, and wet.

'Where's your other mule, Sister Sara?' yelled a man out of his car window. I didn't have the patience. 'I don't know what you *mean*!' I shouted back with pathetic defiance, grabbing Chico and stalking off. It's a film, I know now: *Two Mules for Sister Sara*. I'll watch it one day.

'No Camping' said the two car parks, and although I filled up my water bottles, I didn't really fancy contravening their request. When a woman and her three daughters pulled over on their way home from school, I wasn't as polite as I meant to be. Chico wouldn't stay still, and we were both tired but walking fast, on a kind of agitated autopilot, without destination. They invited us to stay – I'm not at all sure *I* would have – and we had a mile or two to soften ourselves before we arrived.

Becky was from Nottingham, pretty but camera-shy, thin with the effort of feeding the family. She had married a local farmer, tall, broad, cheerful Ieuan, who farmed the one estate farm that they could never buy – it was held in trust for the estate owner's daughter. They'd had their three daughters in quick succession – Bethan, Lauren and Megan, full of spark and spirit. They played 'guess my name': Katie? Jane? Josie? They settled on Marion for me, and weren't at all convinced by Hannah. 'She hasn't guessed *your* name yet, Bethan!' said the littlest, Megan. 'Oops!'

The girls showed me the hay barn – I'd been dreaming of staying in a hay barn, but this one was open to the northeast, and there was a rare, bitter northeasterly blowing straight in. According to the radio forecast that morning, the wind had originated over the Arctic a few days previously. The girls, their warm young blood flowing gaily now they were free from school for the day, led me clambering around their routes through the farmyard, over walls and bales, and didn't seem to notice the chill. I opted for the offer of the living-room sofa, and came in to find that Becky had swiftly cleaned the house. 'We're not posh!' she said.

We put Chico alongside their own donkeys, a fuzzy bunch that Chico mostly ignored. They couldn't possibly understand the things he'd seen, even just that day. There was probably no point trying. Instead he found the living-room window, and looked in at me.

Staying with farmers and schoolchildren meant the day began much earlier than usual – pre-dawn, in fact. There was tea and telly, and Megan and Ieuan had a cwtsh – Welsh for cuddle – on the sofa. Then Ieuan phoned around the local farmers to ask about stiles along my route, pronounced it all clear, and departed in an enormous lorry, taking Megan to her primary school on the way, with her complaining about the terrible embarrassment.

Becky walked Chico and me down through their fields as the day dawned, to the beach on the west side of the Angle Peninsula, telling me about the trouble that coastal farmers sometimes had with lamping. Lamping is the practice of dazzling and shooting wild animals at night, and the spotlight and noise would sometimes scare livestock right off the high cliffs. A campervan was parked at the beach and a woman in a cow-print pyjama suit with 'Dizzy Cow' on the front was sitting in the morning sun; she lifted her cup of tea to us in greeting.

Another woman in pyjamas walked past us on Angle's high street – this early start thing was a whole other world. We paused by the primary school where all the children stroked Chico's face, and he nibbled the scarf of a young teacher called Misty. 'What sort of silly name is Misty?' I asked Becky as we walked on. She laughed and put me right – she was Miss D, of course.

Becky left me at the edge of Angle Bay, where the tide was right up high, lapping gently at the footpath. The green bay was like a croissant, the headlands on each side curling in and making a sheltered lagoon. Boats were moored, jostling in the choppy little waves. Beyond the mouth of the bay was the north coast of the Milford Haven waterway, just a mile away across the narrow strip of water, with great jetties reaching over towards us from the other side. We were heading east now, up the south shore of the deep-water inlet. It's a busy shipping route, called Man of War Roads, a dramatic landscape of natural cliffs, rocks and islands, overlaid with manmade structures – bridges, Napoleonic forts, nautical bits and pieces, and the jetties, pipes and towers of industry.

It would be 10 miles in that direction to cross at the Cleddau Toll Bridge, and 10 miles back west again to where those jetties began, and we'd walk through the towns of Pembroke, Pembroke Dock and Milford Haven – a change from the solitary cliffs and beaches of the last days. With the early start, I was hoping we'd make it to Pembroke Dock that night.

Becky's eyes shone as she said goodbye. 'You've made my week,' she said solemnly. 'Whatever you do after this walk, you'll always have this, forever.'

I made light of it – 'My grandchildren will be sick of hearing about it!' – but she meant it, and I wished I could carry her along for a while. She'd been a policewoman in Nottingham and had enjoyed the grit and purpose of keeping order in a rough city centre. The relentless, thankless graft of being a farmer's wife and mother – two classic, invisible supporting roles – was leaving something unfulfilled.

FORTY-EIGHT

One of Ieuan's farmers had forgotten a critical stile, and after walking around the sea side of the Pembroke oil refinery for a few miles, we came across it. A killer game-over stile, halfway up a narrow path that was well fenced, and with five feet of steep brambles as backup. We sat by the stile on a patch of grass between the refinery fence and the sea, next to another vast jetty and under a huge sign that said, for the attention of the refinery workers, 'Do Not Obstruct the Coastal Path'. There was a high gate, but it was very much locked and topped with razor wire; beyond it vehicles were driving on and off the jetty, the drivers counting themselves in and out through a turnstile.

When I waved in hope of getting their attention, they waved back. It was forbidden land. As I sat in the sun, eating lunch and working up the energy to go back, Chico lay down nearby, and for only the second or third time on the whole walk, rested his chin on the ground for a proper sleep. Like a commuter on a train, his heavy head dipped and jerked as the waves of sleep slowly engulfed him, and I watched over him, with sunny affection.

When he woke up, we walked several tedious miles back around the refinery and onto the ridge behind it. I took the exasperation of the retraced steps and used it to continue learning the Dylan Thomas poem 'Rage, rage...' as we strode along. We went through fields right by the water, passing two men in bright waterproofs harvesting vegetables for the farmers' market at Haverfordwest – broccoli, leeks, cabbage and cauliflower. Lots of new potatoes had washed out of the earth and rolled down the slope, but I held Chico close and didn't scrump – we left their veg alone.

The backtracking had cost us many hours and the sun was sinking. I began to wonder about the wisdom of walking into Pembroke Dock in the dark. Luckily, Holly and Dave, friends of friends, came to the rescue, and offered to put us up at their farm in Hundleton. I slept beautifully on the conservatory floor and woke up at 6am. Holly and I drank tea and chatted, and when it got light she showed me around their five-acre wood. They'd planted it 24 years before and Holly knew every tree intimately, the struggle each had had against its neighbours, and other confounding factors. She introduced me to a tall, bushy holly tree, so well established that its guard was down and its leaves were now completely without prickles. She told me that years ago goats had got in and eaten a lot of the soft leaves. The following year the prickles had all come back.

Holly used to be a conservation purist, believing in native species only, but we passed three oak saplings that she'd bought more recently, hybrids that would be stronger than our native oaks. 'We need hybridisation for survival in a changing climate,' she said. 'I want this wood to survive.'

Next we met the herd. As with the trees, Holly knew each cow's character, and she pre-empted their reactions to my presence. They were Dexters, small Irish cattle that are very hardy and economical and good for meat and milk. Holly managed a fine balance, caring deeply for the cows but not getting sentimental – she knew what she was keeping them for.

She was vivacious and consumed by the task of farming, edged with sadness about the damage being done to the world but still full of the purpose of working and learning and doing something right. Dave had lived on that land his whole life, and Holly had joined him there. Dave's mother, Joyce, had come as a land girl, digging for victory in the second world war, and had married a local farmer; she lived next door and showed me her old land-girl uniform, her tie and badge and high-waisted britches. The land, and work, was the heart of the family.

I thought about Becky from the night before and hoped that, confined as she was in her role as tenant farmer's wife, she would be able to see her own heart take root some time.

Chico and I walked on, belonging to no place, always passing through. We walked through a place called Lightapipe – a junction and a pub. Holly had told me that it was where the carts from Pembroke Dock to Angle would stop to rest the horses briefly before the next hill. They wouldn't wait for long, just enough for the driver to light a pipe.

It took the whole day to walk the rest of the way to Des and Maggie's in Pembroke Dock – I was glad we'd not tried to do it in the dark the night before. Chico stood in his patch of garden, looking out proprietorially over the sound as the Vikings might have from the same spot in the eighth century, and in the morning Des reported that he'd seen two magpies perching on his back.

We didn't have anywhere planned for the next night. Dad and Christine had arrived in their van, and took it in turns to walk or drive, appearing every so often in laybys with tea or exciting snacks. A friend called Demi and her little terrier Monty turned up in a camper too, tear-stained from a crisis involving menacing neighbours, police and a sleepless night. We all crossed the Cleddau Bridge, high above the dark blue water that shone and puckered like crushed velvet. There was a toll of 35p for horses and horse-drawn vehicles, but the man in the booth waved the donkey through.

I worried where we'd camp; a crowd of that size wouldn't be discreet. Christine drove ahead and returned with bad news – a campsite was closed for the year, a car park had a height restriction so that vans couldn't get in. A girl of about 12 appeared on a scooter, announcing herself as Abby, and directed us to Gelliswick, a nearby beach. It was perfect – a bowl of thick green grass running down to a narrow pebble beach, the western outskirts of Milford Haven to one side, and the jetty we'd seen from Angle Bay on the other. Christine and Demi parked their vans at right angles to each other, making a sheltered square, the other edges of which were a toilet block and a corner of the great grass area where I corralled Chico.

With aplomb and skilful use of their tiny kitchen, Dad and Christine make home wherever they like, and that Saturday night they entertained us in style, setting up their fire pit and bringing out all sorts of delicious dishes – fried chicken and squirrel, salad and potatoes, and then an amazing pumpkin pie, followed by Christine's trademark tea with whisky.

Abby had scooted off to ask her mum, and then stayed with us to eat – the only one to finish her squirrel. I walked her home in the dark after a flaming sunset, the lights of the jetty winking on as the sky faded to black. Then I slept across the front seats of Demi's camper, rolled in all of her spare bedding, as cosy as a hotdog in a bun. Another campervan had parked up, and then a tiny sports car, the owner of which erected a tiny pop-up tent in the space between his car and the next. I didn't see our neighbours, but I was pleased with the quiet tribe of weekend wayfarers.

Milford Haven was founded in the 1790s when Quaker families from Nantucket were invited to settle and establish a whaling port, providing oil for street lighting. The town has a New England look to it, set out on a grid, and the old Quaker meeting house still thrives. I was brought up a Quaker: my family on my mum's side were philanthropic industrialists from the Midlands. The social conscience and firm moral compasses of those old Quakers sit well with me – the whaling not so much. But times change, and it was so recent that human beings felt themselves to be the plucky opportunists of the bountiful globe, instead of the lamentable custodians we seem to be now.

While everyone slept, I packed up and readied the steed, and we walked back into Milford Haven to the Sunday morning Quaker meeting. When we arrived, Granny's old next-door-neighbour, Anne, helped me lead Chico through the meeting house and into the garden, where he showed an immediate interest in their new saplings. 'If he eats the trees, he eats the trees,' said Jean, the clerk of the meeting, with welcome insouciance. She ushered me in, a friendly, no-nonsense woman with hair like golden candyfloss and a green, handmade kaftan.

Dad and Christine arrived by van, with Demi and Abby too; we all settled on the wooden benches in the 200-year-old building. The diffused sunlight glowed through the high windows, shining off the simple wooden floorboards, polished by whalers' boots, and the big wooden table that sat in the centre of the circle with a small bunch of roses from someone's garden.

Quaker meetings take place in silence. The central belief is that there is God in everyone; no human being is more qualified than another to interpret God, so there is no preacher. Everyone sits in a circle and, in silent contemplation and a state of listening, has their own time with God, whatever they perceive him or her or they or om to be. Sometimes someone will speak, passing on what they have received from above... or inside, or amongst...

Since everyone is equal, there is a strong emphasis on social justice, egalitarianism and pacifism, on living kindly and acting fairly in this world. Quakers tend to be politically engaged and liberal. Although the Nantucket lot were involved in hunting whales, their ships would have employed many escaped black slaves as sailors, including as captains.

The silence settled – it's a very specific sort of silence, the purposeful quiet of gathered people, actively listening. It's a place to recharge, calm down, remember what is important. I remember once telling an elderly Quaker that I felt bad because I always fell asleep when I went to meeting, and found myself spending at least half the time digging my nails into my palms to try and stay awake. 'Meeting gives you what you most need at the time,' she said. 'Maybe what you need is sleep.'

On this occasion I was kept from sleep by worrying about Chico in the garden. Halfway through, he brayed from outside, and everyone smiled to themselves. A woman spoke, telling a story she had read in old letters. A Quaker was visiting her son, a conscientious objector, in prison during the war. On her way home, late at night, a man had come up behind her on the road, and she'd said, nervously, 'Oh, thank heavens you came along – I'm so tired I can hardly walk. Will you help me to my house?' So he did, and at her door she invited him in for some tea. He said, in distress, 'No! For I meant you harm!' and ran off in shame, into the night. It was her expectation of help, her appeal to the humanity in him, her quavering faith, I suppose, that had caused him to respond with kindness. I was busy expecting help all over the place; I hoped my regular impositions left some good behind.

Chatting afterwards, the conversation turned to adventuring. 'An adventure can be as little as meeting a new person, can't it?' said Jean. Abby was certainly an adventurer – in the space of less than 24 hours she'd helped out a donkey and his retinue, eaten squirrel and tried out a new religion, and was completely unfazed.

We had a cup of tea and a biscuit, cornerstone of any sensible religion, and went on our way – saplings more or less intact and donkey glad to return to the usual pilgrimaging. Abby showed us a brilliant shortcut, and we waved her off sadly at the top of her road. It may be that she was a helpful deity of some sort herself, the benevolent gatekeeper of Milford Haven.

FORTY-NINE

Beth came, just in time for the rain. She's an old friend from Carmarthen days; back then, she made art and smoked and roamed around the place with me. She leaned in and smelled me now, and pronounced me a little bit musty, but not too bad. 'Not too leathery either, your skin!'

We walked through rain showers, steamed dry by intervals of hot sun. I was relieved to be with just Beth, no campervans to coordinate or haphazard combinations of people to worry about. Beth was the friend whose ambling gait had worried me in the early days, while I was looking feverishly for a speedy donkey. In pleasant cities all over the world, my legs have got tired while trying to walk below my natural speed with her, but now we walked along perfectly in tune with each other and Chico. Was it that Beth's pace had more to do with her placid and composed state of mind than the length of her legs? Perhaps I'd just always been in a hurry and she hadn't. Or had Chico and I calmed over time, four months on the road causing us to feel at home in mid stride.

We sat on the old Mullock Bridge alongside a new one at the head of the little Gann estuary and the turning to the Dale Peninsula. While we ate cake in the sunshine a taxi pulled up, and the driver got out to tell us a story. In 1485, Henry Tudor landed nearby with 2000 French mercenaries and began marching towards Richard III, who he'd defeat at the battle of Bosworth in Leicestershire. (Richard's bones had been found under a Leicester car park just a few months before I started the walk.) Rhys ap Thomas of Carew Castle had sworn allegiance to Richard III, promising him that anyone who put to shore in Pembrokeshire would have to 'resolve with himself to make his entrance and irruption over my belly'. He was lucky, or clever, not to have said 'over my dead body' because when Henry turned up, Rhys (who likely had been plotting with him anyway) stuck to the letter of his oath by lying under the very bridge we were now sitting on, so that Henry's Frenchmen marched over his belly. Then he dashed to Bosworth himself, gathering Welshmen along the way, and joined Henry in battle, where it may even have been Rhys who put Richard under the car park after doing him in with his poleaxe.

It's about 220 miles from Mullock Bridge to Market Bosworth, via Aberystwyth and Welshpool, and they got there in a fortnight, which means they must have been marching about twice as fast as me and Chico, but across the very same soil, half a millennium ago. It was the sneaky bishop of St David's who'd suggested the technical oath-loophole. We'd be there before long so I'd have to see if he could design me any handy let-out clauses.

As the taxi-driver-cum-local-historian drove away, the wind blew my map off the famous bridge and onto some long reeds. Beth held my ankles while I lowered myself and clumsily chopsticked the map back up with the corral poles, both of us laughing at the silliness. While I was upside down I peeped under the bridge, looking out for the spirit of Rhys ap Thomas, lying belly-up and grinning at his own cunning.

Beth left me in Dale, a small village that straddles the narrow throat of the Dale Peninsula, with beaches on both the east and west coasts. There were brightly coloured houses, a pub, a shop and a church, but on that Monday afternoon in October everything was closed and not a creature stirred. We said goodbye on a bench, looking out over the east bay. We could still see the Pembroke oil refinery across the water; six days earlier I'd first spotted it from the south at Castlemartin, and I'd seen it from every compass point since. We were reaching the end of the Milford Haven fjord; it had been a long and wriggly back-to-front 'S', out to circle the rocky south Pembrokeshire headland and then in to circling the deep water channel, swing your partner! Soon there would be some long straights – I just had to get the Dale and Marloes peninsulas out of the way first.

The whistling brakes of a coach tore through the Dale stillness, and dozens of teenagers – A-level biology pupils – leaped out and were herded off in the direction of Dale Fort. Chico and I followed at a distance; we'd had a call to say we could stay there too. It's one of the many forts that guarded the precious inlet from Napoleon III, and this one has been made into a field studies centre, built into the cliff, solitary at the end of a track. The director, Mark, offered us his garden to camp in, a little way back along the track and more sheltered than the fort's exposed field. I made the corral, tying the webbed plastic tape firmly between trees – Chico had been showing very little regard for the corral of faith recently, and the battery was in Rhys's car so I couldn't remind him with a little shock to the nose.

Mark invited me in to cook my rice and tinned mackerel in his kitchen. He'd only recently taken up the post and the house that came with it was still quite sparsely furnished. The wide picture windows had an amazing view – the red and green lights of the buoys in the mouth of the channel and the dark shape of the Angle Peninsula on the other side – but they were so well sealed that the house was unnaturally quiet. So quiet that my own chewing was deafening, and our small talk was stilted. Mark said that he wasn't yet accustomed to the dark of the countryside and often drove the 200 yards from his house to the fort. I told him that I had got used to it. I'd been 15 years in the neon city, but after four months in the country, I was now calm in the scuffly, crackly dark; even the owls didn't freak me out.

I bolted the rest of my dinner down as I stood at his sink, and we headed out to the little bar in the fort. As we passed Chico I saw a funny look in his eye, and moments later I spun around in the road to see him following us. Damn! I'd tied the corral to a dead branch and he'd snapped it clean off. I took hold of his headcollar and slung him in the fort's field, next door.

The little bar was being propped up by three students from Bath who were on an introductory residential course in travel- and nature-writing. Along with Mark and the staff member on duty behind the bar, we passed a merry few hours inventing ghost stories to scare the A-level pupils with. A new piano had just been delivered, and Mark spun us a yarn. It had gone down in a shipwreck in the haven, he said, along with a little girl. The piano had been recovered and brought to the fort, but the little girl's body had never been found... until now. Visitors to the fort had reported seeing her, he claimed, climbing up the sheer cliffs and over the fort's high walls in the silent midnight hours, wet through and draped in seaweed, trying to get back to her beloved piano. Listen! Couldn't we hear it playing, softly?

We all shuddered and laughed and made lots of noise. Perhaps if Mark had less imagination he'd not be so scared of the dark, I thought. We walked back to his house together and stopped by the field to find Chico. That was enough darkness for Mark – he excused himself and went inside. Chico was in the furthest corner and I thought I'd remake his corral next to my tent again; after all, he'd only wanted to be with me. But he wouldn't get back into the corral, and just stood, very watchful. I let go of his headcollar to reach into the tent for his rope, and in an instant he turned and walked very fast, out onto the track and back towards the village. I sped after him, trying not to run and encourage his fear. It was past eleven, and when I got to him and we both stopped, breathing heavily, there was no sound at all. The track had a hedgerow on one side with a field beyond, and the other was a strip of wooded bank that fell away to the sea. The sky was black, the road was black, the trees were black, and a low, bright moon drew silver outlines around strange shapes. Chico turned around but wouldn't take a step. Our pupils were dilated, big, black holes, looking hard but seeing nothing. Our ears listened hard but heard nothing.

'Come on, Chico! Come back. There's nothing scary there.'

I stared at the moonshadows so intently that they began to shift around the place. There was nothing to distract myself with, and I realised I was totally scared of the dark still – it was just that usually I was busy with night-time activities, culminating in sleep. Who wouldn't be scared of the loss of vision, the sense most heavily relied upon? A daytime creature is vulnerable in the dark. I put my arm around Chico's warm neck and we stood together. I tried to be a comforting presence for him, hoping there wasn't a good reason why he was spooked. I thought of the dogs at the Prince of Wales pub in Kenfig – they'd been filmed looking intently at a ghost, but apparently someone had been holding a pork scratching just out of shot. Good! Good, Hannah – think about substantial earthly things like pork scratchings and jokes. *Definitely* don't think about the little girl and the piano – for heaven's sake, we just made that one up!

For 40 minutes we stood together on the track, still and alert. Stars glittered in the trees, and after a long time I could make out the shape of the headland beyond. Then a dry leaf fell noisily just behind us, scaring Chico into moving a few steps back towards Mark's house and the fort. Two or three steps at a time, we slowly made it back. I put Chico into the field again, where he released a loud fart of relief. He stayed in the corner nearest to the tent, and in the morning there was a flattened patch, so he'd calmed enough to lie down.

I was woken by one of the writing students, who said their lecturer had thrown his hands in the air and told them off for not interviewing me. Would I join them for a bacon sandwich and a friendly interrogation? Of course I would – being asked my opinion and being fed are my two favourite things. We discussed donkeys and writing, and their lecturer told me his favourite suggestion for keeping a plot moving along: 'When in doubt, have two men jump through the window with guns!'

I fetched Chico and we set off along the coast path around the peninsula. The three students and Mark were coming for a walk, and everyone was fairly sure there were no stiles. Jean, the clerk of the Quaker meeting, was expecting to put me and Chico up in Marloes that evening, and although the village was only two miles from Dale, the coast path traced two peninsulas first. We strode out with confidence and company, but it was to be the day of the three defeats.

The first defeat came within five minutes. The path descended into a little gorge and crossed a stream with several steps and a tiny footbridge at the bottom – too narrow for Chico. I admired him for trying, and followed him back to the fort. That was that for the Dale Peninsula – the only other route was the road that went from Dale to the furthest point. We'd have had to come back the same way, two miles there and two miles back just to see the wretched oil refinery yet again.

Mark went on, and the students turned back with us. We cut across to West Dale and headed for the coast path there. Straight away there was a stile. The second defeat. It seemed a good time to sit around and share our picnics, especially since the sun was so hot. Dale, they say, is the sunniest place in Wales.

After a while a single cloud, hardly bigger than the sun, passed over it, and in that October way we were all suddenly cold and leaped into action. The students left us to it and we chose the next route, a road up onto a disused airfield. It was a strange place, huge and flat and littered all over with round, black balls of sheep poo. In some places thick slabs of the runway had been broken off and piled up, like abandoned icing after drunken guests have picked at a wedding cake at the end of the night.

At the far corner we managed to get onto the coast path that would lead around the Marloes Peninsula – things were looking up! And then, four fields in, came defeat number three – the route was covered in keen-looking cows with very big and pointy horns. We turned around on the narrow path and headed sedately back, cows on one side, precipice on the other, minds very tightly under control.

Screw the peninsulas, I thought. We walked to the other corner of the airfield and into Marloes village, exhausted after managing just three thwarted miles. It could have been the after-effects of all the visitors too; either way, I was finished – all out of energy.

Jean and her sister Grace were in their garden. It was busy, full of towering peas, beans, raspberries and maize, and Jean was as relaxed about it as she had been about the meeting-house saplings. I was less relaxed – the lawn was covered in a thick layer of cut grass, juicy and heavy and half rotted, and harbouring the occasional decomposing apple. Chico would have loved it, like a giant buffet of colic, so I tied him up at the far end and spent a long hour raking whilst cheerfully trying to discourage Jean from helping. Their neighbours turned up carrying a full-sized metal gate which they tied across the gap by the side of the house.

By the end of the hour I'd cleared half of the garden. I corralled Chico into it, away from the grass, apple trees and the tenderest of the veg. It seemed hardly likely that he'd stay in, but I couldn't rake any more. Jean and Grace looked me in the eye and with some pragmatic maternal instinct declared me overtired. They filled me with tea, curry and apple pie and sent me to bed, very early, via the shower, forbidding me to check on Chico or worry about the variety of things that could go wrong.

Just before collapsing into a feather bed, I peeped out of the attic window. I couldn't see the donkey, but Jean was sprinkling raw bacon on the lawn.

I woke at 5am to the sound of the first raindrops on the window and snuck out into the dark garden to put Chico's mac on him. Since it had got colder he no longer minded and, like feeding a baby in the night, we didn't make eye contact; I just got the job done and snuck away again. I was glad I had – a wild storm followed, the wind whisking the rain around in a frenzy. By the morning the garden was waterlogged and lots of the maize stalks had come down, like the middle pig's house made of straw. Chico hadn't done any damage, but there was still time.

Jean and Grace were local community powerhouses, that day doing the catering for an over-60s lunch, churning out several different mains and puddings, as well as elaborate homemade biscuits and sweets. Everything had a brilliant retro look about it, especially the paper bowls of caramel pudding with neat swirls of piped cream and glacé cherries on top. Every surface was covered with bowls and trays of food, protected with fly nets. Those women were professionals. I carried a few polystyrene boxes and giant saucepans to the boot of their car, but wasn't much use. They directed me to a little table set with boiled eggs and a teapot. The elderly of Marloes, the bacon-eating midnight badgers, and me – we were all very well looked after.

The fractious storm had blown itself out suddenly and the wide sky was now perfectly blue, but amidst all of the activity Chico had turned wild. It might have been the wind overnight, or eagerness to get going, but first he tried to follow me and bashed through the sisters' garden gate, breaking the bolt right off, and then – having learned that barging worked – he began throwing himself at the big metal gate round the front, churning the soaked earth into mud. His power was alarming, and I was agitated. I slapped him on the nose: 'Chico! Stop breaking things!'

While I took down the corral he managed to take several big gulps of the cut grass, so at least I knew all the raking had been worthwhile. The moment I opened the gate and Chico could see me, he was as calm as the clear blue sky. But I was still tired and felt irritable and claustrophobic. This new habit of breaking things to be near me – it was too much.

FIFTY

M y auntie Bridie arrived. She was going to walk with us for a few days, and it was a nice coincidence that she had come just as we reached St Brides Bay. Neither of us had been there before. Brides in Brides – I took photos of her posing under the road sign. She was a bit worried about the camping and the carrying and the cold, like Naomi had been, but was keen not to miss her chance and arrived well prepared.

St Brides Bay was beautiful. It's a semi-circular west-facing bay and looks like a cartoon bite taken out of the very end of Wales's westernmost corner, as if some fearsome fishy monster with jaws seven miles wide and 10 miles deep had come from the middle of the Atlantic, swimming powerfully through the deep, dark water with Wales in mind for lunch, and snap! it had taken a great big munch out of the tufty green cliffs and swum away again, chewing on rocks and cows and ice-cream kiosks.

It took us three days to walk around the bay. The main roads were further inland, so the winding lanes were quiet out of holiday season, and we plotted a course that linked farm tracks with bits of bridleway, pitching and soaring through the hills. We were frequently brought to a standstill by sudden views of the shining bay and its spectacular cliffs, and the huge tankers that hung silently in the water, waiting for their turn at Milford Haven, or perhaps for the market price of their cargo to nudge a little higher.

Halfway up a steep hill, a man with a tapering foot-long beard, feathers in his waxed hat and a huge wooden crucifix around his neck introduced himself as Father Andrew. In one hand he held a perfect hawthorn branch with bright red berries on it, which he tried to keep out of reach of Chico's insistent teeth. 'He can eat hawthorn,' I said. 'Not this one!' Father Andrew replied. 'I've chosen it specially for church!' He snipped his secateurs at me in explanation.

At the top of the hill, we found Adam's field. Adam, in his 20s, was friends with someone we'd met on the road a few days before, and he lived in his field in a big, square bus, along with some bright white goats, various chickens and geese, and dozens of very comic piggies in a pen. The pigs careened about, squealing madly and bumping into each other, and Chico looked at them from a safe distance, wide-eyed with deep disgust. Adam showed us the well he'd dug and lined – 15m straight down by hand – and told us about his idea to get a mule and some saddlebags to do the run to the local shop.

Bridie and I set up camp in the sheltered lee of a gorse bush, boiled up some pasta and went to sleep early, Bridie rolled up in a silver-foil space blanket that rustled every time she drew breath but kept her cosy.

Next morning, after just a few miles, we reached the Druidstone, an unapologetically ramshackle and idiosyncratic hotel high on the cliffs, the heart of the arts community around there. People had been telling us for weeks to stop in. It was only early and we'd hardly made any progress, but when the owner, Angus, offered us a night in the house, on the house, we couldn't resist. 'We had donkeys,' he said, his bright, expressive eyes turned admiringly towards Chico. 'My mum used to pick me up from school with them. Great fun in primary school, less so in secondary...' Chico got to stay in the old donkey paddock and Bridie and I settled into a homely room in the eaves. I walked down to the beach for 'one last swim', which turned out to be more of a terrifying pounding and dragging on the rocks. I scrambled out quickly, bruised and genuinely frightened for my life.

The weather forecast was for heavy rain all the next day, so we wrapped everything we owned in bin bags and headed out.

We had an offer of a caravan at some stables for that night, and the prospect of rain was much less daunting with the prospect of shelter beyond it. Chico wasn't keen to come with us. He huddled by the door of the hotel with a pub local who'd introduced himself as John the Ghost. John the Ghost had fallen for Chico – he missed Angus's mum's donkeys, who had gone to live further up the coast. He tried to persuade me to take Chico to visit the old jenny and make some little Chicos. I explained he'd been denied fatherhood and John the Ghost said sadly, 'I know; I had a check,' but didn't elaborate and I thought it best not to ask. 'I visited him last night,' he offered, 'and gave him a pinch of tobacco.'

That, along with the unexpected testicle check, possibly explained the basis of their new friendship. I managed to coax Chico away from the hotel; John the Ghost's great yellowish beard flapped up and down in the wind, and his rheumy eyes were moist and tender as he saw us off.

The rain held off for most of the day, and at Newgale beach we stopped to eat cupcakes and tangerines. The two miles of flat sand were almost deserted and the flags snapped in the wind. All of the colours changed minute by minute – now the sand was dark and the sea a steely grey; moments later the sea was blue-green and the sand like buttermilk. Where the waves had soaked the beach, it shone like polished silver, then became matte and white like zinc. The restless wind seemed to be harrying time itself. Two horizontal stripes cut through the changing scene – the dark frowning line of the bay's north and south headlands and the horizon linking them, and the bright white cuffs of the breaking waves.

'Is this one of the most beautiful bits of the whole walk?' asked Bridie. 'It must be! It's as good as anything in New Zealand!' Bridie is famous for exaggeration ('Oh yes! I exaggerate *all the time*!'), but she was right – it *was* wonderful. And all ours. At the other end of the beach we stopped for tea at a cafe, but sat outside in the drizzle rather than abandon Chico. Warming my hands on the teapot, I had the distinct feeling that we were gaining more through Chico's company than we were losing by having to sit outside. The cafe staff gave me a blue latex catering glove with which to throw Chico's poo, nugget by warm nugget, into the reeds alongside their garden – an inspired new piece of kit.

The rain began in earnest when we were only half an hour from our caravan; by the time we got there it felt like an ark on the top of the hill above Solva. Mic was our host, and after conversing solely online I was surprised to find her female, Mic being short for Michelle. She owned an Icelandic horse stud, and some of her horses greeted us on the road before we got there – beautiful creatures in amazing colours. I fell for a deep rusty red one with wide nostrils, and a black one with an extravagant silver mane and tail. Even in the rain their hair was like the softest of bristle brushes, standing straight up, and their faces were wide and sensible. They stood still and looked at us with sober curiosity; even with Chico alongside there was none of the crowing and huffing that most horses did.

Mic and her partner Maria showed Chico into the stable, where we made him comfortable but left the gate open. It was raining so hard that my waterproofs had long ago been breached and the water ran freely inside and out. We went into their house for a cup of tea and a towel, and when I looked up, Chico had come out of the stable and was standing in the rain where he could see me through the window. I went out again and led him back into the stable, but as soon as I left again he took up his previous post. '*Chico!* Get in the dry!' I called from the door.

But he wouldn't.

Everyone surely wants to be loved, but to be loved is to have power, and with power comes – as everyone knows – great responsibility. I'd had responsibility for Chico from the start, from the first day when he'd somehow cut his eyebrow inside the borrowed horsebox on the way home from Stonehill and I'd been racked with guilt. Then there were all the ways he could die, the hoof worry, the endless attempts to establish why he was being the way he was being. But this was a whole new world of responsibility; now we seemed to be playing for higher stakes, for his heart. And mine was implicated too.

FIFTY-ONE

More and more often I got that flutter of joy in my bosom that I considered to be something like love, especially when Chico laboured up a hill behind me, looking intent and purposeful and totally committed. Even more fluttery was when he wasn't paying attention and I walked out of sight. Then, sometimes, he'd trot to catch up, jiggling around the corner with the bags bumping against his sides, head up and ears pointing forward. 'Where is she? Where is she?' His big, usually unreadable, dark eyes would be full of the fear of being alone in the world. I melted a little.

But was it love? On his side it was provoked by the fear of being alone. I was the only constant in his ever-changing life. I was the one who fed him, and I made him feel safe. By now I could at last calm him down, sometimes, if he got upset. I was forcing upon him the impression that the world was a big place, and my face, amongst the myriad landscapes and admirers, was the sole feature that remained the same. He didn't want to lose me, but did he *love* me?

On my side the flutter came from being needed, followed and trusted, and from being valued above other humans. No human being would ever have followed me around the country, someone they didn't much like or trust at the beginning, with no idea of the purpose or direction.

So he was frightened and I was flattered – not exactly the stuff of love songs.

People had talked about the bond we'd make from long before we'd even first met, and I'd looked forward to it. I'd imagined it being a bit like it would be with a dog – all frantic, cuddly and enthusiastic, although hopefully less spitty – but

Chico always played rather more hard to get than that. When he did catch up, he'd never trot all the way over: he'd spot me, slow to a halt, and drift into the nearest edible foliage. A few days earlier he'd been startled by a tractor and had dashed towards me, but he quickly felt comforted by the proximity – 10 feet will do, thanks – and didn't need to get close enough to be touched.

It took me a long time to read the signs of affection – his quiet guarding, and his ears twitching when he heard my voice – but it still looked to me like he didn't want to let on that he liked me. Perhaps that's just a donkey thing, but I suspected it might be a Chico thing – he is a bit of a diva. And if there's one thing people really love, me included, it's when the object of their affections is a little aloof. Anything hard-won is more precious.

This might be why people liked feeding him so much; having him munch a piece of carrot from an outstretched palm was a satisfactory sort of enthusiasm. It was a transaction of sweetness – he'd get a sweet nibble and the feeder would get a moment of sweet whiskery affection. If they were really lucky he'd even go nuzzling for the next munch. It did look like donkey love, but there could be no denying it – the love was for the carrot.

Later, while Bridie was wondering where to spit her toothpaste, I looked up love on the internet. Biological models pointed out that love in mammals could be a response like hunger or thirst, to keep creatures glued together for mutual support, defence and the saving of energy through cooperation. Psychological models focused on the types of bond that make up love – intimacy, commitment and passion. Intimacy is things shared, and perhaps the exclusion of others; commitment is the expectation of longevity; passion can be infatuation as well as romance. Intimacy and commitment without passion is companionate love.

Ours was a slow-growing companionship. I'd got used to the responsibility, mostly, and it didn't scare me as much as it once had – I was starting to expect that he wouldn't die, unlike six months ago. My affection for him was based on familiarity with his little ways, his wobbly chin, his pretty hooves, his chatty snorts while we were walking along. I gave him rubs, and he appreciated the fuss. The day before, for the first time, there had been a breakthrough – he'd let me stroke his tail. He'd kept it firmly tucked in until then, so that was quite exciting.

But there was this new clinginess. He'd got needy, and I'd hardened my heart a little. Maybe that was just how love went, the ebb and flow of a relationship, of dependence and dependability, in which often one party likes and needs the other more. One strides out into the world and the other runs to catch up, one turns away just as the other craves a moment of sweetness and reassurance. Sometimes sweethearts are all out of step with each other.

Bridie left, Rhys arrived, and Mic let me ride one of her beloved Icelandic horses. They can walk in a whole different way – it's called a tölt. During a trot or a gallop there is a moment when all of the hooves are in the air, the horse's body rises and falls and the rider's body jiggles up and down. When a horse tölts, their front and back legs move in unison, both of the left legs, then both of the right legs. Because there are always two hooves on the ground it's very smooth – the horse's body doesn't rise and fall. It's also very strange looking. Mic demonstrated and it was hard not to laugh; it looked a bit like a pantomime horse in a hurry, head back, knees up.

There was apparently a time when all horses could tölt, but the trot was better for pulling carts, and for firing guns while riding, so the ability was lost. It's the isolated horses that can still do it. The Icelandic parliament decided in the year 982 never to allow new horses into the country, so the breed has been kept separate ever since.

Chico had been in a field with a miniature pony called Eddie and they'd got on well, racing about at dawn and dusk like the young lads they were. Mic and Maria were surprised by Chico's gallop – he puts his nose to the ground and lays his ears back, flat to his neck, very different from a horse. Mic asked what I'd do with Chico when the walk came to an end and said that although Chico had got on with Eddie – donkeys are famous for successful interspecies friendships, which apparently include ducks and goats and even a rhino in Tbilisi Zoo in Georgia – he would always prefer the company of another donkey. I heard her talking, but my mind had got stuck on the very first words: '*when* the walk comes to an end'. I hadn't yet managed to stop thinking of it as an 'if'.

I felt sorry that Chico didn't get much running around time with me – this mission was constant toil. I tried chasing him around the field a bit, but felt silly and tired out before he'd even broken into a trot. Chico just thought I was being weird, and when Mic and Maria arrived to help me catch him I was too out of breath to explain that I was trying to be *fun*.

We set off across another second world war airfield, just the same as the one at Marloes, only this one had an enormous pile of turnips on it. We were right next to RAF Brawdy, and in a few days we'd reach Aberporth. These had both been destinations of peace marches in the 1980s. Naomi and I were wheeled to them in the Peace Pram – a huge, ancient, leaf-sprung pram decked out in rainbow flags – to protest against American military presence in the area. At Brawdy the US Navy listened for Russian submarine activity in the North Atlantic during the Cold War. It was their largest listening base in the UK and the land there had for a time become a small piece of America.

I was an 80s child, born into a mad time when the future was counted in mere weeks. Nukes were more than a spectre, they could have been right there on the other side of a chain-link fence covered in rainbow wool. The protests were in outrage that Wales was being used, without public awareness or consent, as an important pawn in a tense political game. Those remote, quiet villages would have been high on Russian lists of top military targets. The marches were important – a time-consuming public show, a pilgrimage of conscience; marchers showed that they knew what was going on and that they did not want to be part of it.

We passed the turnips, and then a house already displaying an unwelcome plastic snowman and Santa on the roadside. The sun was bright, and clouds like cotton-wool balls skipped across the wide blue sky.

We found a road of three campsites, all in a row and looking back across St Brides Bay. The first was open – a few people came out of caravans to meet Chico – but the reception building was locked. I called them and the answerphone message was in Welsh, we'd re-crossed the Landsker Line and it really was distinct. I left an enthusiastic but halting message; my Welsh had rusted over again.

At the second campsite the owners had reverted to being farmers – the camping field was full of cows that rubbed themselves against a solitary portaloo. The third campsite let us in. Rhys worked out how to switch on the electrics for the toilet block – it was all or nothing, so the whole row of toilets and showers blazed all night long and the owner put the enormous boiler on despite our protestations. The outdoor shower was bracing, the hot water steaming in the crisp air. We dried ourselves very fast and put all of our clothes on in layers, woolly hats over wet hair. There were spiders in every sink and summer's flies were dead on top of the cisterns, lying in state on their brittle wings, legs in the air. A few dry leaves had blown into the toilet stalls – autumn was encroaching.

I'd sneezed hard all day, often making Chico jump on the narrow coast path. My face was sore and my ribs were aching. I'd not been quite right since the Gower. Was I allergic to autumn now? Mushroom spores, perhaps? I looked up what I could do about it, my nose dripping on the screen of my phone. Steer clear of the outdoors, was the first tip. I shifted in the damp grass next to the tent and moved on to the next one. Wash your pillowcase in case you have transferred spores to it from your hair. I looked sideways at my sleeping bag – unwashed, ever. It was my magic weapon, the source of all my powers – a really good down-filled one. They're just not the same again if you wash them; I'd rather be disgusting than cold. I tried not to think about the sweaty nights of the north coast heatwave. 'Consider rinsing off your pet,' was the third tip. 'They carry pollen and spores.' I caught Chico's eye and he gave me a look that said, 'Rinse me? Really? I'd like to see you try,' before rolling defiantly on the ground.

We walked into St .David's, the size of a big village and famously the smallest city in Britain. We were heading for the cathedral, and Rhys had got ahead of us as we were distracted by a woman showing off her barn owl outside the town hall. 'There's a woman here with a mouse in her car too!' said the owl woman, and a little further on I met her, having an early glass of wine while the AA man evicted the mouse. He'd also found quite a lot of dog biscuits inside the battery cover.

The cathedral, built in a hollow so as not to be visible from the lawless high seas, was also invisible from amongst the teashops. 'Turn left by the two women chatting in the street,' Rhys texted – directions that wouldn't work in most cities. The women were speaking Welsh, and it felt strangely like home. I caught a sentence as we passed: 'Ma storom ar y ffordd, glywes i.' Storm's a'comin.'

The cathedral is the holiest spot in Wales. Two pilgrimages to St David's equalled one to Rome – that was a whole pilgrimage less than Bardsey. The Celtic monk Dewi (Welsh for David) chose the location for its remoteness, founded a monastery and set an austere example – he was nicknamed David the Water Drinker, ate only bread and herbs, and for some reason chose to stand in cold water for long periods of time too. Perhaps because his chosen hollow was so marshy. He's often pictured with a dove on his shoulder; one settled on him once when he was preaching to a noisy crowd, at which time he also performed the miracle of raising the ground he was standing on so that everyone could get a better view.

Canon Dorian Davies came out to meet Chico. He looked brilliant – short and round and wearing a long black cassock with red piping and little red buttons all the way down the front to his toes. He was friendly and enthusiastic about Chico, who milled around the place, nibbling the long grass from the base of the gravestones and peeling ancient moss off the walls. 'Throughout time they've played an important symbolic supportive role, donkeys!' Canon Dorian said. 'Imagine arriving here on a pilgrimage. It's a place with serious spiritual might – the remoteness, the reverence of the sea cliffs.' And then, 'Well done. I admire your journey.'

We agreed to disagree about whether the world was fundamentally a bad place (him) or a good place (me). I reminded myself that I'd been walking firmly on the sea side of tough places like Newport, Swansea, Llanelli and Milford Haven, my optimistic eyes turned towards the beautiful view. Canon Dorian blessed me and Chico, drawing crosses on our foreheads, and warned me to take shelter from the storm.

And we were off again. At Whitesands beach we met up with Tracy the owl woman – she'd been excited to walk the two creatures together in the beautiful setting, and we'd gone along with it. Lucy the owl seemed pretty relaxed too, as Tracy tied her leg leash to Chico's packsaddle. We chatted and walked along the beach and back, promenading for the sake of it. Poor

Lucy got blown off her perch, which rolled back and forth with Chico's steps. He didn't seem too concerned, even with all of the hopping and fluttering she had to do to right herself again. I held him close in case the sand gave him the idea of rolling – he'd flatten Lucy and it would quickly become a very bad day.

As we walked, Tracy told me that she'd found art at the age of 38 and it had saved her from all sorts of misery and trauma. Her eyes shone as she enthused about her salvation, and her long, heavy skirt swished in the wind, dappled with little speckles of Lucy's chalky white droppings. She'd come to Pembrokeshire when she ran away from an abusive partner, along with four small children, a suitcase and a Persian cat. She said that she had re-created herself, been set free. She painted and wrote poems, but to me it seemed that most of all she was a kind of living performance. She'd made a film of herself as the Pembrokeshire Princess and showed it to me on YouTube: dressed in high-waisted, low-neckline princess dresses, she danced about in meadows, wended her way through woodland, walked out of the sea and looked thoughtfully into the middle distance. There were sunsets, a castle, a stocky, swarthy handsome prince, a peacock, a huge moon racing across the night sky. It was some sort of self-healing fairytale, and although it was thoroughly crazy, it didn't seem much more so than the stories and icons that got Canon Dorian through the difficult days. My favourite scene was when a butterfly landed on the shoulder of Tracy's shiny polyester bodice and she looked at the camera with total, unrehearsed joy. I thought of St Dewi's dove.

Everyone in St David's knew each other, as you might expect in a city of 1600 people. They all knew the Buicks too – a family who had walked a long way with their donkeys, when their children were young. For days people had been asking if we were on our way to stay with them, but I'd not managed to track them down. At last, in the beach car park with the light fading, someone dug out their home phone number and I called them up. A house-sitter called Yvon answered and said she was sure they'd be happy to have us stay, even in their unfortunate absence.

Rhys went back for his vintage automobile and Chico and I set out for the Buicks's. The land out there was fairly flat, stacked on cliffs about 50m above the waves, but with a couple of striking hills on the northern horizon, their far sides falling into the sea. In the gloaming they were dark cut-outs, and the little lights of distant houses lit up one by one. We made good progress along a quiet back road, despite a bracing headwind. Behind the wind there was a strange pumping, whistling noise, and it took a while before I thought to look up. It was a swan, exactly the same lilac colour as the high, flat clouds, and it was labouring along into the wind in the same direction as Chico and me, its wings pounding through the air and groaning with the effort. Its absurd, heavy body followed its long neck, which pointed intently ahead. It did not look like an animal that should be suspended so high in the air, its progress so slow as to be unfeasible. In the flat, dusk light I had to keep my eye on it or I'd lose it, grey on grey, where it became just the disembodied sound of determined toil again.

We three journeyed on together for a while, and then suddenly the swan changed its mind, turned its course, and flew back the way it had come, from Whitesands beach or beyond. With the wind behind it, it was gone in seconds, riding out the turbulence. All that effort for nothing!

I'd spotted the little light that I thought might be our destination, and as Chico and I carried on, we felt like a traditional scene, walking through the gathering dark towards sanctuary and promise in that windswept, craggy landscape.

FIFTY-TWO

Yvon was looking after the Buicks's many creatures – ducks, chickens, doves, cats and dogs – for a few weeks. In her 60s, she was just embarking on a new life – a second footloose freedom, but with heart and responsibility. Her next stop was going to be volunteering at a nearby community organic agriculture project. She was caring for the Buicks's animals very tenderly, chatting to them and getting to know their characters.

In the kitchen were two enormous dogs – an old and smelly black Newfoundland, her thick woolly fur covering her eyes and weighing her down, and a very young Great Dane called Tolly. Tolly was far too big and strong for his complete inexperience; he seemed like a firework in a shoebox in that lovely old family home, yet to grow into his enormous feet and skull.

Yvon put Tolly in the living room, beyond a baby gate several feet high, but he sailed balletically over it as if it wasn't there; he wanted to get back to where he could see the donkey, who was parading in the garden. Tolly was terrified of Chico and so had growled at Rhys; Rhys was scared, which was very unlike him, and that put me on edge. It was like a quick-spreading virus.

Yvon, little and round and quiet, comforted Tolly, who leaned his giant body against her and trembled. Yvon was worried that Tolly might throw himself at the glass doors and smash them, so we pushed the sofa up against them, only for Chico's huge head to appear behind it, leering through the glass, playing a menacing game of peepo with the petrified dog. We piled cushions above the sofa and hoped Chico would get bored. Eventually we all settled down a bit, and I, with the witless engrossment of exhaustion, carved a little pumpkin to hang on the packsaddle. It was nearly Halloween. When I'd finished, Rhys intervened, made me a potion of honey, lemon, ginger and brandy, and sent me to bed.

In the wild and murky morning we walked out, heading up one of the little hills that we suspected we couldn't pass; we wanted to see the view of the coast to come. It was a moment worth marking – our last new bearing. It was still over 100 miles to Aberystwyth, but after all of the winding and twisting of the previous few weeks, we'd now turned northeast, and northeast we would walk until finally the sea cliffs yielded Aberystwyth. It felt good, but it didn't feel like the final descent; none of the place names there meant anything to me and I didn't know what was coming up. We were still far from the familiar.

'Ah, it is *always* worth walking to a lookout post,' I said with gusto. Rhys had wanted to come up and I had wanted to get on, so I was apologising, in a way. Rhys smiled wryly at me and my oscillating moods, my spasmodic energy levels. I shifted my gaze from the far cliffs on the horizon, and there in front of us was a brand-new stile, still gummy with creosote, planted in freshly stamped earth, and with a padlocked gate alongside.

The landscape was deserted, the last traces of the summer buzz still there, but the people gone. At Abereiddy, a beach black with slate, there was still an ice-cream van, a woman inside reading her book and the hotdogs and tea probably selling better. We were determined to have an ice-cream, even when it began to rain as we were ordering. The heavy drops splashed in our rum 'n' raisin. 'You know there's a big storm on the way?' asked the van woman. 'A couple of days…'

We walked around to see the Blue Lagoon, an old slate quarry right by the sea, like a great submerged amphitheatre. The water was bright blue, strangely so on a day when everything else was grey. As we stood on the high diving ledge above the quarry, it began to rain furiously, like a tap had been turned on above us. We could hardly have been wetter, and might well have been warmer, if we'd leaped into the chasm.

Chico was unimpressed, and so were we. Along the clifftops the wind blew hard enough to dry us off, pushing the flesh on our faces around into the bargain.

That stretch of coastline was so achingly beautiful that I almost felt I couldn't look – my eyes were full. The dark clouds just heightened the beauty, as did the debris of the quarries. The village of Porthgain had made a bid for post-quarrying survival by turning to brickmaking, and red-brick gables and columns stood around, strong enough to weather everything but the whims of supply and demand. There was a sentry on either side of the steep, narrow harbour to help guide the seamen in. The one to port was a smooth obelisk of field stones and mortar, recently whitewashed and as beautiful as any public artwork. Porthgain was now immaculate, with pleasure boats and art galleries, strings of twinkling lightbulbs and cheerful fenders brightening the place up, and not a person in sight. It can't have been very nice there when rock was being crushed, poorly paid men were pulling trams, and the quarry was under constant threat, yet there was sadness in the tidy finality of it, of a place swept of industry. All that energy, all that purpose. A mission dead and over.

A bright blue boat on the harbourside was called *Onward*, so I obeyed.

We camped at Trefin and Philine came for another stint, but I was not a good person to visit. I'd been giving Rhys a hard time but couldn't stop myself – now at least he had company for a day or two. They sat up and drank hot chocolate but I felt so rough that I crawled into the tent and that extra level of sweetness that comes from sleeping when other people are talking softly nearby. Rhys spoiled it when he got in, rattling everything and shining his headtorch in my eyes.

Mum had called to tell me that there was a 'storm special' on – she held the phone up to the radio so I could hear snatches of forecasters saying, 'Tightly packed isobars, deepening area of low pressure… Maybe gale force 11. Amber warning for very strong winds and travel disruption… Could be the worst since the storm of 2007 that killed 11…' and then, 'Heading straight for Pembrokeshire.'

I hadn't heard the news for months, but this item was going to be unavoidable. The storm was forecast four days before it had even formed, and was due to get to us on Sunday evening – by now it was Saturday morning. I'd already received dozens of texts and messages on Facebook, all along the lines of, 'I hope you've got some shelter planned? Bricks and mortar, for you and Chico?' I hadn't. The sense of expectation felt oppressive.

I woke up early and lay in bed, in the dim dawn. The clocks would go back that night and the dark evenings would begin even earlier. We'd walked right out of British Summer Time. I felt briefly triumphant, and then had a little cry, a boiled egg and a hot shower. This great adventure seemed to be tailing off in a weary, unremarkable, anticlimactic trudge. I wondered if I should take the writing teacher's advice and arrange for two men to leap into the tent with guns.

We set off and Philine was impressed to see Chico walking unroped; she'd not seen him since just pre-Clun, when the borderland days had suddenly got much harder. He was a very pleasant travel companion now, but I didn't seem to have any control of myself at all.

The coast went on being beautiful and Rhys and Philine's fresh eyes soaked it all in. They took photos and suggested good spots for wild camping another time. But with the rocky terrain our progress across the map was slow. We clambered 50m down off the cliffs, then 50m up the other side. My muscles felt like they'd been tenderised in salt water, every vitamin washed away. I was as anaemic and insubstantial as the limp toilet paper that was decomposing in my pockets, coming out in damp transparent ribbons whenever I dug about for it as my nose ran in the wind.

'Come on!' said Rhys, striding up the cliffside with Chico in front of him and Philine out ahead. 'Good exercise!'

'FUCK EXERCISE!' I yelled at him. 'I've had enough exercise!'

We had lunch on a high headland, burrowed into spongy hummocks of grass. They headed off before me; I was on the phone, calling around and looking for somewhere to stay the next night that had some sort of cover for Chico. My clammy map scrumpled and tore as I forced it back into the map case, and I howled. The wild headland seemed somehow sympathetic, so I made my plea, shouting as loud as I could: 'I WANT TO GO HOME NOW! PLEASE! THAT'S ENOUGH ADVENTURING!'

The wind took my words and flung them all over the place; the others didn't hear me, except perhaps some meaning caught by Chico's long ears, and my thinly disguised secret was safe with him. Did I really want to go home? I was scared to, too.

I caught them up and we descended to Abermawr beach, where there was the little dark nobble of a seal's head bobbing in the light grey sea, under the light grey sky, beyond the light grey pebbles. We all watched, holding our breath. It was joined by a few more seals, all gazing at us as we gazed at them. Chico was suspicious and watched them too.

After 20 minutes we stopped talking softly. The seals weren't going anywhere – their stamina for surveillance outlived ours, and we went on our way.

Now I seemed to be thinking about endings. I asked Rhys and Philine, 'Do you think it will be two more weeks, or three? I think some people want to come and see us arrive, so it would be nice to get back there for a Saturday, wouldn't it? It's going to be dark an hour earlier from tomorrow. A week is too little…'

'Who needs a party?' said Rhys. He is not a man who makes plans – no doubt one of the reasons that he sails along so calmly. 'I guess it just depends how much energy you have left.'

Another yell came out of me – I was as surprised as they were. 'NONE! I've got none! The idea of two weeks is too much! Tomorrow, even! I want to go home. I'm tired!' I was half laughing and half crying; it was all a bit much. And then it started raining, hard. Chico wandered off quickly in the wrong direction, although with no place to stay, my direction wasn't really any more right. I struggled into the tight, cobwebby shelter of a phonebox to look at the map.

We came to an open field with a very simple, very welcome laminated sign – 'Tents and Caravans Welcome' – and a phone number. I called it, trying to shelter my phone inside my hood. 'Yes!' The voice on the other end had to shout to be heard over the roar of wind on the line. 'Set up wherever!'

All of a sudden it began to rain in a way that made the previous rain seem pleasant. The air was so thick with water that we could hardly see each other, and the sideways wind joined in – I could feel it pushing the water into my clothes from behind. The backs of my legs were soaked, the creases of my knees waterlogged. Yuck.

I thrust the phone into my knickers, hoping the three wet layers might save its life, and bellowed to the others, pointing at a hay shed. It was open on one side but closed on the prevailing side and as we stepped in, the roar stopped completely, our ears ringing. We stood in silence, recovering, amazed by the simplicity of our salvation. The low, long-suffering shed had weathered those exact same winds for years – it wasn't complicated. A few feet to the side the weather raged on past us. After a while we sat down on some nice dry bales. No one dared suggest that we go outside and set up the tent. I was shivering.

'Perhaps we could ask…?' Ahead of us was a very attractive farmhouse with a vintage Airstream trailer in the garden. Suddenly a Land Rover pulled up from the other direction, and wound down the window – it was the farmers I'd phoned.

Their farm was back the way we'd come, and the place we were admiring belonged to Griff Rhys Jones, who was, apparently, 'famously a bit grumpy'. I dropped some heavy hints about the shed, and they said we could stay in it, and invited us for dinner. Rhys and Philine were tired (at last!) so I left them and went for tea. The farm was much further away than I'd expected, and as I walked in the dark, the sky cleared and stars came out. I warmed up with the striding and my own heat began to dry my clothes. When I got back Rhys had laid out our beds. The small hayshed was very full, it being the beginning of winter, so we were perched, the three of us in a row, four bales up, just under the corrugated roof. A Dutch couple from the next house along had stopped by with a bottle of wine. We sat in our tiny shed, Chico keeping watch, and felt deeply content and perfectly at home. Why would anyone need anything more?

We slept pretty well. I was at one end of our bale bed, my body slightly aware even in sleep of the eight-foot drop onto farm machinery. Philine was at the other end, worried about mice and rats and bugs; in the small hours she shrieked in her sleep and woke us all up when a piece of straw settled on her face. It rained and blew some more, hammering on the metal. Chico stood at the foot of the stack, occasionally helping himself, munching loudly in the dark – I hoped he wouldn't destabilise us all. His dark shape in the first smudge of dawn was comforting.

We woke up for a breakfast feast – eggs and bread and a foil tray of brioche with an opportunist snail in it ('Euw!' said Philine), and apple jam made by Grace and Jean, the Marloes sisters. I didn't want to leave, possibly ever, but Rhys and Philine chivvied me mercilessly. Philine is German, so it's possible she didn't fully understand how saying 'chop chop' to a very tired person could lead to inadvertent violence.

We were out on Strumble Head, a great knuckle poking out to sea. The coast path ran all the way around it and would take all day, but it would be very muddy after all the rain, and the precipices might be tricky with a donkey in high winds. On our farmer hosts' advice, we decided to plot an inland course. We would go to Garn Fawr first though, the highest point out there, in order to look out over the land.

The wind was fearsome and the clouds raced over our heads. We climbed up to the very top – a trig point on a rocky outcrop – creeping up like cautious crabs on hands and feet, laughing in the wind. I stood, blown flat to the concrete pillar, clothes whipping against me. It felt like I was being ironed out, rejuvenated by the exhilaration and the beauty, king of the castle and a mere heartbeat in time, all at once. Every sort of weather was on show. The bright sun in the blue sky made sharp shadows, but the sea horizon was fuzzy. Behind us was thick, low cloud. Rain spat and sunbeams twinkled through the mist, coating the rough grasses with silver. The fields were laid out like a picnic blanket of reds and greens and little whitewashed buildings clung like limpets to the landscape. Ahead in the distance was the lighthouse of Strumble Head, its light flashing and huge waves looming straight into the air around it, staying suspended for a moment before falling back into the sea, much too far away to hear.

Back at the bottom, Chico stalked around, starting when my hat blew off in his face, dropping his bags and running about, treading on me. The wind caught my backpack and blew me over onto the springy ground – it was all a crazed chaos, but superb, and as we walked on I felt lighter for the sheer joy of it all.

FIFTY-THREE

At last, a port in a storm. Gilly and Jim were friends of Rhys's Mumbles hosts, and their neighbour was happy to have Chico in her shed across the road. We were in a hurry though – they were still a long way off, and night would be an hour sooner today. As we hurried through Goodwick, a car stopped and out climbed Tracy the owl woman, glamorous in a full-length silver cocktail dress with black flowers on it. She had been expecting to see us. She gave me an envelope, and inside were five pound coins and a leaflet about Jehovah's Witnesses – she was on the lunch break of an all-day assembly. She sat me down on the sea wall and I looked at the leaflet. The cover showed a bright utopia with tidy shrubbery and a small East Asian girl feeding blueberries to a bear while her mother looked on happily. I made some barely veiled rude comment and Tracy said with practised tolerance, 'It is there in the Bible.' Is it? Bears being fed blueberries by little girls? 'The lion shall lie down with the lamb,' she said.

Why is the promised land a place where animals' natural behaviour is curbed, I wondered. I couldn't imagine the lion or the lamb being very happy with the arrangement. Tracy took my arm and said in hushed reverence, 'In the Kingdom of God you'll be able to walk all the way around the *world*!'

'I don't want to!' I said. 'At least, not with a donkey...'

'Well, what then? A zebra? You can, you know!'

'No!' I cried. 'I'm tired! I want to go home! I don't want to walk around the world with a zebra. Please.' This was getting a bit surreal.

We changed the subject to art, and Tracy brought a painting out of the car. Russell Crowe had the other one of the set, she said; she'd given it to him while he was filming *Robin Hood* at Freshwater West. She wanted to give this one to me. I was touched, but declined. I couldn't carry it with me, we'd only destroy it, and I didn't really know where we were going to live when we finally got back to Aberystwyth. *If* we got back. She was gracious and returned instead with a warm, chunky pair of handwarmers she'd knitted herself – a gift I was wholehearted about. They were the first non-edible thing I had acquired since the merino jumper I'd bought in Hay-on-Wye. There were now holes in my tent, in my preferred long-sleeve T-shirt and in my map case, and another shoelace had rotted through. So had another lead rope – it was now short and unravelling, and Chico and I had to walk very close to each other.

Gilly and Jim were like old friends, instinctively companionable. Jim and I made dinner, both of us crying from the onions. Gilly came running into the kitchen, slammed the door behind her and threw her back against it like a fugitive on the run. 'Drink!' she gasped. She'd been upstairs doing the accounts for her mother, a tricky, bossy woman with dementia. 'How can someone who failed maths O-level *three times* be doing this?'

Gilly called us all into the garden in the evening to see how completely still and calm it was on the evening of the 'big storm'. The eye had passed right over Wales and it had gone on to cause havoc on the far side of England – a double-decker bus toppled over in Suffolk, a crane fell onto the Cabinet Office in London, and the helter-skelter collapsed on Clacton pier. Pembrokeshire often got the weather early, they told me, and the worst of the storm in Wales had been over Strumble Head that morning. I felt furtively pleased that though dozens of people had advised us to run for shelter, we'd headed instead for the highest, wildest ground we could, and clung on, whooping.

Rhys and Philine left, and then Mum and Naomi arrived – I think I was being escorted again. The landscape offered up beautiful bridleways and back roads and progress was good. Mum and Nao and I walked from Dinas Cross to Moylgrove, and then on through Cardigan. Now that the sun set before 5pm, I was sleeping earlier and waking earlier and felt a little more refreshed. Chico was easy, walking along with us, the earlier gate-smashing madness of love calmed. I didn't know why, and maybe it was arrogant to assume I could find a simple answer. Some days I felt needy, and some days I felt self-reliant – why not so with my companion?

We'd heard about a campsite on the other side of the river Teifi that had a resident donkey population. The first bridge was in Cardigan, and just before it was a sign marking the Pembrokeshire border. We'd walked into Ceredigion – my home county! As we passed through a farm, the farmer looked at us in surprise and said, 'Where the *fuck* are you going, then?' with an enormous grin on his face. 'Home,' I thought.

We were wet through again, and Gordon, our host for the night, invited us to stay in the hay barn. This one was huge, two stories high, and we put up the tents inside for extra warmth, amongst the bales and beyond the mud. Chico's lodgings were a field next door, in with a 33-year-old mare called Princess. She was ancient, bony, toothless, and dignified, and she and Chico ignored each other.

Naomi began to settle herself in, sitting on a stool, wrapped in her foil space blanket and wearing multiple hats. She looked quite mad. I went to talk to Gordon, who I found in the farmyard, wearing a pair of wide braces with pictures of tractors on them. He came from the other side of the country, from near Longtown, where Chico had first walked alone.

I'd seen a single donkey in with some cows at the end of the track, and asked about it. Apparently a donkey in with cows protects against abortion, possibly something to do with donkey pee. Gordon also used homeopathy on his herd, putting a bottle of something in their trough every so often to boost their immunity. He seemed very sympathetic towards the creatures in his care.

'I'm going to become the owner of a donkey that lives in a field soon,' I said. 'That will be a whole new learning curve!' I hadn't called Hazel about her Aberystwyth field yet – the future still felt too nebulous. I'd also have to think about finding a field companion for Chico. It was too much to dwell on yet.

In the morning Gordon appeared at the barn we had colonised and called to us to jump on the back of his quadbike. We were going to meet his donkeys.

'You're welcome to borrow one of these, to be friends with Chico over the winter,' Gordon suggested nonchalantly, and generously offered to bring it over to Aberystwyth in a horsebox. Then, a few minutes later, he said, 'In fact, why don't you just take one with you?'

It had taken months to find Chico. There had been endless driving around the country, vets' visits and long conversations with Carol and Tamlin. This seemed too easy.

'Take whichever you want,' said Gordon, opening the gate. His donkeys jostled around us. There were eight of them, all different colours and sizes, living together in a big field on the clifftop. 'Well, except you can't take my jack, Ned. He's in that field over there. And you can't take the three foals as they're too new to be away from their mothers. So you can't take their mothers either.' We were down to two. 'You could take Snowflake, if you like,' said Gordon. 'Or this one.' He gestured at the other. He couldn't remember her name, so we all called her 'This One'. We herded them up the track to meet Chico.

Snowflake was a hit with Chico. She was young and small, the runt of Gordon's herd. Her white hair was tightly curled, she had an earsplitting bray, and she ran about, playful and friendly. Chico ran about with her. 'This One' was Snowflake's mother, a dirty whitish colour. She was wide and woolly, disinterested in Chico and in us.

Snowflake it was! Was I really going to do this? She certainly looked lively enough. I steeled myself and tried to pick up a hoof, and then my heart sank. It was awful – weak and broken. Gordon had said she was a sickly creature; she'd been very dehydrated as a foal, and he'd had to get the vet to put her on a drip. She had plenty of spirit, but I didn't think it would be fair to take those hooves on tarmac – we were still 50 miles from Aberystwyth. I looked at This One as she nibbled the grass from around the gatepost.

Could I really take her? Take her away from Snowflake, her own offspring? And from the whole shaggy crew, galloping around their clifftop field? I packed up and when I came back to see how she and Chico were getting on, Gordon handed me a headcollar and lead – bright pink and brand new. 'Try it,' he said. 'Try taking her.' So we did. As we departed, Gordon came out to wave us off and tell me that his wife had remembered: This One was called Floss. Chico tried resting his chin on Floss's back, in what was presumably a little shot at affection. Floss shrugged him off, curtly.

And so we set off. I was worried about passing the field – I wasn't sure I could bear to wrench Floss away, but she walked right past and kept on walking, without any sign of having noticed or cared. We continued along the coast path, Chico untied and watching proceedings with interest. I had a little chat with Floss. 'You don't seem flossy to me. That's far too ethereal. You seem to be an earthly creature. Do you mind if I call you Flo instead?' She had neat little hooves and slender ankles, and placed them close together in a tidy mincing walk that was comically at odds with her great, wide body. Her back was flat and wide on top – there was something rather sofa-like about it. Her coat was thick and hefty, greyish, with long soft white hair under her belly and chin. Whenever I stroked her nose she'd twitch her head and peel back her lips and try to bite my knuckles.

We walked down to Mwnt, a conical hill right by the shore, with a sandy beach tucked in below its cliffs and a low, stalwart, fourteenth-century church on the saddle above. It was a charming little place, like an aesthetic, poetic grouping of three objects: hill, beach and church. Hiding discreetly in a little gully was a kiosk for all of the other human needs – change for the parking, frisbees, hot chocolate and postcards. The path crossed some exposed rock and Flo slipped a little. I chastised myself; I'd have to remember that we didn't know what she knew, or what she could do. She was being so well-behaved, calm and constant, I allowed myself a full lungful of air. This was something new! We were doing it!

Naomi was beaming. She had fallen for Flo, who was very good for the self-esteem. The two of them strode on up the coast path, and I hung behind for a moment, making a plan with Mum, who was going back for her car. Chico was off the lead, walking along with all of us, but as we thinned out he stopped, halfway between Flo's retreating rear and me. His sudden moment of dilemma was very obvious, as if there was a cartoon question mark above his pointed ears. He looked up at her, and back at me. His donkey brain whirred.

And then he turned uphill, walked quickly to catch them up and fell in step behind the new donkey, his nose to her tail. Nine hundred and fifty miles of hard-won companionship and he'd switched allegiance to this simpleminded, matronly donkey after half an hour. I stood and watched them round the corner and felt a wave of relief, bittersweet but unmistakeable.

FIFTY-FOUR

We'd been stupid to leave Gordon's so late, but after the peculiar donkey transaction I'd felt the need to move on. A pony on Twitter called Tiny Tim had offered us a place to stay, but it was too far away – it was getting dark fast. As we walked away from Mwnt, two cars slowed behind us, both packed full of people, sandy and boisterous from a day at the beach. A boy was poking out of the sunroof. We held them up – wrestling one donkey out of the way of traffic on a single-track road was hard enough, but two was nearly impossible. As we walked on, Flo setting an unhurriable pace, the two families held a powwow and then invited us to stay at their holiday home on the seafront at Aberporth. We were saved!

I was a bit worried. I didn't know how Flo would cope with her first night as an itinerant animal, I didn't know whether their garden would be suitable, and I didn't have the battery for my corral of faith, so Flo would have no reason to observe it. We paraded down to the seafront in the dark with no option but to somehow make it work. Flo wouldn't walk on the left-hand verge and moved her unyielding bulk out into the middle of the road. We held her tightly, aware that she might surprise us at any time. Cars tried to pass us too quickly on the narrow road; we were an unexpected cavalcade. Mum found us and escorted us in with her hazard lights on. Very bizarre. I was apprehensive and nervous again, uncertain and in need – all familiar feelings. In a strange way, it felt good.

There was dinner – a banquet with all of us crowded around their table and passing dishes about noisily. The two mothers, Rachel and Ali, discussed second children, laughing about Flo. 'It's all different when the next one comes along!' Then came games and music, everyone calling out requests and singing along to a guitar, banging makeshift drums. I gave my pumpkin lantern to the kids – despite the rough treatment of the road it was still more or less intact; we lit some birthday candles inside it and they took it out for a trick-and-treating circuit of the twinkling little town. It was wonderful, warm mayhem.

I leaned on the ornate wooden veranda of the 1920s beach house and watched the donkeys. They stood alongside each other at the bottom of the steps, not touching, but probably near enough to feel a little of each other's body heat. It was the last night of October, five months since we'd set out. I lifted my eyes to the chilly blackness beyond the shush of the waves breaking on the sand. There were lights on the horizon, to the right. Rachel, wrapped in a blanket, leaned out of the door and saw me looking. 'Yes, that's Aberystwyth,' she said.

By the morning the donkeys had churned up the strip of grass alongside the house and the wooden fence on one side of the garden gate was broken. Chico was showing great interest in the gap, but Rachel said it wasn't the donkeys who'd done it. It was quite rotten anyway, and a boy in a mask had tried to climb over the night before. The donkeys had just given it the last nudge, she reassured me kindly.

Tiny Tim the pony had sent his owner's friend Sarah to walk with us that morning. Mum and Naomi had left the night before and I had quickly realised I was going to need company all the way now. I didn't dare walk two donkeys on my own.

Sarah took Flo and I took Chico and everyone waved us goodbye from the veranda. We crossed the beach – had Flo been on sand before? She seemed as nervous as Chico had been in the early days but shrugged it off, almost as if she'd made the decision not to let it worry her. There was a stream pouring through the town and across the beach and Sarah and Flo walked right through it. Chico followed and I hesitated a moment – it would go over my shoes! But I didn't want to break Chico's resolve. I ploughed through too: wet feet at the beginning of the day, what a calamity! St David really must have been saintly to have voluntarily stood in cold water without getting grumpy about it. I was soon distracted when the morning's mean drizzle mustered its full brawn and poured as hard as it could, all over us four. Now the wet feet were in perfect harmony with the rest of me.

I didn't have a rain mac for Flo. Gordon had said that when it was wet he left the gates to the hay barn open but that the donkeys rarely sought out shelter. Flo was a tough year-round cliff-dweller, and even in the downpour she didn't flinch or look sorry for herself. Her thick hair just coiled up in kiss-curls. We walked along the path from Aberporth and by the time we got to Tresaith the rain was coming sideways off the sea so hard that I couldn't open my left eye. For some reason I felt very cheery.

Tiny Tim's owner, Sally, took us into her house, where I discovered that every single thing on me was wet – my bra, my legs, even my armpits. I had some dry clothes buried deep in my backpack, but only one change, so I was saving it for the evening.

We'd put the donkeys in Sally's stable, where she had asked me, 'Short feed or long feed?'

'Um…' I said, as if I was trying to decide. Then, 'No, it's no good – I don't know what that is.' A short feed, Sally explained, was anything concentrated – like the alfalfa stuff. A long feed was grass or hay – pretty obvious really. I nodded and decided to forget this new information right away. I allowed myself a little grin at the thought that I'd have been really abashed at such a faux pas half a year ago. Now I emitted a warm glow at the thought that having kept a donkey alive for 960 long miles meant that maybe I didn't have to get the terminology right. The glow steamed my bra dry from the inside.

Sarah left us and Sally took us the next bit – we were being passed along the coast. Tiny Tim came too. He was more like a big dog, and very excited to be going for a walk with donkeys. He'd had a grim start. Sally used to work for the RSPCA and had rescued him from the boot of a car. His legs had been tied together and his hooves were long and curly. No one thought he'd pull through, but he became the local mascot and was a sprightly thing. Sally – unsurprisingly for a woman who'd seen so much animal suffering at the hands of humans – was very energetic about welfare. She'd left the RSPCA and was writing her own blog, or rather, as she regularly mentioned, Tim was writing it. The whole thing was in Tim's voice, as were his tweets to the 'twitterherd'. 'Hoof circle for our friends!' he'd tweet to encourage remembrance for animals used in war, or support for RSPCA week.

Sally must have seen me wince because she said, 'I know! I know it's silly, but I love it. There are *loads* of animals on Twitter!' It was true – I'd been befriended by a terrier that tweeted in some sort of baffling rasta patois. Sentimental *and* kind of racist!

'Ah, am I a joyless curmudgeon, Tim?' I asked as we walked up a steep, drippy bridleway – I'd palmed both donkeys off on poor Sally (hey, let's swap!). 'It's just that even after all this time I've got no idea what Chico's thinking about anything. I couldn't begin to put words in his mouth. To me that would seem… a bit presumptuous.' Tim trod on my foot.

'And it's twee, isn't it?' I went on, gathering pace. 'Caring so deeply about animals, but sort of dismissing their wild, essential animalness. It's the lion lying down with the lamb again, isn't it? All furpals together. Hoof circle!'

'I wouldn't fuss about it too much,' said Tim. 'She does a lot of good, you know. She saved my life and now she cares for me by the book – she can tweet what she likes, I say.'

Tiny Tim and Sally bade us farewell and turned back, and I had a mile or so to walk with two donkeys. Nothing bad happened.

I carried on mulling. There seemed little that was healthy about the relationship people have with animals. Of course,

Sally was doing nothing but good, she was making a huge difference, one maltreated animal at a time. But the scale of the problem seemed vast, and much bigger than the easily vilified animal abusers who made the headlines. Weren't we all absolutely incriminated?

Human beings had a meddling hand all over the globe: pedigree pets with features over-exaggerated to the point of health problems; vast domesticated herds medicated to stay alive in artificial environments; animals used for sports and discarded when they were no longer fit.

And our intervention had knock-on effects on the lives of other animals. The species silently lost to deforestation so we could eat cheap beef, or the many billions of birds killed every year by domestic cats. What really got me cross was the animal apartheid – that there were animals for eating, animals for loving, and animals for killing out of sight. And that people were so sentimental about some of them and wilfully blind to others – going gooey about a puppy but then feeding it the most appallingly treated, mechanically recovered, unidentified flesh. There seemed to be a fundamental indictment of human beings in it all, and it got me hissing a one-sided argument to myself. I didn't doubt the enormous human capacity for genuine compassion, but it seemed scrambled by sentimentality, double standards and compartmentalisation.

Chico and Flo left me to my silent ranting, and then there we were – at an unoccupied bunkhouse above Llangrannog. I put the donkeys in the field, made a cup of tea, draped my clothes over all of the storage heaters, climbed into my sleeping bag and watched the place at the field gate where Chico would, up until yesterday, have been standing to get a glimpse of me.

Another storm was mobilising. Outside the wind was tearing the leaves off the trees prematurely. This one was sudden and worse for Wales than the previous one – trees and power lines came down, trains stopped, bridges were closed, 10,000 people lost power. Huge waves and 80mph winds battered the Mumbles, Amroth, Little Haven and a whole list of other places we'd been to, and flood warnings were in place across the land. At the bottom of the hill, Llangrannog was having a hard time. Bits of the prom in Aberystwyth were torn up.

I didn't know any of this, from my sofa, but when there was a powercut and the lights went out, I put my woolly hat on and stayed where I was, listening to the roaring wind as the room got dark and cold. After a while Dad and Christine arrived – the next in the emergency escort rota – and Dad found the meter and put a pound in it. How embarrassing.

We feasted, as we always do when Dad and Christine appear. They cooked up burgers (deforestation! Hypocrisy!), potatoes and salad, and brought forth pie and fudge and more whisky-tea.

I checked on the donkeys – they'd found shelter in a corner between a tall hedge and a caravan. 'Flo! Are you okay?' I stroked her nose and she tried to nibble me, as usual. She was surely in some physical and emotional turmoil – torn from her clifftop buddies and made to do exercise for the first time – but she didn't show it.

Dad and Christine had their van, and I slept all alone in the converted cow barn – a single long attic with eight empty bunk beds and one and a half empty double beds.

We walked to New Quay. Christine, an osteopath, kept a professional eye on Flo's gait. She was right, Flo looked uncomfortable on the downs and the flats and picked her feet up high. I led Flo, leaving Chico to follow on his own, looking back at him and trying to say with my eyes, 'I'm sorry! You're my main man, Chico! It's you and me all the way, but this new one needs a little looking after. You're a big boy now...'

At New Quay the campsite offered me their little camping pod, and before Dad and Christine left again, Eric from Cae Mabon up in Snowdonia joined us. He was on his way home from playing Prospero in *The Tempest*, in an outdoor production in the Black Mountains, complete with pyrotechnics. Prospero! His face was tanned, his hair and beard long and wild – he hadn't quite been released from his audience's applause yet. Wild seas, tempests, a triumphant homecoming, the ending of the story, the releasing of two indentured sidekicks – all of these things I would have known about if I'd ever seen *The Tempest*. It was good to see him.

Christine fed us from the van, calling, 'I'm not coming out there!' from inside. It *was* particularly chilly, up on the hillside. Tea, hot chocolate and homemade cheese straws were all passed out. 'You should be careful,' she said to me, 'you'll get diabetes. Another piece of fudge?'

And then they all departed, driving away through the dark, their headlights lighting up the dark lanes, as Dad and Christine went back to Machynlleth and Eric went back to the foot of Snowdon. As Flo and Chico's night vision was slowly restored, another pair of headlamps appeared. It was Rhys, arriving for the final furlong. We settled down on our mats on the floor of the wooden pod, lit the gas stove and soon warmed up our hearth and hearts.

FIFTY-FIVE

Rhys introduced himself to Flo, who tried to bite him. Thanks to her, the walk had got a little shot of the old adrenaline back, if just as a consequence of not ever having quite enough arms. But two donkeys, in many ways, were easier than one donkey – certainly easier than one donkey called Chico. As we strode down the hill to New Quay we remembered Tamlin's warning, back during my bollocking in Tywyn: she'd said he wasn't a lead donkey. He was taller, fitter, faster and way more experienced than Flo, but he didn't try to overtake her. I discovered that I just had to direct Flo around, and Chico would follow. If we were standing still, waiting for something or looking at the map, Flo would stand still with us, and Chico would stand still with Flo. He'd demoted himself without a moment's hesitation, and seemed happier for it. 'Go with the Flo!' we said to him, often.

New Quay was so pretty that we hung around. The tide was out and the puddles in the harbour reflected the deep blue sky and the towering white clouds. Little boats and orange buoys sat in the puddles at jaunty angles, and we tied Chico and Flo to bollards while we bought calamari in the posh chip shop.

'I *love* donkeys!' said a woman who appeared suddenly at Flo's side. 'I always have!' Flo was a bit on edge – I suspect she'd not been tied to things very often, and this woman had quite a high-pitched voice. Flo boffed her, accidentally, I think. 'Oh!' said the woman. 'I don't have very good balance! Oh, I'll keep my distance from *her*!' She glowered angrily at Flo. 'I didn't know donkeys were like *that*!' As she ran away, I smiled to myself and thought, 'You and me both, lady!'

We ate our calamari looking at coast to come. I couldn't identify Aberystwyth. I spent 40p on the coin-operated beach binoculars, thoroughly gloss-painted in the same blue as the sky, bolted to the ground and pointing in the direction of home. I still couldn't be sure which collection of rectangles was Aber, but I saw two enormous starlings in a bush three feet away.

We were now in the tricky peripheries of the A487, the coast road that has very beautiful views but is fast, no good for donkeys, and commandeers more than its fair share of the precious narrow strip between the sea and the mountains. Avoiding it would be a challenge. It was a frustrating stretch of stiles and impenetrable bridleways, but for a while at least I was enjoying the lightness of a burden shared that I always got when Rhys arrived. On a farm track we let Flo off the rope and she followed along – it had taken 500 miles to try it with Chico, and only 20 with Flo. We expected her to fall in line, and she did.

We found ourselves in a field of cows, escaped from there into some woodland, and then had our hopes dashed by a deep ford. It was also fast, wide, noisy, opaque, brown and cold. I took my shoes off and put a foot in, and Flo ploughed past and straight across, with Chico right behind her – it was clear he didn't want to think about it for himself. Brilliant donkeys! We cheered their bravery, and they looked pleased with themselves.

We had to come out onto the road, and went into a petrol station for some terrible pasties from a self-service microwave. It began raining bitterly outside. 'Poor donkeys,' said the woman behind the counter, disapprovingly. 'Don't worry,' I said testily. 'Only three more days and they'll be able to get bored and fat and start devising ways to escape, like most donkeys.'

There weren't many camping opportunities, and we got to Aberaeron without really meaning to. There was a campsite, closed but with a farmhouse alongside. I knocked and said, 'I know you're closed. We don't need facilities, but I was wondering if we could stay because… we don't have anywhere else to go!' I didn't like doing that. The worst thing about the onset of winter wasn't the cold, particularly – it was the need.

Back in the glorious summer days we'd walk until nine or ten at night and sleep where we fell. If we camped somewhere indiscreet at least we knew that there probably wouldn't be anyone about to mind, until the advance dog-walking guard. Now it was dark even before people left work, and our things were often wet. I craved the indoors. And now that I really needed help, it felt harder to ask. I was an exhausted guest, and probably exhausting – too apologetic, too grateful, simpering.

Dorothea was a retired doctor, brilliantly down-to-earth. She showed me the pig's ears she'd just been baking for the dogs – big, crispy triangles. 'There's the hole where I took out the tag, you see? And that's a bit of snout stuck to it.' I made approving noises, and she pointed proudly at the rows and rows of jars of stock that she'd been making, from boiling the pig's head. The saucepan was still on the stove. 'It's very good – you're allowed to do it at home, a slaughterman comes.'

I did approve, although I was a bit squeamish about the chunk of snout. They were huge ears – the family must have had that pig for years. I remembered Mic from Solva telling me that in Iceland, where they love their horses as friends and companions as well as the most useful of servants and, in Norse mythology, even as deities, they nevertheless eat horsemeat. In 732 Pope Gregory III kicked off the taboo against eating horse in Christendom, because it was associated with heathen paganism, and it stuck in many countries. It hadn't been some natural, intuitive truth, but a decree from above, deliberately imposed for a calculated purpose, and then incorporated into culture.

I set up the tent, feet into the vigorous wind that was coming from the sea, and wondered if the reason I didn't want to eat Chico was because he was my friend, or because of my culture, or because of his intelligence and our communication. I was pretty sure that Flo was less intelligent, and I'd definitely rather have eaten her. If I had to choose, you know.

FIFTY-SIX

It rained so hard at three in the morning that Rhys and I both woke up, laughing in the face of the sheer deafening ferocity of it. And then it stopped, as suddenly as if someone had held an umbrella over the tent outside. I looked up the weather forecast for something to do, since I was wide awake, and wished I hadn't.

I'd often noticed, on rainy days, how many moments of beauty there were –sunbeams, cloudscapes, lightshows through green valleys of mist, all the smells and sounds of grateful earth. Often I was amazed how little rain there actually was on days I'd have dismissed as no good from behind a window. These were sometimes the most magical moments of living outside. Walking a line meant seeing all of the in-between bits of space, the land between the destinations, like the unexpected beauty of the red cliffs behind the docks in Barry, or the exceptional blackberry haul of the Newport industrial estates. But it also meant feeling all of the in-between bits of *time* too – the rainy days especially. There hadn't been a single rainy day without its moments of arresting beauty.

Until today.

It was raining when we packed up, which was never fun. Chico ran away from the packsaddle and I didn't really blame him. We walked up the hill out of Aberaeron and a lorry swerved towards Flo and me – the driver appeared to be trying quite hard to hit a puddle. I laughed. I was already so wet, it made no difference. I stuck my middle finger up at the retreating lorry in case it had been on purpose, and grinned widely in case it hadn't.

We turned off the main road – a long two-sides-of-a-triangle detour inland and up a hill, on a road that was just a little bit too narrow and frequently used for us to walk together. We advanced in single file along brand-new tarmac, one donkey each, unable to pass the time with chatting. It was neat and clean, I thought, softly rolled at the edges like miles and miles of black molasses flapjack. Mm, flapjack… A very heavy drizzle gave way to an out-and-out rainstorm – at what exact moment, I wondered, did drizzle become rain? Was it to do with downward velocity? In Welsh it was raining 'hen wragedd a ffyn' – old ladies and sticks.

I was chipper. Somehow, like laughing at the ferocity of the rain in the night, being cheerful seemed the only option. When the road widened a bit, we pulled alongside each other and began a game of Animal, Vegetable or Mineral. Mine was horse nuts – Rhys got it in seven guesses. His was difficult: sort of a mammal, smaller than a shoe box, not microscopic, doesn't live in trees, burrow in the ground or swim in the sea…

A penis, it turned out. Nice.

We got to Pennant, at the top of the hill. I'd hoped for a surprise pub, but would have been happy with a bus shelter. There was neither; we walked on.

The fog was thick and unbroken in every direction. As we began to descend again I saw the most aesthetically pleasing sight of the day so far – a line of telegraph poles heading boldly off across a stubbly field, each one a little paler than the last until, like some sort of fog gauge, they faded to white. The grass verges had become sodden so suddenly that they were holding puddles above the level of the road, and on the tarmac itself the rain poured downhill in waves. In the ditches, bright autumn leaves floated and spun.

We had a break standing by a junction, bags off and an apple for the donkeys. Flo still didn't have a jacket, but she wasn't concerned, or wasn't showing it. I dug my fingers into her soggy hair and her skin underneath felt warm and fairly dry – a well-adapted Welsh creature. Both would stop grazing when the rain got really hard, but started again as soon as it went back to just ordinary downpour levels. There was nowhere dry to sit; everywhere had inches of water on top. I tried crouching, but after a while we walked on.

In Llannon, back on the main road, I tried to refold the map to consider our meagre options. Everything was so wet – my hands, my sleeves, the whole world – that the map was becoming papier mâché; place names were rubbing off, rips were appearing. Rhys tried to help, but our hands were so numb that our fingers couldn't grasp. We tried to handle the precious thing gingerly but kept failing, swearing and laughing and retrieving it from the ditch.

We got down to the sea, and picked our way along to Llanrhystud beach and some incredible knobbly headlands I'd never noticed before, in all the years of passing the place on the main road. They were kind of beautiful, beyond the brown sea, and the brown clouds, and the brown sand.

In Llanrhystud, Ann and Andy took us into their old mill. It was dark by the time we got there, so we could only just make out the shape of the waterwheel alongside the building. We hurried past it and into the house, where our backpacks made great puddles on the living-room floor and the map crisped up on the rail of the stove. We were fed casserole and wine, and very soon I was yawning so hard that it made my jaw ache – there was no hiding it. I slunk off to bed, borrowing an old shower curtain so my bag wouldn't soak the carpet, and draping wet things all over the room. The cold had got deep into me; I wore all of my clothes to bed.

Ann and Andy had bought the place as a family home for their seven children and Ann's mum, and it was only after they'd been there a while that they began to fix up the mill. It was 150 years old, and the most beautiful machine I'd ever seen. Our tour began with a walk, up beyond the donkeys, to the far corner of their triangular woodland. Down one side of the field the river was flowing fast with all the rain, and Ann opened the sluice, letting water into the leat that ran down the other edge of the field and into the millpond. We greeted the donkeys on the way back and Flo bashed through the corral to see us – perhaps the electric shock didn't penetrate her shaggy coat. We let them loose in the trees, reassuring Ann that they wouldn't fall in the river, and they ran around in delight.

There was time for coffee while the millpond filled, and then Andy let the water from the pond fill the first few buckets of the wheel. For a long time the wheel stayed still, and then slowly it began to turn, like an old soul, confident in its majesty, refusing to be hurried. The wheel's axle was turning a vertical shaft, the teeth of the gears folding into each other and rotating the great millstones inside. The whole building shook with the power of the mechanisms.

Inside the three-storied mill, Ann was busy. She poured grain into a hopper that fed it between the stones; soon the flour would flow through a chute into a sieving machine downstairs, also powered by the wheel. Ladders led through trapdoors in the floors, via lattices of rough-grained beams and lintels, and everything was made of honey-coloured wood so well worn that the imprints of millers past were all around us. Ann said that often, halfway through a task, she'd look up, thinking, 'I really need some sort of…' and there would be the perfect tool, hanging on a nail on the wall. I felt it too – as I climbed a ladder I put out a hand for support, and at my fingertips was a knot of rope for exactly that purpose.

There were no right angles; everything felt settled, organic, built for function, and yet immensely elegant. Next to a stool was a picture of a ship, drawn right onto the wooden wall, above which was a shelf with old cigarette cards on it – Ann and Andy were leaving them alone. But it was far from just a living museum; after a lot of mending and learning, they were milling flour and selling it.

Ann said that visitors sometimes asked where the off-switch was. She and Andy had caught themselves thinking that way too – once, during a powercut, the lights had all gone off and they'd been surprised when the stones didn't stop turning. It's so deeply lodged now, that power comes from pushing a button and paying a bill. That wires are hidden in the walls and the power station is far away. Who could be expected to correlate charging up a phone with the restless turning of a wind turbine on the horizon outside? While I'd stood in a hot shower at the Anglesey campsite, just out of hearing range of the humming of the nuclear power station, there had been nothing to link the heat of my shower to the dark molecular magic going on a mile away, day and night. Clean domestic switches and sockets couldn't be further removed from the coal thrown on the power station furnace somewhere else, or the tankers in St Brides Bay and the oil and gas pumped through Milford Haven.

I imagined trying to grind flour by hand for one loaf of bread – how quickly I'd have been impelled to look for another way. People must have been so grateful to that living, noisy mill, bringing their own grain along to be ground. It would have been the heart of the village. The family who owned such awesome energy must have been powerful. And yet it was just down to the opening of a little sluice on the river Wyre, a few minutes' walk away. It was so beautiful, it made me want to cry.

I began raging against the cheapening of the light. How far modern humans are from living our lives according to real needs. Electrical energy that had burned a path of so much dread to get to me – environmental misery, oil wars, out-and-out corruption and skewed political priorities: I should consider every amp an enormous privilege. At least when whale oil lit the streetlamps people had the grace to know where it came from. How dare we squander such a precious miracle?

I was scared at the thought of inventing unnecessary needs again once I'd finished the walk. I didn't want the hard edges of my fierce gratitude for every comfort to soften, didn't want to be slowly taken over by habit and routine. To buy stuff! To own more than I could carry! I didn't want it. It would probably take a few months, maybe even longer, but the time would come when all of this would be put away. There would be a time when I didn't get giddy with delight at an unexpected chance to wash my hands, when the soap didn't froth up a satisfying grey. I'd fall asleep in front of a TV, or let food rot in the recesses of a fridge, or be seduced by adverts and fashions.

Living outside, desires and priorities seemed to have returned to some sort of sound foundation, and I prayed I'd at least remember this raw and simple thankfulness.

FIFTY-SEVEN

It wasn't far to Aberystwyth, in fact it hadn't been far for days. We were going deliberately slowly in order to hit the prom on Saturday afternoon, but somehow the days still didn't feel easy. We left Llanrhystud on the old road, then headed through a gate onto a very muddy bridleway. Flo hadn't got Chico's skill with gates. She would begin by coming right up to each one, swivelling her head 90 degrees to the side so that she could poke her soft, silvery white nose as far through the rails as possible and then reach even further with her wriggling lips. Backing her up whilst opening the gate and balancing on disintegrating clods was a challenge that we mostly failed at, all the while trying to keep eager Chico back until the gate was open wide enough that he didn't catch his bags on the latch. On this occasion he knocked a bag off into the wet mud. I swore.

Our progress along the bridleway was blocked at different times by a gulley of gorse, a temporary lake, a barricade made out of pieces of gate, and a London taxi rotting quietly to itself in a murky copse. It was also hampered by strike action, when both donkeys refused to walk along a flooded farm track until we went back and coaxed them most tenderly.

After all that it was a relief to see the road. It was a narrow back road that I didn't know, so when it rolled over the crest of a hill, the sudden view took me by surprise. It was Aberystwyth.

'Oh look, it's Aberystwyth,' I said at first, and then, as it sunk in, I whooped a bit. From the south, the town was hemmed in by Pen Dinas, a hill with an unmistakeable column on it, something to do with Wellington. There was an Iron Age fort up there, and a Bronze Age burial mound, and evidence of Romans too, but none of them could possibly have been as pleased as I was to see its familiar old shape. We diverted swiftly into a field with a bridleway down one side and began digging out the wherewithal for a celebration – cream cheese, cherry tomatoes, rolls, and the stove for tea and brandy. While the billy boiled, we walked into the field to take some photos. The grass was green and rich, the middle-ground hills were golden, and in the distance Aberystwyth was dark blue and deep green, with white streets of houses under high, heavy purple clouds. It was a majestic tapestry of a scene. While we watched, the distance became yellow and luminous. In fact I could no longer see Aberystwyth at all, and the knotty trees on the golden middle-hills were suddenly in the picture, backlit like an atmospheric silhouette scene for shadow puppets. Then I couldn't see the trees either! I realised suddenly that it was a thick, glowing raincloud, racing up the hill from the sea, waiting until just the right moment to… And yes, that was the moment. It reached us, and rained, hard. We ran back to our bags and feast and donkeys – the pan wasn't even boiling yet. We tried to cover things up, but too late; the rolls soaked up the rain, the cream cheese tub filled with water. Very sad.

Rhys took some tomatoes and went to eat them under Chico's rain mac, lifting the edge to make a tiny awning and crouching under it, leaning companionably into Chico's side. I stumbled around getting into my waterproofs. Poor Flo still didn't have a jacket but didn't seem fussed. Moments later the rain stopped and I ran back over to see a gap in the cloud right over the town, full of sunbeams like a chosen land. By the time the tea was ready, the clouds had assembled themselves into great white meringues on a bright blue sky, dappling the hills with sunshine that lit up the red bracken and distant green hillsides. The whole display had taken just 30 minutes – it felt like a showreel of best moments, or as if the town couldn't decide what to wear for our big reunion.

Chico tried to eat a huge spiky branch that was lying on the ground and dragged it over his rope, getting himself stuck. 'Need some help from the humans, do you, Chico? Of course, any time!' Rhys unhooked him cheerfully. 'But if I want something in return – a little hug, a little affection...' Sure enough, Chico swung away from his advances.

We walked on, reaching Pen Dinas with time to spare, so we decided to climb it – we'd look down on the grand finale from a safe vantage point and consider our achievement. Several bay horses, each with a white stripe on its nose, leaped about in excitement, and we scrambled past their field, up the narrow, slithery path. I tried to keep ahead of little Flo, who raced along; by the top, my lungs were burning. If we'd had her, I thought, I'm sure we'd have managed Snowdon.

And then suddenly there *was* Snowdon! And the Lleyn Peninsula stretched out along the horizon, and Bardsey Island like a full stop at the end, and to the south the coast all the way down to Strumble Head. And at my feet was Bronglais, the hospital where I was born, and my old secondary school, Penweddig. And Dad's house and Mum's house, and all of the old shapes and roofs of the town, the castle and the old college, the pier and winged Victory on her column, looking out to sea. Above us circled a red kite. It was all fantastic, perfect. So familiar, but from a different angle – from the top of Pen Dinas, but also from the context of the long, long build-up to get there. I looked across at Constitution Hill on the north side of the town. I'd been working up to this moment since I'd dithered, in tears, at the bottom of that hill, five and a half months before.

'We shall not cease from exploration,' I said to myself – I'd looked up those words of TS Eliot's the night before. 'And the end of all our exploring will be to arrive where we started and know the place for the first time.' I said it a few more times, like a little good-luck charm. We'd decided to live in Aberystwyth for a while, borrow Dad's spare room, burrow in and see what happened. I'd get to know it for the first time.

A few small flocks of starlings were beginning to come in. They shuffled and spun, gathering to head down the hill and join their crowd at the pier, to make something bigger than themselves. It was mid-November, and they were starting to file into Aberystwyth for the winter, to fluff in and see the cold months out together.

I needed a good-luck charm – stopping would be hard. 'To make an end is to make a beginning,' said Eliot. 'The end is where we start from.' I said that to myself a few times too.

Mum appeared on the top of Pen Dinas, ready to escort us in – she'd guessed we'd be up here. She was wearing a carnival flower garland on elastic, in rainbow colours and all fluttery, and she had one each for Chico, Rhys, Flo and me too. We got ourselves ready for the prom. Harry was down there, busy tying rainbow-coloured helium balloons to the bar at the far end. We were going to kick the bar a second time, the town tradition, with 1000 miles of Wales between kicks.

Mum strode across the top of the hill to investigate a route down, and without warning Flo ploughed off after her, and Chico after Flo – bored of waiting while we mooned around up there memorising poetry, and ready, as ever, for adventure. Rhys and I laughed, grabbed our bags, stopped marvelling at the view, and hurried down after them to the end, or the beginning.

Above left: The 'game-over' stile behind the Pembroke oil refinery. *Above right:* Tenby's old greengrocer's courtyard. *Below:* Looking south from St David's, back over St Brides Bay.

Above left: Rhys sharing Chico's mac. *Above right:* Flo, a little donkey with great confidence.
Below: The bar in Aberystwyth, ready to be kicked again .

EPILOGUE

Slowly, over the following weeks, I put away the things of the journey. It was much harder than I expected. I hardly looked out of windows – a strange part of me felt I wasn't entitled to enjoy the view if I was going to be some sort of part-timer.

But ordinary life became normal and I eventually stopped sneezing, wore other clothes, came to care about having clean hair, and got to know Chico and Flo as pets. They still live in Hazel's field in Aberystwyth where I visit them every day. Flo comes trotting over, wheezing her ear-splitting greeting each time, and Chico hangs back awhile and watches through narrowed eyes. Occasionally he comes right up, puts his great big nostril to mine and smells me thoughtfully. Sometimes he goes for a scamper around the field, nose to the ground, ears flat along his back, kicking his hooves in the air. Most often he just swings his head away in the usual mild contempt. But sometimes when I get close he lifts up a hoof and lets it hang in the air until I oblige him by cupping it and having a look, thanking him enthusiastically.

I still don't know what they're thinking, but if I had to guess I'd say that Flo was mostly asking for more horse nuts, and Chico was chiding me gently, saying, 'All that counts is how you spend your time, Hannah.' Often, from my warm and ordinary bed, I want to send him a text to see if he's alright out there in the wild darkness. But there's no cheating possible with his affection – all that counts is time.

THANK YOU

HUGE THANKS TO EVERYONE WHO HELPED GET THIS SHOW ON THE ROAD

Chico, Rhys, Flo, and my brilliant parents, Jo and Alf

Superb editor Lucy Ridout, designer Isobel Gillan, artist Lee Wright, Jasia Warren and Ffion Rhys, packsaddle-maker David Evans, donkey-host Hazel Fairplay, Tamlin Watson and the Donkey Sanctuary, Carol Limmer, Gordon at Nant-y-Croi, Bill Doyle, Louise Peeters, Peter Muckle, Dave and Margaret at Stonehill Donkeys, Naomi Engelkamp, Annette and Oscar Wallis, Harry Durnall, and Christine Conroy

EVERYONE WHO WALKED WITH US AND WELCOMED US IN

The Judd-Olsen family, Lois and Austin and the Adventure Travel Film Festival, Gemma Kirk, Susie Ennals, Michael Thomas, Rhodri and Sarah of Moelgolomen, Philine von Guretzky, Amy and Dee Ellen, Maria Gandy, the Llanddona wild camping crew, Deborah Good, Mandy Cartwright, Mike Taylor, Steve Webb and Liz Morris-Webb, Chris and Chantelle, John Jones, Kate Lemoine, Polly Rubery, Gareth Wood, Tom Murrells, Andy and Abby, Jasia, Georgie, the Webbhardts, Beth, Bridie Wallis, Tracy Hadley, Cat V, Tiny Tim and Sally and Sarah, Long Linda, Hanwag, Coleman, Nikwax, and the Volvo Amazon, Aberystwyth allotments, Jane Burnham and Gerry, Billy Langley, Gareth Vince, Frongoch Boatyard, Kath, Bill, Norma, Jack and everyone at Chickenshack, Dave and Chenda Moir, Bryn and Lizzie Roberts, Eurliw Jones, Iain and Lindsey Crosbie, Natasha and Iona Gwyn Jones and family, Dafydd Davies-Hughes and Alice Midmore at Felin Uchaf, Pete and Sue at Penrallt Coastal Campsite, Stuart Webley and Ty Coch Inn, Andi and Will Chell, Marnie and Wyn, Mandy Sutton, Kay Laurie, the Mundle/Garratt family, Della, John, Paul and Shan at Moelyci, Pete Baars, Coed Cottages campsite, Point Lynas Caravan Park, Tafarn y Bont, Eric Maddern and Cae Mabon, Jan Loxton and Steve, Mark and Nicola and Paul at Bodafon Farm Park, Paul and Angie Board, Janette Craven, Anneke and Tom Philips, Sandy Lane Farm, Ruth and Ray at the Farmers Arms, Mari at Cae Adar Farm, Wern Isaf campsite, Pat and Godfrey Williams, Holly Thomas and Nick, Steve and

Sue at Spring Hill Stables, Anne and Andy Bennett, Llanfyllin Workhouse, farmer Arwel, Severn Caravan Park, Mellington Hall Campsite, Tess and Ben at Lower Spoad Farm, June Tabor, Teddy Bennett, Emma and Dan Price at Cosy under Canvas, Ros and Geoff at Racquety Farm, Charles and Kathryn Mackintosh at the Bull's Head, Lyny and Billy Wood-Cole, Lynn and David Price, Anna and Tim, Warren, Jez and Jo and Jeanie, Joe and Sandie Hill, Nonn Vaughan, Gaynor at Rosedew Farm, Glyn and Phillipa George at Heritage Coast Campsite, Rob Williams at Ogmore Farm Riding Stables, Gareth and Julie Maund and all at the Prince of Wales, Gail and Gareth and Lisa Needham, Fran, Ann, Margaret and David Christie, Carolyn Llewellyn, Bank Farm Campsite, Chris and Anna Stevens, Caroline and Morgan in Burry Port, Kay John and Ma and Pa, Aurelia and Colin Reynolds at Cwrt Mawr Campsite, Ali Barlow and Bearnice, Adrian in Laugharne, farmer Rob at Pendine, Abi and Marcus in Tenby, Stuart and Lisa at Freshwater East, Abby the angel of Gelliswick Beach, John and Georgina Llywelin, Lawrence and Marcia at Trefalen Farm campsite, Becky, Ieuan, Bethan, Lauren and Megan Preece, David and Holly Harries, Des and Maggie Thomas, all at Dale Fort, Grace and Jean in Marloes, Alex at Broadhaven, Angus, Beth and John the Ghost at the Druidstone, Mic, Maria and Linnie, Glan-y-Mor Campsite, Yvon at the Buick's house, Norman at Arymwny, Peter and Olwen George, Gilly and Jim, Rachel, Paul, Ali, Charlie and kids in Aberporth, Pob, Andy at Ty Rhos, Christine at Quay West, Dorothea at Camping on the Farm, Anne and Andy at Felin Ganol, Maz and Mitch

THE 831 MOST EXCELLENT PEOPLE WHO FUNDED THE WRITING OF THIS BOOK THROUGH THE CROWDFUNDING CAMPAIGN. YOU ALL ROCK!

Jeff Lee, Julie Morgan, Nigel Baker, Val Wood, Anja Hertzberg, Graeme Agnew, Nicky Kirk, Sandra Pillans, Aline Denton, Kay Laurie, Mark Davies, Lewis Packman, Emily Wallis, Fiona Hopkins, Jackie Smith, Elaine Hughes, Sue Freeman, Louche Theatre, Colin Robinson, Denise Dudley, Manu Franken, Anne Pole, Heather Nicholls, Joanne Tinsley, Jenifer Morgan, John Plumb, Suzanna Klein, Sam Bracegirdle, Susan Mann, Susan West, Rachel Martin, Iain Nicholson, Stephaney Cox, Samantha Minas, Maggie Thomas, Juls Sims, Michelle Lee, Bill Evans, Anita Barnard, Susan Sawade, Abigail Kegg, Andy Gray, John & Helen Milbank, Marie Dempsey, Carolyne Carter, Alan Kirby, Jessica Myra Green, Laurence Rolleston, K. Kendall, Ali Gaskell, Kerri Thomas, William Richardson, Penelope Rance, Matthew Gompertz, Scott Alexander, Natasha de Chroustchoff, Emma Read, Zoe, Susan Mace, Gemma Kirk,

Sarah Talbot, Natasha Jones, Ruth Turner, Kathleen Coles, Mark Clark Holter,
Anthony Rees, Lorraine Hill, Joan Tincher, Sheena Thomas, Mathias Urban,
Jan van Gulik, Catrin Simpson, Ingmar Clarysse, Dorothy Reilly, Sue Laver,
Eleanor Hunt, Lisa Jakobsen, Jasia Warren, Brigit Thurstan, Katie Vasquez,
Jodie Ferriby, Jason Hufton, Jane Burnham, A.W.Engelkamp, Stace Martin,
Dominic Lemoine, Sara Ayliffe, Rahul, Crystal Phelps, Alex Minton,
Bobi Harmon, Nathan Cooper, Barbara Smith, Christopher Baird,
Chris Mayfield, Helen Craven, Paddy Dillon, Timmon Milne Wallis,
Emma Halstead, Julia Fox, Paul Christie & Pete Boyd & Elaine Franks,
James Bryant, Richard Hiscutt, Susan Stark, Carlton Solle, Amanda Rolleston,
Lois Pryce, Semaeopus, Diane Slaney, Jennifer Morris, Frances Robinson,
Paul Board, Stewart Doig, Deborah Good, Janet Sanders-Hill,
Vivienne Rickman-Poole, Polly Pearshouse, Roger Hickinbotham,
Tom Allen, Lisa Hamilton, Zoe Wathen, Steph Oneil, Klimskady,
Catherine Mary Aylward, Claudia Linse, Tamsin Weatherly, Linda Carson,
Indra Morris, Sarah Pinnell, Linda in New Mexico, Sue Catling,
Patricia Mary Rubery, Paul Buttle, Joe, Liz Woods, Jackie Clark,
Matthew Shanahan, Thomas de Vries, Gill Pearson, Marion Griffiths,
Tim Platt, Janet Joel, Darren Griffiths, Maria Hay, Janet Davies,
Lizzie Roberts, Madeleine Wenyon, Carol Limmer, Arry Beresford-Webb,
Katherine Pan, Michal Rosenn, Garfield Southall, Helen Southall,
Carol Quillévéré, Tim Hewes, Richard Shipman, Julie, Luca Ometto,
Mariasu, Hugh Welchman, Denzil Broadhurst, Robert Parkhouse,
Christopher Floden, Chris Stolte, Clare S Brindley, Laura Hartman,
Helen Jacob, Dan Rodemsky, George Julian, Rebecca Anderson,
Kate Bremer, Stephen Caldwell, Francesca Daniels, Joe Hill, Rhian Perridge,
Luke Williams, Jens Bunte, Julia Silvis, Nick Sanders, Nova Clarke,
Wyn Jones, Kool Carine, Abraham Lewis, Pete & Marguerite wallis,
Naomi Engelkamp, Aloysia, Emma Lloyd, Gail Diefendorf, Katerina Pavlakis,
Lucy Burrow, Ross Buckley, Cynthia St Clair, Caroline Parr, Sarah Steinhardt,
Jill Kwan, Nor'dzin Pamo, Jan Harvey, Victoria Rogers, John Dix,
Winston Hall, James Clark, Samantha Kidd, Catherine Maris, Jean Tyrie,
Alex Fryer, Fran Christie, Jacquie Blake, Liz Morris, Claire Antoszewski,
A C Robinson, Renee Yanik, Barbara Techel, Paula Hannett, Maria Gandy,
Robert Thorwald, Christian Leigh Dunville, Alex Montgomery,
Kathy Haranzo, Beverly Frankeny, Rebecca Miles, Marcel Van Der Stroom,
Victor Marsden, Martin Granville, Rhian Lewis, Tom Newman,
Michael Reik, Morten Moen, L Newman, Lawrence Hourahane,
Thomas Perridge, Marylou Terryberry, Declan Connolly, Dee Lynes,
Margaret Moss, Sara McAleese, Iain Fox, Kyla, Tamara Jane Habberley,

Dan T., Sonja Daniel, Jeff Woods, Graham Elias, Alison Walker,
Susan Johnson, Stephanie W Davies, Cath Sherrell, Anne MacDonald,
Gerelyn, Ann Ham, Eric Maddern, Marianne Aamot, Emily Riggs,
Anne Riley, Joanna Grace, Rob Simpson-Jones, Astrid Piepschyk,
Emily Lenker, Maya Alberta Horton, José Ángel Lara, Neil Kirk, John Davies,
Peter Watts, Rebecca-Lorraine Egan, Marianne Steele, Daniel Wittberger,
Katie Simmons, Anneke, Laura Louthan, Tom Murrells, Philine von Guretzky,
Scott Ellis, David Philomath, Norman Sharp, Isabel Rogers, Tiny Tim,
Vikki Gardner, Doune Fairfax, Kathie Lester, Graham Roche, Paul Bankston,
Nicole Green, Kathy Seckinger McTyre, Melanie, Laurie MacDougall,
Steven Dunbar, Nikki Simpson, Diana Calder, Sam Griffin, Gabriel Morgan,
Mare Wakefield and Nomad, Mad Martigan, Anders Nilsson, Jack Osborne,
Mindy Grusin, Dan Robinson, Shahob Hosseinpour, Mathew Key,
David Darling, Damon Cogman, Ben R, Paul Knights, Erika Guerra,
Sean Bonnette, Math Heinzel, Glenn Menein, Abdalla Alshamsi, Steve Cody,
Derric, William Howell, Dean Cooney, Rosemary Collins, Carol Smith,
Sarah, James Cullen, Laura Frost Gilbert, Sheridan, Wendy Rowe, Tom,
Melanie Walker, Petra Beresford-Webb, David, Janette Caroline Craven,
Rhiannon Lloyd-Williams, Emma Price, Judith Law, Caroline Neller,
Ralph Whittington, Sebastien Dufresne, Derek Kwok, Carol Coe,
M D O'Malley, Emma Joy Fulford, Abby Yates, Jenny Swann, Allan Tyrie,
Kevin Maynes, Debbie Brown, Catherine Griffiths, Alice Briggs,
Mariamne Briggs, Grant "Max" Wellington, Lee Wright, Rhodri Shore,
Anne-marie Beseke, Dorothy Bell, Mark, Steven Moule, Linda Hall,
Steven Despiegelaere, Abigail Hook, Susan Greaves, Pat McDonnell,
Rorie Smith, Lori Hutchinson, Mary Engdahl, Trish Young, W. H. Rockey,
Lynne Johnston, Bengt Eliasson, Fritz Nordengren, Aureta O'Conner,
Shirley Pickersgill, Corinna Vigier, DonkeyandaCart.com, Richard Swaine,
Mike Beckingham, Nicholas F. Russell, Ruhi Behi, Kar Rowson,
Shannon Callahan, Margaret, Andre Egger, Della Cremin, Diane Banksy Banks,
Philippa Mack, Lisa Crispin, Iain Donaldson, James Holloway,
Michelle Kuzak, Jackie Lewin, Cat, Kate Whittaker, Fiona Macready,
Andrew Cremin, Nick Warlow, John Sharples, Jill Wallis, Jonathan Phillips,
Liz Baines, Andrea Chell, Steve Holt, Akyra Moto, haveyouseenthisgirl,
Mei Tan, Kat Hone, Jo Engelkamp, Ben Young, Beth Alexander, Gavin Baily,
Stuart Young, Scott Kramer, Sam Alexander, Cathryn O'Connell, Nat Doyle,
Daniel Martin, Megan Parsio, Matthew Cashmore, Sarah Heyworth,
John Quinn, Will Brimmer, Caroline Clark, Karen & Tom Thwaites-Jones,
Marcus Ainley, Colleen Koenig, Gareth Wood, Rose Deakin,
Jacqueline Croxford, Sandra Souza-DeSimone, Gill Baldwin,

Cathryn Lloyd-Williams, Dominic Murphy, Sarah Louise Pugh,
Gilly Thomas, Robert Relph, David Morton Lloyd, Ros Phillips, Amy Ellen,
Simon Edwards, Mrs Miriam Morgans, Katy Green, Rhiannon James,
Danni, Hazel Griffiths, Mathias Urban, Kristin Otto, Michelle Freeman,
Julie Fetherston, Jody Veith, Sue LeDieu, Louise Foley, Khaiti French,
Al, Michele, Susannah Porsz, Derek Swale, Amanda Stone, Lynne Stanley,
Maria Mathews, Clare Fellows, Mary-Ann Shoubridge, Sue Harris, Kristin,
Pat Shaw, Randa Zenthoefer, Lauri Michael, Eva Rios Castillo,
Ann R Bruns, Leah Griffith, Krishna Maxwell, Mandy Cartwright,
Delma Jones, Marie Bjork-Haugen, Rebecca Spalton, Michelle Anderson,
Pete Appleyard, Mary Jo Swaner, Linda Clinker, PiwiWiwi Surf Campervans
NZ, Craig Edmondson, Theresa Adams, Jenn Lopez, Jeremy Ricketts,
Leanne Survivor Myers-Baines, Maggie O'Regan, Katherine Dunn,
Andrea Budimulia Schmid, Eric Damon Walters, Jennifer Samson,
Petra Aydin Barberini, Christina Locke, Jean King, Patricia E Lyons,
Richard Scrase, Philip Harlow, Uta Kohl, Harriet Ann Judd, Caroline Roberts,
Cookiedo Twos, Hilary Matthews, Jacqui, Laura Atherton Briggs,
Seraina Manser, Patricia Jones, Nicky Toop, Richard Balchin, Sarah Williams,
Mike Wilson, Tony McNicholl, Jeremy Harmer, Lorna Fillingham,
Cheryl Owen, Gareth Tucknott, Savannah Marie Kemp, Erica Whitcombe,
Doug Alexander, Matthew Trembath, Chris Moreton, Jacqueline Rafferty,
Jessica Harmer, Clare Hieatt, Gareth Jenkins, Bethan Jones,
Heather J C McLean, Chloe Redfern, Nerys Welch, Storme Winfield,
Naomi Keevil, Merris Griffiths, Josh Kinnersley, Tom Walker,
Mr William G Tetlow, Norma McCarten, Edward McCarthy & Lizzie Coker,
K.M. MacKinnon, Gavin Reading Rainbow, joe937rich, Gloria June Edwards,
Alf Alderson, Jolien Veneman, Andy Middleton, Kate Saner, Mark Diacono,
Simon Redding, Andrew Churchill, Stuart Bird, Hannah Doyle, Andy Evans,
Jenny Lambert, Sally Johns, Jon Langton, Retha Ritter, Wiard Sterk,
Osian Davies, Lindsay Semple, Carolyn Black, Cheryl Westbury,
Kate Macdonell, Jan Newton, ö-Dzin Tridral, Sarah Walter, Gloria Alderson,
Susan Girdwood, Angharad Closs Stephens, Suganya Sivasundaram,
Catherine Magda Boucher, Sophie Barrett-Kahn, Valerie Warburton,
Mali Hill, Jocelyn Keshet-Price, Joe Steinhardt, Katrina Adam,
Andrew Mackay, Sam Gosling, Sue Beesley, Paul Coleman, Bridget Osborne,
Ged Lynch, Anthea Harvey, Frankie Fenton & Des Kelleher, Nick Ross,
Deb Smith, Phil Catling, Caroline Black, Susan Sedlmayr, D Morris,
Susan Taylor, Lynda Wilson, Michael Scriven, Jolly Clothing,
Dorothy A Gibbs, Isobel Lewis, Peter John Caldwell, Kevin W. Kulp,
Todd Corley, Joseph Cairnes, Valeda Scribner, Svend Andersen,

Stefan Gazdag, Dorothy Williams, Neville Whitton, Lynne Hewitt,
Eryl Crump, G Booth, Bija Knowles, Sue Thomas, Leonie Turner,
Kay Wilson, Elizabeth Thorne, Joanne Harris, Paula Dower, Morven Telling,
Louise Adamson, Rachel Devlin, Vanessa White, Charly Massey,
Huw Robson, Jacqui Watson, Adam Aharon, Toby Stanwell-Smith,
Clare Meaney, Alice Monfort, Stephen Fenner, Robyn Kinsman-Blake,
Lee Gavin, Helen Lloyd, Mary Brocklebank, Brian Blevins, Nest Howells,
Ben & Kathryn Whitworth, Ken Corey, Sheila Haswell, Matt Dickens,
Rhona, Kelli Russell Agodon, Verrinia Rees, Valerie, Milena Buyum,
Evin Grano, May Umi, Darren Cooper, Jane Tarini, Ben Mayers,
Hoani Horsfall, Sean Flaherty, Chris Zygmant, Helen Picknett,
Jeneene Brengelman, Zenguitarguy, Ellie Hamilton, Lisa Firke, Patricia Wogan,
Patricia H Flagler, Anne Mears, Audrey Kalajian, Mel Jones, Cynthia Hodgson,
JSBusque, Robert Moore, Maryann Conner, Catherine Phillips,
Gemma Pearson, Anna Hughes, Rebecca, Bob Obijiski, Katharina Rayner,
Korie Endicott, Tony Janssens, Henley Johnson, Kirk Weaver, Emma Chan,
Emil Petrinic, Ilya Gulko, Monica Reeve, Kara White, Miriam Rieck, Carey,
Mark Mosher, T Kottavitty, Anne-Sophie Wulff Hoffmoen, Tessa Morrish,
Jo Falcon-Cross, Emily Semple, Julian Kigwana, Karen Naylor,
Patricia Mitchell & Drew Heles, Dominic McHale, Debbie Scott, Jeff Dixon,
Annette James, Becky Aitken, Barb Paulini, Mary Gordon Hanna,
Grace Brouwer, Kirsten Swanson, Ruth, Kat Lochmann, Bas Dekker,
Samuel Reddick, Richard Fortune, Matt Harris, Rebecca A Johnson,
John Dunn, Trish Frizzell, Mary Herbert, Steffi Engelken, Melissa Messer,
Paul Zarn, Susan, Amy Louise Walker, Peggy Harvey, Bill Farquhar,
Elizabeth Eirlys Cartwright, Brianna McLellan, Danielle Oggy, Linda Moore,
Natasha Gilmore, Martha J Flynn, Robin Lindemann, Peg Kocevar,
Brian Clarke, David Möritz, Sherry Schwabacher, M. Bibi,
Marjan Baxter-mondt, Lisa Barrow, JWhiz, Rosie Patterson,
Cheney Creamer, Alana Simpson, Alexandra McClellan, Rebecca Trilsbach,
Susan Sweeney Smith, Lisa J. Geiger, Caitlin Tarvet, Sue Caldwell,
Dawna White, Daniella Schulte-Wilke, DD Ra, Sarah Davies, Emily Kerr,
Pamela Barker, Charles Cooper, Jane West, Dianne Nacson, James Boulter,
Tracy Germaine Crouch, Jerry Sullivan, Sarah Rowley,
Maureen Constantine Lett, Debra Gilbertson, Susan Cleary, Xeph Grand,
Catrin Roberts, Matthew Koch, Gail Whiffen Coyle, Martha Haynes,
Owen Watson, Adele Walshe, Chris, Terresa Cook, Amy McGehee,
Melanie Hedlund, Amanda Smith, Jessica Hill, Simon Wadsworth,
Margaret Benjamin, Steve Bremner, Michelle Hall, Sarah Brunt, Rowan,
Claire Smart, Birgit Deubner, Lorri Noble, Brooke Bolte, Larissa L.,

Jessie Fischer, Elizabeth Visco, Angie Gerrey, Experiencing Life to the
Fullest – Da Wolf, Anne Jennings, Anja, Julie Simpson, Margaret Birch,
Vicki Rowe, Diane Anderson, Darren Coulson, Stuart Radford,
Lara Pressburger, Zoe Dashwood-Evans, Chris Rixon, Rachel, Amy Parlo,
Helen Austin, Andy Hyde, Chenda & Dave Moir, Rebekka Harrison,
Mark Tobin, Tim Wilkinson, Matthew Ledbury, Fiona Winter, Joe Tristram,
Christine Helfrich, Sion England, Cathrine Plumridge, Tim Olsen,
Charlotte Wolff, Alison Wade, Eve Wittenberg, Sue Clapham, Norm Fasey,
Bethan Williams, Lucy Dancer, Amber Ellis, Demelza Jones,
Heather Elizabeth Hall, Paul Vickers, Dan Mason, Carol Reid, Ann,
Chris Petheram, Ruth Adams, Kendra Chilcoat, Hayley Beckley,
Rachel Ridge, Alison Clegg, Mike Grenville and Forest Row Film Society,
Jennifer Vachon, Lizzie Spikes, Laura Nailor, Orla McConville, Katie,
Rebecca Sturgeon, Jennifer Roy, Sue Dumpleton, and Tina Ridd